ALL WEATHER YACHTSMAN

Dedicated to my crews—
who usually came for the love—
or the hell of it.

All Weather
Yachtsman

PETER HAWARD

ADLARD COLES NAUTICAL
London

Published by Adlard Coles Nautical
an imprint of A & C Black (Publishers) Ltd
35 Bedford Row, London WC1R 4JH

Copyright © Peter J. Haward 1961, 1990

First published in hardback by
Adlard Coles as *All Seasons' Yachtsman* 1961
This edition published 1990
Reprinted 1991

ISBN 0–7136–3560–6

A CIP catalogue record for this book is available from the
British Library

Printed and bound in Great Britain by
Hartnolls Ltd, Bodmin, Cornwall

Contents

Charts

Foreword to the new edition

These stories are from the many voyages I made during my first thirteen years of boat delivery work, which I began immediately after the war. A good sea yarn may result from venturing out in an old, unsuitable, or poorly maintained yacht in the face of difficult weather. At the time such craft were plentiful. When war broke out all the boatyards round the coast ceased yacht-building and concentrated entirely on naval harbour launches, air-sea rescue craft, MTBs, MFVs and diverse other little vessels to sustain the armed forces. At the end of it all the once treasured yachts that had been hastily stowed away in obscure hiding places (which were not necessarily conducive to their preser-vation) began to be unearthed. By taking some of them to sea I soon began to understand the effects of five years of neglect.

Other peculiarities coloured those early days. New yachts were in demand, but the war building programme had drained the world of seasoned timber. Some brand new boats went quickly rotten, to the frustration of their owners and the trepidation of those who were to sail in them. Petrol was still rationed and by delivering a petrol driven motor cruiser one quickly developed an in-depth understanding of the coupon system. With the sailing craft, at least the wind was free, though nature has always imposed its own inscrutable rationing system.

One solemn reader has doubted the sense of some of my delivery voyages, suggesting that they were merely foolhardy. He questioned my temerity in even writing about them. In reality, I always aimed to ensure that there was a valid margin of safety within which I knew I must stay. Foreseeing the worst eventualities and having the necessary if perhaps makeshift equipment to deal with a problem is a key to safety. Nobody is infallible and my one deep regret is only belatedly devising a safety harness—although I was the first to design and market one for yachtsmen.

I was attempting to develop a business, and customers wanting boats moved were thin on the ground. Every commission was valued and I always felt an enthusiasm to finish a job properly, both for the owner's satisfaction and my own. Something of the "no case too difficult" ideal was as necessary as it was challenging. However, not everything in life goes exactly as planned, and I have faithfully recorded differences between aspirations and performance. I now perceive a naivety on my part which perhaps invited extra problems. Yet, on the whole, I think I learned sufficiently quickly to have a go at the next difficulty. Usually I was able to provide the service I offered, at the same time gaining from a series of gently graduated lessons. In presenting the book again I hope the yarns may still raise a flicker of interest, even if only to make the modern sailor thankful that there has been an improvement in boat design and construction.

A delivery voyage often revealed a boat's condition to be different from her owner's description, but on the whole most of my clients sincerely believed they were sending me to sea in sound craft, fit for the voyage. However, I remember one occasion when an unguarded comment hinted an owner's penchant for research. When I had delivered his nailsick yacht (an 80% pump job) to him, he reminded his wife excitedly of his conviction that if a delivery skipper could get her round safely she was worth the hard bargain he had struck. I remain curious about that purchase price.

When my stories were written yacht voyages were often regarded as amazing feats. Today, even transocean passages are considered in a matter of fact way. Much more sailing is done now, and a modern, well found yacht is usually easier to handle and more comfortable than her predecessors. Nevertheless, seagoing in any small craft, particularly in the stormier, higher latitudes, should not be taken lightly.

I devoted two chapters to bad weather, much of which discussed Capt. Voss's faith in sea anchors, which I thought misplaced. Perhaps less emphatically, I still do not think a sea anchor warrants space on a small yacht. Nor do you often come across this gadget now.

Diesel engines today deliver such power that every sailing yacht is a motor sailer. The concept of the "auxiliary" motor has gone. Far from being helpful only for manoeuvring in harbours or during flat calms, the engine is a boon during headwinds and general lack of progress—Humphrey Barton mentioned the "irresistible combination of sail and power".

In bad weather the engine, together with a trysail or a close reefed main, will enable a yacht to avoid being driven on a lee shore, a peril which a sea anchor was supposed merely to postpone. With her engine a yacht can now lie-to happily in heavy weather, the only proviso being that if she is carrying any sail, oil pressure must be monitored carefully. Excessive heeling may result in intermittent loss of oil pressure which, if the pump is badly worn, could initiate complete lubrication failure and severe engine damage.

Among the many changes in yachts since my book was written, none has been more obvious than the alteration to keels. An old timer might be forgiven for saying that yachts no longer have keels. Instead they have ballasted, fixed dagger plates. The development stems from the quest for ever more speed. In 1928 Uffa Fox designed and raced a dinghy that was able to plane and which won fifty-two races out of fifty-seven. It was to take nearly forty years for such development to be applied to offshore racing but by the mid-sixties it was the fin keel, planing hulls that were winning open sea events. Cruising yachts followed the trend.

The weatherliness of these new craft is different from the old long keel breeds. Beamier, flatter bottomed, with fin keels, usually they are of lighter displacement. Initial stability is greater but the ultimate righting moment is likely to be less. They enjoy the advantage of modern materials and design and the strength of their superstructure and general watertight integrity is frequently of a high order. Under bare poles they will tend to blow down wind. Directional stability is small and bilge sumps are often very shallow. These characteristics should be kept in mind when considering heavy weather.

Spared the total capsize experience myself, I recognise it to be a very serious test of morale, but if it is a more frequent event today it seems to inflict less than the terminal damage that frequently occurred when wooden craft turned over. Abandoning ship need not be the automatic response. Liferafting is an adventure of great peril—the last card. Unless it is obviously impossible to prevent the boat sinking you will be safer doing everything you can to keep her afloat. In the Fastnet race disaster of '79 many of the abandoned yachts rode out the storm unaided and were subsequently salvaged.

A refreshing change today is that modern, well built boats seldom leak. Both hulls and decks are well sealed and even vessels with large windows are remarkably good at keeping out the marauding sea. Today, life on a yacht at sea is less disagreeable. The business of removing water from surging bilges that so frequently used to require persistence and not a little experience is seldom the pastime of the modern sailor. Modern bilge pumps are more effective, diaphragm hand pumps have replaced the less reliable semi-rotaries and the advent of the electric immersion pump is a boon. Of course things do go wrong. Shaft and rudder glands leak and skin fittings can fail. It is now the rarity of serious leaking that can take a skipper by surprise. Once a boat is full to the floorboards the cause of the influx may be harder to establish.

Crews sometimes register shocked surprise when boats leak, and even more so when bilge pumps fail to live up to their promise (or cannot cope with a bouillon of debris-infested bilgewater). The fainter-hearted conclude that it should not happen, castigate the pump manufacturer and even abdicate their duty. Some recent losses of yachts, just like others before them, can be blamed at least in part on failure to routinely check bilges and on what I call a dearth of good pumpmanship.

Modern technology now makes it easier to ascertain a position at sea with great accuracy, but the importance of voyage strategy is no less pertinent. Newly included in this edition are hints on passage making between various UK ports and to the Mediterranean, with comments on the weather patterns that may be encountered, including that disagreeable local wind in the Gilbraltar Strait called the Levanter.

Preface

I hope many amateur yachtsmen will be among the readers of this book. I mean "amateur" in its correct sense—i.e. one who cultivates a thing as a pastime or a pleasure, and not, as it is sometimes used, wrongly to my mind, to indicate a limited proficiency. There are many books describing yacht voyages and those I have read I have enjoyed. Such seagoing has been described by amateurs because their passages were undertaken primarily for pleasure or, as the French happily put it, for "the sport". Thus enthusiasm for their adventures is flavoured with the outlook of men doing something for reasons other than that old mundane requisite of earning a living.

At one time I went sailing as an amateur and I understand and am in sympathetic agreement with the compulsion that some men feel to challenge the wind and the sea and the elements. However, there would be very little point in my describing some enjoyable holidays on the Norfolk Broads. Chapter 1 of this book is called "Amateur turns professional" and, without apology, I kick off from there. The flavour quickly becomes that of the professional, with much of the drive behind the adventures being what in Yorkshire is romantically described "brass". I trust the amateur will bear with me during these brief barbaric discourses.

I like my job. I like the sea. I like yachts of all types. There are easy delivery voyages to be undertaken, difficult ones, arduous ones, and sometimes, for one reason or another, hazardous ones. I like to do my best whatever the challenge but that does not mean I do not like proper financial reward, fair pay for fair work; nor do I dislike holidays, walks in the country, green fields, tall trees that measure the wind by its whine in their branches, or bright city lights. Happy is the man who likes his work, yet all work and no play makes Jack a dull boy. . . .

Textbooks on yachting state with dignity the value of a professional survey before you buy a boat. I have outlined two examples of what can happen when such advice is unheeded. I hope the sea stories involved are entertaining but if the lessons in the background are sordid I trust the reader will not think I include them in any spirit of vindictiveness. I am sure there is something to learn from this kind of boat trouble and I am certainly not qualified to throw stones at the scholars—my fellow students, I ought to say.

Most yachtsmen are secretly proud that big ship mariners say that if you go yachting for pleasure you would go to hell for a pastime. I am. I am also vain in that my yachting is forced (financially) to continue when the amateur sensibly hauls his vessel out of the water. Hence this book is written from a slightly different angle from most yachting books and I hope that adds to its justification.

P.J.H.

Acknowledgements

In Chapter 4, some of the descriptions of voyaging in the yachts *Sceptre, Misha, Cohoe* and *Janabel* have already appeared in the *Yachting Monthly* magazine. The editor has kindly consented to these inclusions. Among the books on voyages which I have read the following have been of special interest and have helped me in arriving at the conclusions I have expressed relative to the handling of yachts in heavy weather: *North Atlantic* by K. Adlard Coles (Adlard Coles); *Vertue XXXV* by Humphrey Barton (Adlard Coles); *Deep Sea Sailing* by Erroll Bruce (Hutchinsons Technical); *The Venturesome Voyages of Captain Voss* by Captain Voss (Rupert Hart Davis); *Cruises of the Joan* by W. E. Sinclair (Edward Arnold); *Wandering Under Sail* by Eric Hiscock (Adlard Coles); *Atlantic Adventurers* by Humphrey Barton (Adlard Coles); *To the Great Southern Sea* by W. A. Robinson (Peter Davies); *Once is Enough* by Miles Smeeton (Rupert Hart Davis).

Also I wish to acknowledge reading Edward Young's *One of Our Submarines* (Rupert Hart Davis) and express my sympathy with him concerning thunderstorms.

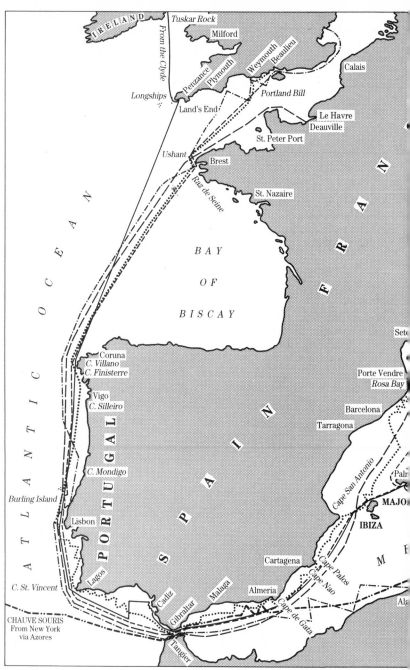

CHART I

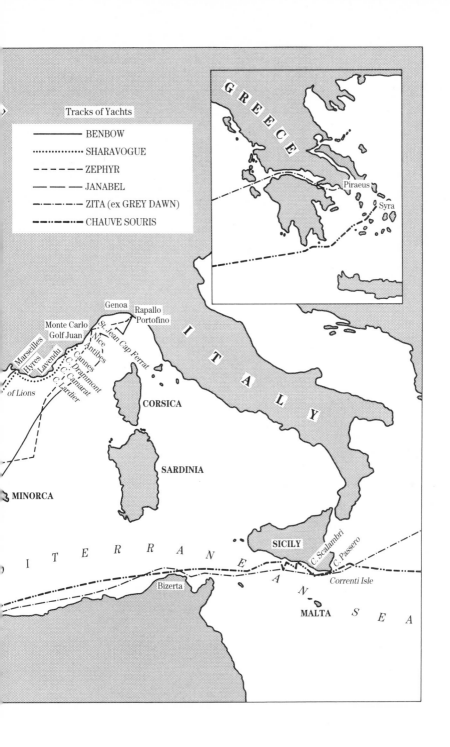

Tracks of Yachts

——— BENBOW

············ SHARAVOGUE

– – – – ZEPHYR

— — — JANABEL

–·–·–· ZITA (ex GREY DAWN)

–··–··– CHAUVE SOURIS

GREECE

Piraeus

Syra

Genoa

Rapallo
Portofino

Monte Carlo
Golf Juan

St. Jean Cap Ferrat

Nice

Marseilles

Antibes

Hyres

Cannes

Lavendu

C. Drammont

C. Camarat

C. Lardier

of Lions

ITALY

CORSICA

SARDINIA

MINORCA

SICILY

C. Scalambri

C. Passero

MEDITERRANEAN SEA

Bizerta

Correnti Isle

MALTA

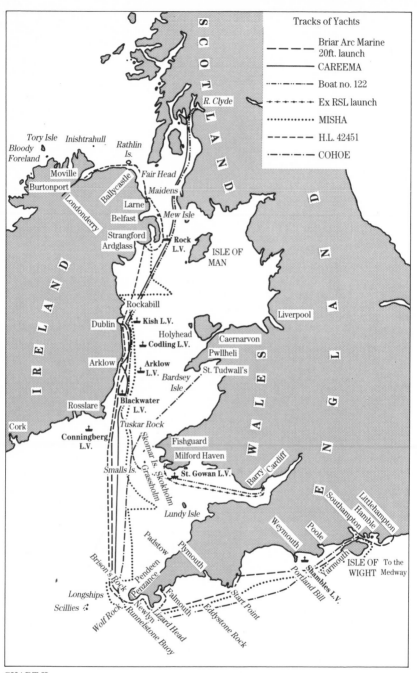

CHART II

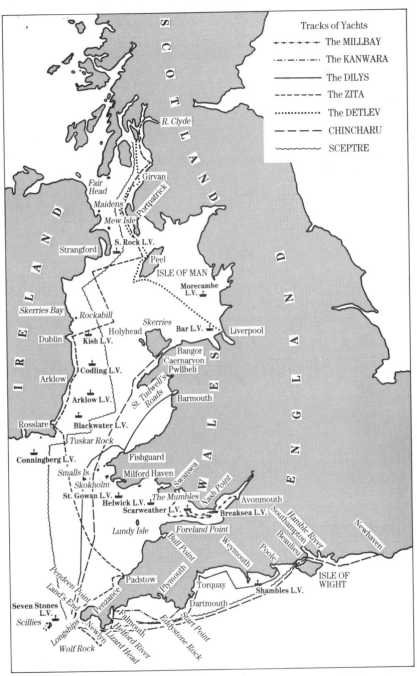

Tracks of Yachts

+·+·+·+·+·+	The MILLBAY
·—·—·—·—	The KANWARA
————————	The DILYS
– – – – –	The ZITA
··············	The DETLEV
— — — —	CHINCHARU
∿∿∿∿∿	SCEPTRE

SCOTLAND

R. Clyde

IRELAND

Fair Head
Maidens
Mew Isle
S. Rock L.V.
Strangford
Girvan
Portpatrick
Peel
ISLE OF MAN
Morecambe L.V.

Skerries Bay
Rockabill
Holyhead
Skerries
Bar L.V.
Liverpool
Dublin
Kish L.V.
Bangor
Caernarvon
Pwllheli
Arklow
Codling L.V.
St. Tudwell's Roads
Barmouth
Arklow L.V.
Rosslare
Blackwater L.V.
Tuskar Rock
WALES
Conningberg L.V.
Fishguard
Smalls Is.
Milford Haven
Skokholm
Swansea
St. Gowan L.V.
The Mumbles
Nash Point
Helwick L.V.
Scarweather L.V.
Avonmouth
Breaksea L.V.
Southampton
Hamble River
Beaulieu
Newhaven
Lundy Isle
Foreland Point
Bull Point
Weymouth
Poole
ENGLAND
Pendeen Point
Padstow
Plymouth
Torquay
Shambles L.V.
ISLE OF WIGHT
Land's End
Penzance
Dartmouth
Start Point
Seven Stones L.V.
Scillies
Longships
Newlyn
Falmouth
Helford River
Eddystone Rock
Wolf Rock
Lizard Head

CHART III

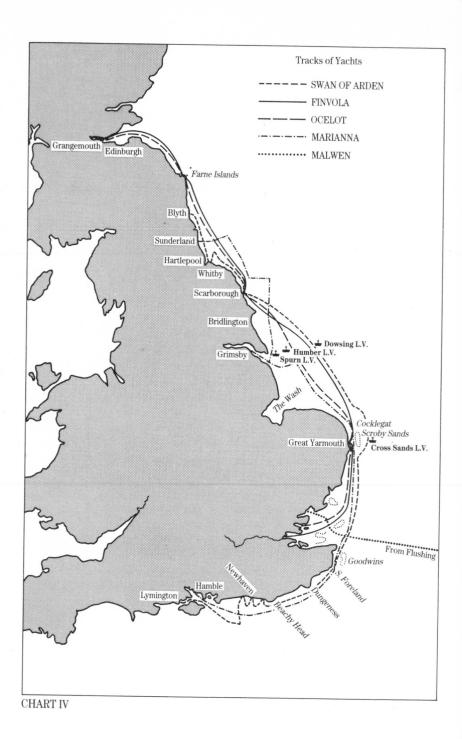

Tracks of Yachts

- – – – – – SWAN OF ARDEN
- ———— FINVOLA
- – — – — OCELOT
- –·–·–·– MARIANNA
- ············ MALWEN

Grangemouth
Edinburgh
Farne Islands
Blyth
Sunderland
Hartlepool
Whitby
Scarborough
Bridlington
⚓ **Dowsing L.V.**
⚓ **Humber L.V.**
Grimsby
Spurn L.V.
The Wash
Cocklegat
Scroby Sands
Great Yarmouth
Cross Sands L.V.
From Flushing
Goodwins
Newhaven
S. Foreland
Hamble
Dungeness
Lymington
Beachy Head

CHART IV

CHAPTER I

Amateur turns Professional

A KNOCK-OUT drop would have worked wonders. Or a crack over the head: something to make me sleep. I knew that sleep was all-important for the project ahead; yet it was the brain-fever about it that effectively prevented sleep. I tossed and turned through the night in the top floor room of a rough-and-ready hotel near Paddington Station; then I caught the five-thirty morning train for Avonmouth. I had been commissioned to take command of a 100-ton auxiliary sailing yacht, partially converted from an old coasting vessel that had recently finished trading.

It was going to be a brand-new experience. Just out of the Army I had thought a small advertisement in the yachting press might bring me some sailing during my demobilization leave:

"Experienced yachtsman will deliver yachts or help with cruises or passages."

My conscience battled with me over the word "experienced", suggesting it could be misleading or extravagant. I informed it that I had used the word in the literal rather than the implied sense. Though it had been none too extensive, I had had yachting experience before the war. A few trips on a friend's 30-ft. auxiliary cutter around the Isle of Wight, some half-decker sailing in Chichester Harbour, and a number of Norfolk Broads holidays. These latter are an excellent training ground for handling small yachts under sail, but they teach you nothing about the sea. It was a background from which one could sensibly graduate to undertaking a cautious coastal cruise in a 5-tonner, but hardly a basis to claim professional competence to skipper an 80-ft. auxiliary sailing vessel on a voyage round one of the more difficult parts of the English coast.

Thus I had bitten off quite a mouthful, and I do not think I should have taken on the command if the complete proposition had been fully revealed at the start. Such was not the case. I had worked my way up to skipper during the negotiations, and promotion is a hard thing to decline. The business was done mainly by telegram. The first said:

"Will you sail as Mate on 100-ton ketch, Avonmouth to Littlehampton."

A highly satisfactory invitation from my angle. Avoiding captain's responsibilities, I would gain good experience on one of the larger types of yachts. My affirmative reply brought the next telegram:

"Agree terms. Skipper's mother ill, thus he cannot come. Assume you will take over."

I rang my client at this stage, cautiously stating that I had never before taken charge of so large a vessel. His optimism told me I soon would.

"You'll find it quite straightforward. The sail plan is rather unusual but you should soon fathom it out. . . ."

The next day came his third wire:

"The crew are green but don't tell them."

I thought: "That describes the whole ship's company. Thank God we are all the same!" Writing fifteen years later, I still defend the outlook. One thing worse than an inexperienced skipper is a raw skipper, dogged with a crew of critical diehards with salt for blood. As long as I could keep my own council I felt I stood a chance. My confidence sprang from fairly extensive reading on sailing, seamanship and coastal navigation, and, despite the size of the vessel and the weight of her gear, I was eager to put my theoretical knowledge to the test. Inevitably I would set about much of my work inexpertly, with the air of the novice, and the fewer old sweats about, with sage comments on their lips, the better.

Heavy-eyed, as though the previous night had been of wild celebration, I forged my way along Avonmouth Dock with my seagoing gear. The yacht *Millbay* lay at the seaward end near the lock. As I came abreast, a sturdy young woman in slacks and jersey clambered up to the quay.

"Captain Haward?"

There was promotion for you! After $2\frac{1}{2}$ years' alternating between gunner and lance-bombardier I had held the military rank of lieutenant for 18 months, with little prospect of elevation beyond its dogsbody status. Now people were rushing up ladders to call me Cap'n. I warmed to my crew, though greenhorns they must be.

There were four all told. Hutch was the mate, a lion-hearted, charming personality who was, I think, sailing in an amateur capacity. Some time back he had been to sea in cargo vessels, but he claimed little knowledge of fore-and-aft sailing craft or of navigation. Originally he had taken on the third hand's job but, of course, when the first skipper departed, he too went up the ladder of promotion. Of the engineer's background I knew little, nor why he had involved himself in this voyage, because it was soon clear that he viewed the whole adventure with apprehension. On the other hand, his wife held no fear of the sea, and appeared to enjoy everything about shipboard life. She offered proof, if it is ever necessary, that the weaker sex can endure and survive just as unpleasant conditions as the physically more powerful male. The last member of the ship's company was a young fellow of about 17. I can complete his place in my narrative in three sentences. Shortly after leaving Avonmouth he began to be vigorously seasick. After that he completely disappeared, though I was assured that he had not fallen overboard. He came to life again when we made port.

The *Millbay* was a very old ship. She was built in 1889. After many years as a small sailing coaster, she had now been bought and was partially converted into a yacht. She carried a small motor tender which had also to fulfil the role of lifeboat—though my guess was that it would have quickly foundered if anybody were to take to it in rough weather. However, the opinion was that it must be carried in such a way as to facilitate speedy launching. It was stowed on two very springy planks erected across the side deck, their ends resting on the bulwarks and the cabin coach roof. The launching davits were spaced too far apart to help secure this little boat. She simply stood on her highly sprung platform, sparsely secured with dirty rope. Launching might be easy enough; what I feared was that she would come adrift when our vessel started to roll. The whole arrangement ought to have been changed, but I felt reticent about countermanding the orders of my predecessor who, I assumed, must have been more experienced than I was and who, apparently, approved the lash-up. Weakly, I said she must have extra ropes holding her. The inadequate order was carried out in an equally half-hearted manner.

Prior to my joining, arrangements had been made for a pilot to take us as far as the Breaksea Lightship, which is stationed in the Bristol Channel off Barry. This is the normal practice for large ships leaving Bristol or Avonmouth, although for only a part of this distance is pilotage compulsory; and in any case yachts, being generally very small vessels, are exempt from these regulations. We were not obliged to carry a pilot, and as a self-respecting yacht-delivery skipper with a fair practical knowledge of many ports in the U.K. I would now make a point of avoiding pilotage charges for my clients. However, at that time I had no experience of buoyed channels, nor had I ever done practical chartwork nor ever manoeuvred a vessel the size of the *Millbay*; thus I was extremely lucky to be provided with a man used to taking charge of all types of ships, and having an intricate knowledge of the Estuary of the River Severn. I would have no worries until the yacht was safely in the open sea, where bad handling need not spell immediate disaster.

Dusk was falling on the evening of Friday, 13th September 1946, when the *Millbay* left Avonmouth and began her voyage towards the English Channel. The local meteorological office told us that the strong westerly wind would soon ease and veer north-west, and that no further bad weather was expected in the immediate future. As darkness spread over the Estuary, only a faint breeze was discernible, and our sails remained stowed. The auxiliary diesel engine was giving us about 5 knots.

I expect the pilot was amused as he guided that yacht down the Channel. The whole ship reflected the anxiety of tyros right out of their depths. The skipper was surreptitiously checking the course on the chart and only establishing his position when the most conspicuous of lighthouses showed themselves. The many flashing buoys confused him from the start. He felt like a drunkard adrift in Piccadilly Circus on the last shopping day to Christmas. One of the ways in which he demonstrated his inexperience was by referring to the second hand of his watch to check the intervals of the flashing lights. The pilot laughed and said it was easier, and just as satisfactory, to judge the seconds with a slow count.

The engineer crept up to me in the dusk.

"Don't you think it would be a good idea to put in for a night's rest? We could call it a day at Barry."

I was alarmed at having to exhort the crew to their duties at such an early stage. We had only just left Avonmouth and were not even in the open sea. Despite the many matters to be considered, the idea of putting into port before rounding Land's End had never occurred to me.

Should it come, I was convinced that our vessel was capable of withstanding any bad weather, providing her Master and crew served her faithfully. That is what all the yachting books had said, and I was determined that we all should fulfil our side of the bargain. Moreover, we should drop the pilot off Barry, therefore, to put in there, of all places, would be the depth of ignominy.

A powerful factor maintaining this proper outlook, paradoxically, was my complete lack of confidence in manoeuvring our heavy old vessel in a confined space. My experience extended only to 30-ft. Norfolk Broads sloops, and I had no idea of our ship's turning circle, her ability to go astern or the time required to check her way through the water. The thought of entering a strange harbour of unknown size in darkness, without any clear idea of what I should find inside, terrified me. One mistake could create a glorious catastrophe. However, these fears could not be for the crew's consumption because they would effectively undermine an innocent confidence in the skipper.

The engineer sloped back to his machine shop. He could only pursue the matter by exhibiting his fear of the dark night at sea. As long as I kept my mouth shut I remained the intrepid seadog.

The matter seemed settled for a bare 5 min. Then Hutch came aft.

"Engineer told me to bring you a message," he said. "The oil pressure is falling."

Being a suspicious character I read beyond the statement. I had no idea what it meant anyhow, because at that time my mechanical understanding went no further than the operation of the autoloader in a Bofors gun. But I thought that if the engine was in danger of a breakdown I would have been told clearly, and probably in person.

I mumbled an acknowledgement and Hutch went back to the

deck saloon. The pilot had heard the conversation and to me he was the nearest seafarer's textbook. I pumped him.

"What does that mean?"

He gave a non-committal grunt. I think the workings of compression ignition engines was a closed book to him also; but after some thought he said:

"I don't think I would worry too much."

It was not long before we came up to the pilot vessel that would collect him. Pointing ahead, he said:

"The course is due west for Bull Point and that will take you clear of the Foreland." He swung his arm round the horizon and continued. "There's Barry, and that's Flatholm's occulting light on the port quarter. The Breaksea is on the port bow. You are all right now, and you have a good ship." He gave a nod towards the engine room hatch: "Don't worry about him. His job is to keep the engine running, not tell you about it. Keep your own council and you will do fine." Then he steered the *Millbay* alongside the pilot vessel. He shook me by the hand, walked forward a little and jumped on to his parent ship. A moment later the 57 year old *Millbay* was under the command of her most raw skipper ever.

CHAPTER 2

Embayed in the Bristol Channel

HAVING swung the yacht clear of the pilot boat, I brought her on course; then I called Hutch to the helm and went to the deck-house for a serious session of chartwork. Establishing my position on that dark sea, and tracking my course along it appeared an urgent task.

In the Army I had prided myself on my map reading, and I was surprised to find difficulties in sorting out the lights that the pilot had just shown me. This was because I had not noted which way the ship was heading as he brought her alongside the pilot boat. Being back on course the orientation was different. Coastal navigation and map reading are akin, but noting prominent objects at night—lighthouses, lightships and buoys, all giving particular characteristic flashes that must be counted and timed— was new to me. Frequently I had to apply the auld auld adage of Robert Bruce. Eventually, having coaxed a blinker to tally with the information supplied on the chart, I would honour it with a compass bearing, possibly achieving an accuracy of 5 degrees either way. Finally, in triumph, a whole new world before me, I was satisfied with a "cocked hat" position—the small triangle on the chart that was the intersection of three compass bearings.

This settled, I was due to relieve Hutch. Soon, alone at the wheel, the old vessel rolling slightly to the swell that was the aftermath of the strong wind of the day, confidence came surging over me. With it came the romance, sea fever, the yachting bug, the whole force that makes people dream of voyaging in small vessels. It is a veritable infection and few who contract it are ever entirely free again. I have learned to live with my affliction. It has to be like that with most of us; in fact I know of only one case where a quick and final cure was found. This was an amateur crew of mine who once sailed with me on a 31-ton yacht from Scotland to the Channel Islands. The voyage occupied 4 rather rough days and brought considerable discomfort. For him sea-sickness emphasized the hardship and a whole 2 days after our arrival he said: "That's that. I've done with yachting. I think I shall try mountaineering next!"

However, such spontaneous cures are a rarity. Countless patients undergo similar or worse experiences to no avail. At the time they swear never to go to sea again but their oaths are like those of the drunkard, screaming future temperance. An hour or so deprived of their dreadful addiction, the fever reasserts itself. They are planning their next voyage once more.

The magic enchantment departed suddenly—in one wave. Timing its advance for best effect, a swell heavier than usual caught the *Millbay* so that she rolled more quickly and further than before. There was a grinding upheaval, a heavy crash and the crazy erection of planks fell from under the motor launch, leaving her hanging on the outsize davits. On the next roll she swung wildly on her falls, fouling the bulwark but passing out-board and over the sea. Then she started to smash herself up, swinging to and fro against the ship's side.

"All hands!"

My urgent shout brought the crew tumbling out of the deck saloon, but quickly it was apparent that nobody could get near enough long enough to secure the lumbering boat as she crashed about in the darkness. Looking back over the years, I can see how raw and ineffective were our efforts. The situation was beyond our control but a resourceful crew could have coped. As it was, serious damage to the sides of the yacht appeared imminent, and I was also fearful lest somebody should be badly hurt. There was a brief panic party, then I went below and found the bread knife and, standing on the cleat of each davit in turn, I cut through the falls, and the boat dropped stern first into the sea. Semi-water-logged it drifted astern into the darkness. We never saw it again. A sad, expensive way of solving the problem.

Quiet again. Then very quiet. The engine had stopped. I

called the crew and while the engineer set about rectifying the breakdown, the rest of us hoisted the mizen and main staysail. Just those two smaller sails was all we managed because by the time we had them up we were exhausted. I cannot recall the difficulties—even if I ever knew them. Lack of "know-how" probably explains them.

The engineer soon had the motor running again, and we continued with these two sails drawing the light breeze on the starboard bow, until the mizen began to split at a seam near the luff. In order to avoid it parting altogether, we stowed it.

At dawn the wind began to back towards the west and freshen. Our progress through the night had been meagre, although, having made no other voyage with which to compare it, I was satisfied. The tide in the Bristol Channel is strong and between the Breaksea Lightvessel and Nash Point from where the South Wales coast curves north-west towards Port Talbot and Swansea Bay, it will run at speeds of up to 5 knots. Thus, after the ebb tide had helped us, the last part of the night was spent punching into the east flowing flood stream, which at times held us more or less stationary.

Now, using both sail and power, we were having to tack. The engine alone would not have been powerful enough to push our heavy vessel straight into wind and sea. The west wind was dead against us and, paying off towards the Somerset coast, we closed with the shore near Minehead. Then we put about on to the port tack, hoisted the mizen staysail and lay across to the Welsh side of the Channel once more.

The varied business of the night had kept me active, either on deck or at the charts in the deck saloon and, coupled with my previous night of insomnia in Paddington, I was much in arrears with sleep. I went below to make good the deficiency without success. Problems past and possibilities to come had no stowage lockers in my brain. They refused to stay still. I spent 40 min. lying quietly, in unrestful mental turmoil, then Hutch came down and said we were approaching land again.

That had been quick. The wind was still increasing and the very small amount of sail set was helping the engine. We had romped across the Channel. The sun was out and the sea was a sparkling mantle of blue and white. The *Millbay* came round to the other tack and back towards Somerset we went, at the same time making good progress to the westward. Swilled by the favourable tide, we slammed through the overfalls that lie off Nash Point.

By afternoon the yacht was nearly as far west as Ilfracombe but, on the port tack and heading north-west, she was unable to weather the Scarweather Lightvessel. Had this been done we would have sailed into Swansea Bay and remained out of reach of the unfavourable tide that would soon pour back into the Severn Estuary. Before we could close with this guardian against the dangerous Scarweather sandbank our progress diminished, then we even began to lose ground. This was only the start of the flood tide. I had realized that a 6-hr. period of little or no progress must be expected, but I was dismayed when our vessel could be seen sliding sideways towards Nash Point. No navigational ability was necessary to perceive that all our hard-earned gains were being rapidly reduced to naught.

Morale sagged. Dusk revealed the Breaksea Lightvessel that we had left astern immediately after dropping the pilot the evening before. Her flash mocked us every 15 sec. The engineer was the most depressed. He seemed to have a special unreal fear, all of his own. Whatever it was, his solution to it astounded me.

"Don't you think we had better run her ashore?"

I could think of no answer. For a day my whole aim had been avoiding just that. We were approaching the problem from a different angle. In yearning for a comfortable fireside in a great stone house on a mountain he had omitted practical considerations that stood between him and his desire. He could see it was necessary to reach the sea shore, but could not appreciate the danger of a rocky coast or thundering surf. Even if the *Millbay* were of no consequence, to abandon her in such a way would be fraught with peril. Clearly he was at his best out of sight of the sea, down amongst his pressure gauges (which he had managed to stabilize by now) and his other mechanical devices so helpful, if not essential, to our project.

Since joining the *Millbay*, I had kept a log of events, but by that afternoon utter weariness brought an end to these entries. It must have revealed a voyage of incident because later I completed it in retrospect and sent a copy to the owner. He commented that it was a "masterpiece of understatement". Unfortunately I have lost this record long since and therefore I can only outline roughly the subsequent fortunes of the *Millbay* while in the care of her novice skipper.

Night fell. The tide turned and once again we struggled to the west over the same old stretch of sea. The wind had backed to the south-west now and, though it was settling down to a hard blow, the Somerset and North Devon coasts afforded shelter and for the present we were no longer faced with the need to tack. However, the fair slant would only help us as far as Bull Point, the headland 5 miles west of Ilfracombe, because that was our corner where we turned to the south-west for Land's End. Then we should be faced with a dead headwind blowing from the open sea. Even fresh and experienced seamen would find reaching the English Channel a long hard slog. Weather deterioration into full gale would hold them up completely and force them to lie-to until the wind eased and veered. The *Millbay* had no such crew; she was in the hands of tired greenhorns, clearly unable to face such eventualities. We were bordering on exhaustion and, if our ship did not soon reach a safe haven, she would become dangerously under manned—virtually derelict, in fact.

This early experience, and those of other novice yachtsmen of which I have heard, convince me that sleep is the least considered, and one of the most important factors in small vessel voyaging. Careful consideration is rightly given to the essentials of navigation and seamanship, also the gear to be carried, the fuel, water, victuals. But sleep, being intangible and a matter for the individual, is left to each crew member to sort out for himself. Anybody can eat when he is hungry—bread and cheese, if the galley is *hors de combat* through bad weather, and note that you are *never* truly hungry if seasick—but sleep does not come to the man with his mind in turmoil, even when exhausted. Proper attention to comfortable berths, in which a crew can relax safely without being hurled out by rough weather, and an orderly routine will go a long way towards promoting sleep. Beyond that self-discipline is necessary. Each crew member has a duty towards the ship to keep himself up to date with sleep. And for the worried skipper? Possibly sufficient seagoing experience to bring just a little of the contempt of familiarity will help; otherwise the adoption of the one-hurdle-at-a-time spirit is good advice.

Thus my original ideas on progress had to be modified. I examined the chart for a convenient port of call. The experienced coasting seaman, particularly if he has an intimate knowledge of the Bristol Channel, would suggest the safe anchorage under the lee of Lundy Island. It affords secure shelter against sou'westerly gales and, if the opposite wind blows directly into this little bay, it will be fair for Land's End. By sheltering there our yacht would be waiting in the most convenient jumping-off point for rounding England's south-west corner. Swansea lies some 20 miles off course to the north, while Ilfracombe's tidal harbour offers indifferent shelter during westerly gales because a heavy scend runs into it.

For all that, Lundy is a wild almost uninhabited island, and in going there we were likely to be entirely on our own, remote from facilities. Exhausted greenhorns would be better advised to find a thriving, well organized harbour. I settled on Swansea.

By midnight the *Millbay* was feeling the full wind from the open sea. It is hard to be precise after 14 years, particularly because I viewed that bad weather through the eyes of a novice, but I conclude that it was blowing at Force 6 or even 7 from the south-south-west.

The yacht was going very well. I could see what a difference it made having the wind slightly free, and I can remember to this day how impressed I was by the way she rode the big lumbering waves that rolled out of the darkness, lifting her bodily. The threshing spray, the wind in the rigging, the feeling of life in the timbers of our ship, the creaming crests that were dim in the darkness; all this was indelibly imprinted on my mind, the embodiment of that challenge which exists eternally between man and the sea.

Enthusiasm made me wonder whether the idea of putting into port was pure defeatism. However, I could not argue against the truth that we were all dead tired; also that the wind was absolutely wrong for carrying on. Our short burst of progress would only be as far as Bull Point, and we were nearly there already. To continue beyond that corner would mean a dead beat in the open sea, while to make for Swansea involved an easy run before the wind. There would be no struggle to claw up to the Scarweather Lightvessel this time; indeed it could already be seen to leeward, nicely on the starboard beam.

At 0230 I paid off to the north and handed the helm over to Hutch, but my subsequent attempt to sleep was short. The stearing gear broke down. Investigation revealed a rigging screw adrift, the quadrant slamming about as the seas kicked at the rudder. Reconnecting was a very difficult job. In the confined space, Hutch and I had to assume positions that would have interested a contortionist. One of us struggled to hold the steering wires together as the other attempted to engage the screw threads. Several times success was frustrated as the kicking quadrant snatched the two parts of the bottle screw from us, but in the end we managed it.

Under way again the engineer's wife gallantly took the wheel while Hutch and I collapsed exhausted in the deck saloon. For me the effort also induced a vigorous seasickness—my first experience of the malady.

Pulling myself together, I went on deck to fix our position. The Scarweather was coming up abeam and I must set a new course. I noticed that the wind had eased considerably and the visibility, which had been excellent, was deteriorating. I studied the chart carefully and took note of the tidal streams. It was an interesting exercise. The course would not be entirely without dangers. I must consider the cross-tide in case visibility became poor, yet I must avoid making too great an allowance that would bring us up on the dangerous Mixon shoal to the west of the Mumbles, the south-west head of Swansea Bay.

Progressive weariness was now entering the nightmare stage. The reality of our situation became less obvious. It was a dreadful effort to move and unless urgent necessity demanded action all hands were sprawled on the deckhouse floor, indifferent to the wet, the heaving motion and the shambles around them. The female member of the crew was showing her worth. I am not sure of the details, but of the last 4 hrs. of the night the engineer's wife did 2 hrs. at the wheel while Hutch and I managed one a piece. After dawn brought its welcome light, she and I steered for another hour each, and that brought the *Millbay* round the Mumbles.

With relief, I read that pilots were stationed there. As at Avonmouth I was to be spared the task of manoeuvring the heavy vessel into dock. Because of my exhausted condition a wager against a show of skill would have been cheap. We soon sighted the pilot boat, its large pilot jack flying, and altered course towards it. Hutch came out and sorted out a "G" flag, the pilot signal. Then a stocky, vigorous man jumped aboard, and the *Millbay* motored safely into South Dock, Swansea.

The green crew now signed themselves off. This kind of yachting was all very well, but it appeared dangerous to exceed the stated dose. The skipper had only a few days more to the end of his demobilization leave, then he was committed to a shore job. In sending a full report of the passage to the owner, I could suggest nothing better than having another go at Christmas, when I expected more free time.

The offer was not accepted. The *Millbay* must be at Little-hampton as soon as possible, and another skipper and crew did the job. I received a small cheque in full settlement for my services, together with fair comment. The owner could not dismiss the loss of the motor tender as a gratuity to Neptune, nevertheless his remarks were magnanimous. The limitations of the self-styled yachtsmen that he had unearthed and prodded into promotion obviously were dawning on him; yet his yacht lay safely in Swansea Dock instead of piled up on some wild Bristol Channel shore. Progress had been meagre, but now he realized that only by engaging a skipper with extensive and proven competence in small sailing vessels could he have expected better.

For my part I was amazed that yacht owners were apparently prepared to accept a delivery skipper at his own valuation. I was also enthusiastic. With open arms I grasped the fact that anybody wishing to take on yacht movement was at liberty to do so without reference to officialdom. No licence, no Ministry of Transport certificates were demanded or thought necessary; and that suited me, a book-reared yachtsman with a Norfolk Broads background. In this age of essential paper qualifications, here was one occupation where accomplishment, not academic study and written examinations, established competence. Indeed it is clear to me now that none of the existing certificates for mates and master mariners by themselves indicate an ability to handle a small vessel at sea, particularly a small sailing yacht. Of course many merchant seamen are also competent yachtsmen, but apart from general principles their yachting skill will have been acquired aboard yachts.

It was this element of free competition, as well as the sea-going, that appealed to my sense of challenge. I was determined to have a go and discover whether the job could provide a reasonable financial reward. Only then could I justify such a career.

I gave up a chance to attend a Government teachers' training course for which I had been accepted, and planned to set up my yacht delivery shop in the spring of 1947. I wrote to several yacht brokers and learned that on occasions when their clients purchased yachts some distance from their own home ports, a skipper and crew to bring the new craft round were often required. One broker, who appeared to have practical experience himself, remarked that it was a very hard way of earning a living. He did not reveal whether the difficulties were financial or physical, but now I suspect he thought both.

CHAPTER 3

Raw Delivery Man

A FORTNIGHT before my first assignment was to start—delivery No. 1 I had designated it as soon as negotiations had been completed—I was contacted by telephone. Would I join the owner of a 16-ton ketch who was ready to sail for Scotland? Last year he had come south single-handed but, not wishing to persist with the hardships a lone sailor has to face, he wanted a mate for the return trip. I was asked to join immediately for a non-stop passage, Salcombe, Devon, to the Clyde. Again I had the chance of sailing under an experienced yachtsman and in this case, unlike the *Millbay*, there was no risk of cheap promotion to skipper. However, a different factor prevented my gaining fully from the opportunity—that scourge of the small vessel sailor—seasickness.

Within an hour of my arrival at Salcombe the Maurice Griffiths designed *Kanwara* stood seaward out of the estuary, past massive Bolt Head. A mere moderate swell lifted the yacht's bow gently, rhythmically, but even as I coiled the halyards I was aware of unfamiliar internal sensations, in no way pleasant. Doubtless a blood-drained pallor warned my skipper more than I realized, but soon I was painfully aware, the actor of a sorry play. My indifferent competence as a sailor deteriorated amidst dreadful digestive upheaval, and by next morning the yacht was virtually being managed by her owner single-handed, despite my lip service to duty and presence at the helm when it was my turn.

The breeze was so light that we were barely moving, even so I did not steer the straightest of courses. We ghosted erratically to the west while I remained amazed at the material manifestations of my malady, the distress it inflicted and that I should have succumbed at all, especially considering the weather. True, I had been briefly seasick on the *Millbay*, but that had followed exceptional exertion while reconnecting the steering wires, and anyway it was kid's stuff-after-the-party kind of thing, soon forgotten. This was real; an endless hell which took on a characteristic cycle of 20 min. duration. Five minutes comparative relief, then the torment of deterioration towards the next upheaval, a desperate cold sweat finally heralding flash point, then convulsion.

Around 24 hrs. out, still engaged in eliminative effort, supercolossal, I vaguely perceived an increase in the yacht's speed. Crawling on deck I saw that we were close-hauled, heeling, and making excellent speed towards the land ahead.

"Breeze has sprung from the south and is beginning to freshen," said the owner. "Looks to me as if we are in for a blow. I shall put into Helford River and see what happens during the night. The barometer is starting to fall again."

Whether he was concerned more with his suffering crew or, in fact, foresaw a severe gale, I do not know. Probably both matters were considered, but within 6 hrs. of *Kanwara*'s arrival in sheltered water a prolonged and furious sou'wester was established. It lasted nearly a week, and because of my previously arranged commitment (of which I had warned the owner before joining at Salcombe) I was unable to spare the time to complete the voyage. With punctilious thanks for my services, and never a hint of inadequacy, I was paid off, doubtless my skipper thinking that another pot-luck ring round yachting magazine advertisements could hardly bring forth a worse crew. Confidence and self-esteem somewhat shaken but, for a reason I barely understood, no change in determination to pursue my chosen career, I awaited my voyage to North Wales.

The owner of the 5-ton auxiliary sloop *Dilys* met me at Poole Station, bursting with enthusiasm for the project ahead. He had recently purchased this delightful Harrison Butler designed 23-footer and, with yachting experience confined to inland waters in India, had hired me to skipper him round to Barmouth, Merioneth, where he intended to keep *Dilys*. My recent exhibition of seafaring makes it difficult to see how I felt able to shoulder the responsibility—why I did not think of resigning right then. It was a good thing no report on previous conduct was available. But I realized that an immunity to seasickness often can be acquired, and I hoped my experience on *Kanwara* would not be repeated—at any rate not so severely.

The speed at which natural immunity to seasickness comes was once convincingly demonstrated during a trial with soldiers, with a view to finding a suitable anti-seasick drug. After a few days' experimenting the controllers of the test sadly recorded that none of the volunteers continued to succumb with or without their pills.

Despite unfavourable omens, our voyage in *Dilys* went off well in the face of fairly adverse conditions. Realizing the need for proper credentials, I afterwards solicited a testimonial from the owner, who kindly recorded complete confidence in his skipper, and noted that contrasting weather on the trip ranged from a flat calm to a moderate gale. This latter developed as a northerly blow on the first night out.

Norfolk Broads training had taught me how to reef properly, but there you did it with the yacht tied to the river bank. How to reef at sea, with the yacht bucking like a bronco, had been a matter of puzzling concern to me for some time. Therefore I had decided to shorten sail very early on—an important precaution if a novice yachtsman is to keep out of trouble.

Sailing under a press of canvas in heavy weather shatters morale rapidly and makes accident to gear more likely. Several times I have heard people blame their distress at sea on the fact that it was too rough to venture from the yacht's cockpit. This should never be; no competent skipper or crew should submit to such ideas. Excepting a jam aloft, sail can always be lowered given the will, and even if the halyard has jumped the masthead sheave something can be done towards dousing a mainsail, but you have got to clamber about.

Portland Bill was abaft the beam when the serious wind began. It came from the north-west very suddenly, and my work on the second reef seemed remote from Broadland techniques. After that I reefed the foresail and we lay a course north into 50-mile wide Lyme Bay where the weather shore would afford some shelter. Here we lay hove-to until dawn.

The wild night made a deep impression on the novice crew of that tiny yacht, and I count myself fortunate in experiencing vigorous wind off the land before encountering a real blow in completely unsheltered waters. Despite the short fetch the sea was quite rough. I remember the shambles that quickly grew in the cabin, particularly when my rather weak bunk board carried away, depositing me heavily on the cabin sole. The wind veered during the night but maintained its strength. In the morning we sailed along the coast and entered Exmouth in heavy weather. Safe arrival here represented a successful outcome of the first part of the voyage and confidence was boosted fully. Two days later there was a lull and we continued our way down Channel.

By nightfall the wind was piping up again, from the south-east this time, the full Channel fetch, and we clawed past Brixham and Start Point in rough seas. Then, the wind free, we had a grand run to Falmouth, another well deserved port of call in our view.

In those early days I accepted putting into harbour for frequent rests. Later, when family responsibilities made the economics more important, such amateurism became severely curtailed. Nevertheless, the voyage of the *Dilys* seemed prosperous enough. We soon left Falmouth, rounded Land's End and set off across 100 miles of open sea for the Smalls, the outlying rocks of south-west Wales. I claim to have spurned amateur tactics here. Pandering to their reluctance to lose sight of land for long, many novices navigating the west coast follow the shore up to Lundy Island, tending to embay themselves in the Bristol Channel approaches and making a longer passage besides courting substantial additional hazard.

The north coast of Cornwall is a wild, inhospitable place, with Padstow representing the only doubtful haven during rough weather—that estuary having at its mouth a pilotage problem ominously named the Doom Bar. Altogether it is an area to be avoided, especially if inexperienced. *Dilys* did so and rounded the Smalls some 19 hrs. after leaving the Longships lighthouse off Land's End—excellent time for a 20-ft. waterline sailing vessel. I remember the big Atlantic swell, cliff-like it seemed, rolling its impressive way from the south-west, the vigorous sea of the fresh southerly wind superimposed upon it. I remember being at the helm, glancing through the yacht's open companionway which revealed all the cabin and forepeak, and thinking what a little cockle-shell we were in. I remember the damp saltiness of that raw May which had yet showed little hint of summer, and how lack of sleep made it all rather a hardship that second day out of Falmouth.

I felt less enthusiastic about doing such work continuously. Fine for the amateur enjoying an exciting adventure a few times a year, but different when it is routine, summer and winter. After 14 years I am immune to these latter sentiments, but I grappled with them frequently during the early days.

Rounding the Smalls we headed for Fishguard for another rest; thence we had a comfortable sail across Cardigan Bay to Barmouth.

A week later I was adrift some 12 miles south of Milford Haven. Soon after leaving port, both vintage engines of the *Bonnie Jean* had broken down for reasons unknown. From another mysterious cause our 35-ft. motor cruiser began to leak badly and the bilge pump demonstrated a reluctance to do what bilge pumps are supposed to do. My crew and I spent a busy night bailing with an oil drum. The wind was light, the sea calm, but current unsettled weather made it likely that a vigorous sou'wester would soon start, in which case we would end up in smithereens on the forbidding South Wales coast.

At dawn a further inexplicable fact emerged on the credit side. A drill that had previously brought forth only the sound of a tired starter-motor suddenly made one engine burst into erratic life and with this we crawled thankfully back to Milford, where we suggested that the movement to Essex would be best done by lorry.

I returned home to face paternal exhortation to abandon a way of earning a living beset with such perilous snags. Out of concern for my welfare it was pointed out that I had completed only one job in three. Being pigheaded, these truths served but to harden my resolve. A week later I joined the 8-ton auxiliary ketch *Zita*, determined as ever.

Having 9 days' holiday, my cousin Cyril came with me to Scotland and, boarding the yacht in the Gareloch, we squeezed below deck amidst mountains of gear dumped willynilly in the tiny saloon by the caretakers.

Inexperience and continuous rain found us still sorting and stowing 3 days later, and this left my shipmate only a further 4 days for the voyage to the Helford River near Falmouth. The perhaps-we'll-have-a-fair-wind hope turned out 100 per cent wrong, and, with the near dud auxiliary affording no help, we took a day and a half to reach Ayr, barely out of the Clyde and still in the Firth. A day to recover and effect make-shift engine repairs permitted a further leg down the coast, in fog, as far as Port Patrick. We had not yet left Scotland, but here my cousin had to return to his banking routine. With no obvious replacement available, but schooled on Eric Hiscock's charming book *Wandering Under Sail* in which he describes single-handed cruises round Britain, I faced my first lone voyage.

"Peel is only 6 hours away," said the owner of the 50-ft. motor yacht alongside. "We are off this evening and will be there by midnight."

That sounded as good a start as any to my single-handed task, but I realized that 8-ton auxiliary *Zita* would take somewhat longer than the diesel driven vessel towering above me. I set off earlier and arrived in Peel much later—after an 18-hr. sail. The experience gave me confidence. Headwinds might lengthen the voyage but at least they enabled my vessel to look after herself with minimum attention to the helm. Sailing with the wind aft is the tiring time for the single-hander because, unless a yacht is fitted with a special self-steering device, it means steering continuously. Apart from the problem of keeping a look-out, sleep is out of the question.

Peel to Dun Laoghaire, in Dublin Bay, took 30 hrs.; then a beat down the Irish coast brought me to Arklow. From there freshening headwinds forced a call at Rosslare, where I had to take the mainsail ashore for repairs. Then the persistent sou'wester forced me to leeward as I struck out from Ireland for Land's End. I came up a little east of Padstow and entered that harbour safely for a much needed sleep.

Nor did the next hop bring me to the Cornish corner. Faint airs and fuel rationing sent me to Newquay, a tidal harbour only a few miles down the coast, where I had another rest.

Determined to conclude the drawn out voyage, I put to sea once more and stayed there for 3 days. I entered the Helford River one early dawn and handed the yacht over safely and in good order. I remember my considerable pride as I rowed away from *Zita*, a pretty vessel, trim and shipshape on her new moorings. Her delivery had taken over 3 weeks and, the contract having been a lump sum for the job, had brought me no great financial reward. Nevertheless the experience represented capital wealth and was well worth while.

The few jobs I landed that first year, the *Bonnie Jean* excepted, were surprisingly well found craft. I say surprisingly because, having few credentials, I had to be prepared to take on anything, and it was inevitable that I would eventually find myself committed to move something more properly belonging to the scrap heap.

When the British Army drove into Hamburg in 1945, probably many soldiers allowed their enthusiasm for victory to lead to excesses, some ill-advised. Thus in those hectic hours of triumph a young Scottish captain indulged a desire that had lain dormant for 6 years. He bought a yacht—he thought.

Later he shipped his converted German ship's lifeboat to Liverpool. From there the *Detlev* was to be sailed to his home port on the Clyde, but by this time he was back in civvy street and could not easily spare the time for the voyage. Thus came my final job in 1947, which brought the total to five deliveries completed, but although this vessel arrived safely I cannot say the voyage was a happy one.

Detlev's cabin was absolutely empty. She had no berths even, except a small cot in the forepeak. She was to be fitted out properly on arrival on the Clyde. A primus stove, paraffin, cooking and eating utensils and several old boxes to hold food was the sum total of luxury equipment. She had a mainsail and foresail, a bare minimum of cordage, a rubber dinghy, an old compass, a few shackles, odds and ends, and most important, a big bucket. There was an auxiliary motor under the cockpit but this was seized up and useless. Luckily, her spars and standing rigging were in fair order, and the mainsail was quite presentable. In fact, as converted ship's lifeboats go, she was a pretty little ship.

Happy at landing the job so late in the year, the problem of tiding over winter looming ahead, I was perfectly satisfied as I ghosted before a north-east breeze down the River Mersey, assisted by the strong ebb tide. Satisfaction received an early jolt as I passed the Crosby Lightvessel, still in the buoyed channel. An overtaking coaster, whose skipper had heard a yacht was bound for the Clyde, kindly hailed me to tell of a south-east gale imminent in the Irish Sea. A return to moorings would have been prudent but, in the existing light breeze, impossible until the tide turned. Thus I decided to continue, consoling myself that a south-east wind would be a fair one. I knew that a yacht will run safely before heavy weather, providing sail is shortened accordingly. I did not bargain for mine starting to leak!

I must have been about half-way to the Isle of Man when it began to blow. Rain and poor visibility accompanied the wind and, together with considerable compass deviation which earlier I had managed to check only roughly and which was caused by the steel deck, faced me with navigational worries. I also had to bail almost continuously to keep pace with the leaking that developed as quickly as the wind rose.

Fortunately the craft maintained a fair course under foresail alone which, in the prevailing weather, was sufficient to give excellent progress. After what seemed an age Langness Point loomed out of the driving drizzle, some 3 miles distant, and by some means long forgotten I identified it correctly. I altered course for Chicken Rock, the southern extremity of the island, but as I passed Port St. Mary the foresail split. Hauling in the mess, I hoisted the main, duly reefed, and close-reached toward this harbour. I entered safely, to be congratulated by various locals, members of the lifeboat crew, who had sighted me and were expecting a distress call at any minute.

All praise to the owner. On being told the full details, he managed to get time off to join me. If anybody else must share these perils he would be that person.

We coasted round the Isle of Man stopping at Port Erin, then, after reaching half-way to the Mull of Galloway, the foresail split once more, prompting a run back to Peel. The weather persisted rough and when we did reach the Mull we clawed along that rugged Scottish coast in something approaching a full gale. The wind eased off Corsewall Point and Peel to Girvan took altogether 24 hrs., mostly tough sailing and continuous bailing. Even on arrival in harbour the yacht went on making water.

The last leg to the Clyde was peaceful, though steady bucket work was essential. We were winning though, and the poor old ship at least had built a bond of fellowship between her two mariners.

As we sailed past Wee Cumbrae light, the entrance to the

Clyde, I remember a pang of sympathy as Jim completed his umpteenth bailing session.

"There! I think she's taking up a little at last. Didn't seem so much that time!"

But I am afraid he was an optimist.

I earned that delivery fee, but felt sorry to take it.

CHAPTER 4

Crews that have Made it Possible

I THOUGHT the comfort of a 35-ft. "Girl Pat" type motor sailer would be an enticing introduction to yacht voyaging for Joan, and the little vessel appeared spick and span when she boarded her at Greenwich Pier. I had collected *Finvola* from the Upper Thames that morning.

Built to a standard design, the "Girl Pats" have comfortable accommodation for their size, consisting of a small double cabin aft, a large saloon amidships with convertible dinette furnishing, galley, W.C. and a good fore cabin. Full power is provided by a single engine and an auxiliary ketch-rigged sail plan affords progress in a fair wind, enables you to look after yourself should the machinery fail, and steadies the yacht in a beam sea.

Together we would deliver her to the Clyde via the east coast and the Forth and Clyde canal.

Delight became tempered with concern immediately we cast off from the pier and set off down the busy tideway. The steering broke down, putting the yacht under doubtful command.

"Go down into the aft cabin," I told Joan. "And heave on the steering quadrant according to what I say. That will be our only way to get ourselves alongside a moored barge, where we can reconnect the steering wires."

Hastily I showed her the cramped space where she must operate the rudder by hand. It was going to be a rough job because she would have nothing like the leverage she would have with a comparable tiller. I returned to the engine controls and with Joan, the human steering engine, we managed to bring our vessel along-side a moored barge and tie up safely. During the manoeuvre I saw fit to bellow a stock ultimatum to another river user:

"Get out of my way—I can't get out of yours!"

Afterwards Joan said: "That scared me stiff. I thought the end was imminent—underneath a 10,000-ton liner."

"It wasn't so bad as that," I replied. "In fact we would have won out on it. A rowing eight was going like mad, straight at us!"

We soon reconnected the steering wire which had parted at a rigging screw, seized it with wire, and proceeded. We called at Great Yarmouth for a rest and more fuel; then we set out across the Wash in unsettled weather.

Working watch and watch, 3 hrs. each, Joan came up at 0300 in the morning. The stars of midnight had vanished, replaced by blustery rain; the calm of the evening had become a short vicious sea, which gave our little vessel a wild motion. The steering position was in the open, aft of the saloon, and had only a wind-screen shelter. Complete blackness was relieved by the loom of the navigation lights and the dimly lit binnacle. Joan hung on grimly. You had to do that all the time but it seemed hard to concentrate on anything else besides when first coming from the comparative comfort below.

"Lord. . . . He must have had a lot of guts!"

I preferred to tell her the course to steer and the things to look out for, but queried her comment.

"Columbus of course. He had to do all this and not even know where he was going. At least you know when we shall reach the land again—I hope!"

Which makes you realize what we owe the pioneers who left our shores long before there was a lighthouse on Flamborough Head—or a lightship off the Outer Dowsing Bank.

Squalls and rain crossed our path all across the Wash and the Humber approaches but when we closed with Flamborough, Yorkshire's easternmost point, evening sunshine broke through. We plugged on under the rugged coast and entered Scarborough to refuel—there to remain two days because a true gale sprang from the north next morning. On our way again, we completed the next hop to Granton in 36 hrs.; from thence proceeding to Grangemouth to enter the canal. No further time was wasted in delivering the motor sailer to the Clyde where a pleasant reception was given us. However, in a roundabout way we heard somebody had offered the comment: "No wonder he took so long—taking his wife as crew!"

You might think I had been trying to teach Joan to drive a car. That is always a husband's lost cause but there is plenty of evidence to show that yacht voyaging is not the prerogative of the male.

A classic example of the prejudice was revealed at an American Boat Show. The story claims that when transatlantic yachtswoman, Ann Davison, the only one of the fair sex to have completed this crossing single-handed, stood by her 5-tonner, *Felicity Ann*, on display, a male visitor to the exhibition read the caption and turned to her.

"Honey, don't you go getting those ideas!"

As for *Finvola* I still think we made a good passage.

A year later Joan and I collected a 20-ft. cabin cruiser at Littlehampton, a standard boat built by A. R. C. Marine Ltd., which had to be taken to Ireland.

"A comfortable little cruiser, robust, seaworthy, competitively priced."

"A big motor dinghy with a roof over the fore part!"

These are two ways of describing the same craft, according to whether you are a proud owner or a struggling delivery skipper faced with a lengthy coastal passage.

The leg down Channel was comfortable to start with, but after a call at Dartmouth (surprised at the fuel consumption) we encountered a headwind, Force 3, and the ride became purgatory. At Penzance, where we were gale-bound a while, we faced the fact that our little engine's fuel consumption was sky-high above normal and that the next 150 miles hop to the nearest port on the Emerald Isle was going to be a problem. After soliciting inconclusive opinions from local mechanics, our answer was to load a total of 67 gallons of petrol, 50 gallons of which was in 5-gallon oil drums and these completely filled the cockpit, the whole after part of our vessel. Well laden we motored round the Land's End corner and set out across the sea to Ireland. The trip took just over 24 hrs., during which time the calm after the last blow strengthened into another vigorous wind from the south-south-west. Buoyant and stiff, even if uncomfortable, our tiny craft took the rising sea well. Had we been punching into it, a different story would have been told, particularly considering the undiagnosed engine fault which was becoming progressively worse. But running before a big sea in haze and rain, the Tuskar Rock was sighted that following morning. We turned thankfully towards Rosslare with a bare 10 gallons of fuel to spare. Normally this would have run our engine another 14 hrs. but now she was drinking nearly 3 gallons of petrol every hour—an amazing feat for a motor of her size.

Repair facilities at Rosslare for our sort of trouble were non-existent but, receiving all information by telephone, the owner said he would join us if we would continue as she was. We did, and despite the headwind that came as the trough moved north-east, and despite further engine deterioration which eventually snuffed out two cylinders, we struggled into Dun Laoghaire safely.

"Sure I'll be fixing the engine soon . . ." and our client went ahead to fix his delivery crew with a V.I.P. reception—so often my experience when taking yachts to Ireland.

We left the next day. Joan read the Sunday paper and said: "Look, somebody else has just done a trip almost exactly like ours." She read out the paragraph: "While a gale forced merchant vessels to run for shelter, a man and a woman crossed to Ireland in an open boat. . . . They are Mr. and Mrs. P. T. Hayworthy and taking turns at the helm they made the crossing from Land's End to Rosslare in 24 hrs. . . ."

I pondered a while.

"That must be us."

And, allowing for journalese which will promote a strong wind to a gale, call an open cockpit cabin launch an open boat, give people wrong names, describe yachts and trawlers in Rosslare as "merchant vessels" and assume that because they are there they are stormbound, I suppose the report was a fair one.

With teaching still her main occupation, Joan was my crew during the long summer vacations only, but over succeeding years she logged many sea miles. Coasting extended to a voyage to Italy, when we successfully delivered the 39-ton auxiliary cutter *Zephyr* despite a numerous but rather unsatisfactory crew. These consisted of the new owner's permanent skipper, that superlative *marineiro*, Giovanni Scottini, plus Joan and a stomachally unsound English amateur yachtsman, together with two

Italians, friends of the owner and rather non-nautical. Language difficulties added to other troubles; three spoke English, three Italian; none were bi-lingual. Skippers do not count; thus, on arrival Giovanni told his boss that he and Joan alone had brought the yacht out.

The following year we delivered the 25-ton auxiliary schooner *Zita* (ex-*Grey Dawn*) to Greece. After one crew member had to leave at Gibraltar, Bill King, Joan and I commenced a slow passage along the North African coast with strong headwinds and other difficulties prompting calls at Algiers and Bizerta. Then we headed out into the Malta Channel, hoping for more favourable weather. It came with a vengeance, easy to start with, a moderate south-west breeze, but steadily it hardened, finally reaching gale in a series of dreadful squalls. Yet, coming from astern, it was a fair wind and there was no check on progress. Standing the first trick of the night, Joan had the sailing measured up as she steered *Zita* towards the southern tip of Sicily before steep, growling crests. But the onset of blinding, continuous lightning with accompanying thunder began to unnerve her, until she called the watch below in the hope that the skipper had some special trick of seamanship that would keep us secure against this new peril. I poked my head into the torrential rain that mingled with the spray roaring past horizontally and, in drawing my attention to the phenomenon that was almost an a.c. lighting circuit, it was clear she hoped I would not fail.

I am reminded of Edward Young's experience in the same part of the world, described in his book *One of Our Submarines*:

> Feeling an absolute fool I called the Captain on the voice-pipe and told him that we were in the middle of severe electrical storm, that the visibility was nil, and that in my opinion it would be advisable to dive until it was over. . . .
>
> It took me some weeks to live down my decision to dive because of a mere thunderstorm. But in spite of numerous arguments, nobody produced a final answer to the question: What *does* happen when lightning strikes a submarine?

What happens, indeed, on a yacht with its mast reaching 60 ft. into the supercharged heavens, its steel shrouds groping aloft to embrace a million volts and deposit them into her frail hull? Probably wires connecting the shroud plates to the keel bolts would help, but I do not think *Zita* had such an innovation.

43

My only answer was to change the watch; make another of us sit out and witness the electrical turmoil.

In the way honourable discharge may be obtained from the women's forces, Joan stopped yachting that year. Caroline Haward was launched into the world and other crews were required for my voyages. From then on the job had to achieve greater efficiency, the business angle assuming more importance as family responsibilities came into being. No "ticket" for me: we males must soldier on, being able only to offer willing co-operation in these projects.

These last few paragraphs spotlight the importance of the crew in delivering small vessels. That single-handed yacht cruising is a practical proposition has been proven many times, particularly by ocean wanderers. But though I have mentioned two of the various occasions when I safely delivered yachts in this way, for practical purposes, when one trip follows another and a full amount of work must be accomplished, a crew is essential. Too much single-handed work on the coast invites eventual illness through lack of sleep and relating hardships and the jobs will always take longer.

I have enjoyed the company of many capable and agreeable shipmates, many of whom are now my good friends. To them this book should be dedicated. They have endured not just the sea and decrepit yachts, but this author in all his moods, his temper and his sarcasm. Very few have ever taken umbrage but have done their duty to the end—which goes to show the great fascination yacht voyaging holds.

That a good crew member will not necessarily make a good skipper is easily understood but it is less often realized that a good skipper may be dreadful if he goes as somebody's crew. He must refrain from giving the orders, contain himself over those matters that are the prerogative of the captain. If he cannot, a dismal situation results, inconducive to friendship, mental health or safe navigation. You have a yacht with two skippers. A good crew is a competent sailor who does not take a wrong step here.

My classic illustration was given by Bill King when we delivered the 63-ton auxiliary ketch *Ceol Mara* to Italy and were held up by a full-blooded Levanter at the approaches to Gibraltar Strait. Anchored in partial shelter off Barbate in a mere $2\frac{1}{2}$

fathoms, the 55 fathoms of cable veered was bar taut permanently because of the continuous tremendous wind. The yacht never snubbed despite the short, steep sea. She could not; it was as if she was secured to the end of a long, rigid rod. Reports of the wind came over the radio from fishermen who gave up attempts to cross the Straits: 160 kilometres per hour was their estimate.

If our cable parted we should have little time to avoid being blown ashore, or over the Banco de Trafalgar where a dreadful sea could be expected. Setting any canvas in the prevailing weather would be a Herculean task and our auxiliary power could have done little for us. I confided my fears to Bill and, observing non-committal disinterest, I said: "Aren't you worried about the chain parting and landing on Cape Trafalgar in smithereens?"

"Not at all," he replied. "That's your headache. You're the skipper. Don't come upsetting me with it."

And he meant it: which humbled me into realizing that such a superb crew deserved a very special skipper, not one who sowed despondency. Luckily our cable held though, on getting it a day later, all the galvanizing flaked off as it rode over the gipsy. Every link had stretched.

Most of my crews are amateur yachtsmen who come for the trip on an expenses paid basis. They are preferable in many ways to casually engaged professional hands. They facilitate an economic delivery charge and in these days of high costs it assists yacht owners who, in the end, finance the whole yachting industry. Redundancy for professional yacht crews does not come into it. A reservoir of amateur hands exists. Later some will become yacht owners themselves and contribute to the industry. They want voyaging experience. It is fair that they have the chance. Nearly always they give capable service; often they are first-rate crews.

Good professional yacht hands prefer permanent or seasonal jobs and they will only take on a run job to fill in time, but I have sailed with several and know what great shipmates and fine seamen they are.

A real hazard to the yacht owner looking for a crew is the deadbeat barside sailor (saloon or public) whose stirring yarns suggest the great mariner, willing to ship aboard any vessel, yacht or otherwise. In reality he knows little of seamanship, less of yachts and as a shipmate he is strictly incompatible. Often unrecognizable by the landsman or inexperienced yachtsman, even competent skippers, against their better judgement, may sign him on if their need of crew is desperate. Inevitably he lasts only as long as it takes to find a replacement. Then he is back at his favourite place, ill-earned beer money in his pocket and another tall yarn in his head. It is in error and a blight on yachting that such characters are sometimes classified by disillusioned novice yacht owners as "professional yacht hands".

CHAPTER 5

With "Benbow" to Italy

MORE and more people are turning to sailing and motor boating for pleasure: yachting today prospers but the style is altering in this era of the common man. The old conception of the yachtsman with his fabulous wealth, vast vessel and disciplined crew is losing its hold. Sailing must always be more expensive than long walks into the country; nevertheless enthusiasts of the sea swell in numbers and the answer now is smaller yachts but plenty of them.

"What is so wonderful about this yachting?" the land-lubber may think to himself. He may remember being on the promenade at Cowes, Torquay or Hunter's Quay and have a vague recollection of the grace and the beauty of big fellows racing off the shore. Perhaps they were more than just part of the scenery, but he cannot work out how they were operated and does not really believe that those pretty white sails really can voyage any distance or survive any storms. Acceptance of an idea often occurs only after an initial battle against it: disbelief is often a start, something to work on. I shall try to give a picture by telling you of a particular voyage of some 2,000 miles in *Benbow*, now gone from Britain.

She is a fine modern sailing yacht of 53 tons. Designed by Robert Clark and built by Camper & Nicholsons, rigged as a Bermudian cutter—that means she has a single, very tall mast—and her normal sail area totals 2,000 sq. ft. Ocean racing rather than luxurious accommodation was the prime consideration, but she was built with three double cabins and the after one, the owner's stateroom, would do credit to any cross-Channel steamer. Other berths are available in the saloon, where bunks fold out of the panelling above the settees, and there is also room for two in the forecastle—right up in the eyes of the ship. The galley has a gas cooker, "fridge" and sink, and though it is no mean task to prepare food in a small vessel that will take on a vigorous motion in a seaway, an experienced yachtsman or sea cook has every chance of turning out a hot meal.

Tucked under the main companionway is a small diesel engine, powerful enough to help the yacht during calm weather and particularly useful for entering harbour or a congested anchorage. The engine also drives a dynamo to charge the batteries and provide electricity throughout the vessel. It is surprising how many landsmen believe that an auxiliary engine in a sailing yacht will serve some purpose in bad weather, but in fact during a gale of wind, one of these small motors would be as much use as a motor scooter engine in a double decker bus.

My job was to skipper this yacht from Sandbank on the Clyde to Porto Fino near Genoa, Italy. My crew consisted of four experienced amateur yachtsmen, one of whom, Bill King, has sailed many thousands of miles with me on other yacht delivery voyages. Besides these, I was to take an Italian professional yacht hand and two guests of the new owner—also Italians. One only of the Italians could speak a little English and none of us knew a word of Italian. Shades of *Zephyr*, briefly mentioned earlier, but this crew was a good one; yet the Tower of Babel had nothing on us!

Alex Robertson's had fitted out our vessel for sea and on joining there was little to be done other than check the sails and gear, buy stores for the voyage and have a compass adjuster attend to our compass and make known such errors that he could not eliminate.

At dawn on 9th August 1957 fresh squalls with rain were blowing into the Holy Loch where we lay at a mooring, our preparations nearly complete. The weather was not ideal, but for once the Scots were being let off lightly compared to the Sassenachs. A deep depression in the Atlantic was heading for glorious Devon, causing dismay (though probably not surprise) to those thousands of holiday-makers who reckoned that part of Britain stood the best chance of sunshine. The Meteorological office was already issuing gale warnings, but in area Malin, which includes the Clyde, the terms "fresh or strong" were considered appropriate.

We left in the afternoon. The rain had stopped and the wind obliged by shifting more to a northerly point, thus blowing behind us when we set our course out of the Firth of Clyde. When voyaging under sail the direction of the wind, no less than its strength, is of great importance. It will make or mar: prosper your journey or subject you to torturous progress coupled with acute discomfort. A modern sailing yacht can go against the wind more efficiently than any of her forebears, commercial, naval, or otherwise. She can lie a course to within 50 degrees of the wind (some will manage even 45 degrees) and by changing tacks—going from side to side against the wind—she will gradually move up towards her goal. It is a slow game, however, compared to heading straight along a desired course; therefore we on *Benbow* were lucky with our following wind as we surged past the Cumbrae Islands and down the Firth, leaving Aran Island to starboard. A good beginning—but our fortune soon changed. We were becalmed at midnight and turned to the auxiliary engine for progress. All through Saturday we plodded down the Irish Sea in faint airs and drizzle.

The wind came again on Sunday at midday, after we had cleared the Tuskar, a rock some 6 miles off the south-east tip of Ireland. We were entering the part known to the weather men as "sea area Lundy", and were on a course south-west for Land's End, the westernmost extremity of England, 130 miles distant. It blew in strength from the west-north-west and at last our yacht began to show what she could do. The noisy, petty engine was stopped and under full sail she heeled over, picked up her skirts and was off. Leaping and bounding buoyantly over the rising sunlit seas, her foredeck thrust through the creaming crests or glistening in the sun when she lifted above them. Her crew were robbed of the easy, even-keel life and had to hang on—whether above or below decks. Harnessing the power of the wind, our little vessel was careering along faster than the average coasting steamer. The patent log—the instrument that records distance run by towing a fin rotator on a long line—was spinning merrily astern, and soon disclosed that we had travelled 29 miles through the water in 3 hrs.: 9.6 knots. That means good going for a vessel only 50 ft. long on the water-line.

Often a fresh breeze will ease at sunset, but it can be a brief lull. Darkness may find all hands shortening sail just when they thought a comfortable night was their lot. On this occasion, however, I had a hunch that our wind would not persist all night, and we hung on to our canvas, revelling in the progress and the ship's newly found vigour. With her fine racing record, *Benbow* was obviously used to hard work.

At dawn the breeze dropped light; then faint. We were closing the Longships Lighthouse that stands guard over a reef of rocks $1\frac{1}{4}$ miles off Land's End. The tidal stream divides here, flooding up the north Cornish coast as well as into the English Channel. Cooked up by a heavy swell, the legacy of the fresh wind—now gone—tumbling seas marked the demarcation point: a boiling inferno of white horses that crashed about willynilly, without rhyme or reason.

The yacht entered the area without wind to steady her and sails, mast, boom and gear flogged wildly, as though a huge demon was intent on shaking her to bits. Slamming to and fro, a heavy bronze slide holding the mainsheet fractured and the triple pulley block shot out to the end of the boom. Robbed of adequate purchase, it took three of us to haul the sail flat and control the spar. Until repairs could be effected, trimming the mainsail would now be a difficult task.

Once through the Longships overfalls, we bore away for the Runnelstone Buoy; then towards Mount's Bay. Soon we tied up in Penzance, and set about final preparations for our departure from Britain.

England to Gibraltar in one hop was the intention and this leg involves crossing the notorious Bay of Biscay, wide open to the North Atlantic. Gales may spring up from any direction and a yacht could be caught far out of reach of shelter, with no alternative but to ride it out. This is not so bad as it sounds because a small vessel is safer lying-to in a gale far out at sea than if she were running for port in bad weather. Visibility in gales is often poor and a landfall may be bad. On closing the coast a sailing craft may run into shoals or reefs before finding out where she is, and when the weather is really bad she will have a hard job to claw off such dangers into the teeth of the wind. That is the time sails blow out or rigging gives under the strain. Disaster will follow.

Unless a skipper is completely confident about making port, the correct action in gales is to avoid the coast and ensure there is plenty of sea-room. Sail must be reduced or stowed completely in good time and the ship will then ride the seas like a duck, making relatively slow drift with the wind.

We rushed through our jobs in Penzance. Fuel and fresh water tanks were topped up, extra Calor gas bottles bought, rigging overhauled, the mainsheet slide replaced by a new fitting and attention was given to the dynamo on the engine that was not working properly. We were ready on Tuesday afternoon, but the B.B.C. cried "halt". A south-west gale was brewing in the Channel approaches: headwinds would increase to Force 8 during the night and, were we to set off, we should soon be denied progress unless we risked damage and condoned the certainty of hardship. We stayed where we were, thankfully avoiding both possibilities.

The gale was short and sharp and, because winds tend to blow anti-clockwise round the depressions that are generally the cause of our rough weather, as it passed eastward it veered north-west and eased a little. That was the signal to be off, and on Wednesday, 14th August, *Benbow* motored out of Penzance, hoisting a double-reefed mainsail and small foresail. Soon we were thrashing to the south-west, across the mouth of the English Channel towards Cape Finisterre, north-west Spain, far distant across the Bay of Biscay.

Besides our two Italian guests, who did not stand watches, we were a crew of six. This enabled us to work 4 hrs. on and 8 hrs. off and have a companion while at the helm. By splitting the evening 1600–2000 watch into two parts we avoided standing the same watches each day. This is called working the dogs, and I carried the idea further. Every other day the second hand in the first dog watch worked right through to 2000, thus finding a new mate on these occasions and it meant that Natalie, our Italian yacht hand, had to practise sign language on a new student every 2 days. Not receiving an explanation in Italian, it was a long time before he believed that we had a system at all.

On most voyages, when I carry two or more as crew, I like to establish a cookery and ship's chores routine as early as possible. Seasickness troubles often disorganize things on the first day out because, although most people can struggle with watchkeeping duties while under the weather, preparing food, or in fact any job below decks, is nearly always beyond them. Unless an enthusiast can be found, or the luxury of a professional sea cook indulged in, cookery is best shared; but it is pointless fixing a daily rota only to find that the first candidate is permanently holding the rail to his chest in the traditional seamanlike manner. Alternatively, a robust, horribly healthy pirate will roar "Come and get it!" and learn that a bunch of green-cheeked, bunk-addicted farmers must have eaten something that disagreed with them.

Provided you do not try nibbling to "keep up your strength" while your digestive processes are in reverse, seasickness will generally clear up in 12 to 48 hrs. and you will then enjoy complete freedom from it for at least the rest of the voyage. This is a considered statement, knowing the distress of the immunization period—when faith in recovery is at its lowest ebb. I emphasize that taking even one dry biscuit during seasickness will only prolong your agony and do nothing to nourish you. Eat nothing and drink only what is absolutely necessary until you *relish* food. Simple you may think, but in fact, being habit-bound to meals at set intervals, many force themselves into taking biscuits, barley sugar or dry bread. The result is generally a digestive tragedy which interferes with what is usually progress, however slow and obscure, towards immunity.

Many experienced yachtsmen will disagree with this, maintaining that they themselves have warded off seasickness by forcing themselves to eat. In my view they have recovered from a slight initial tummy tremor *despite* their ill-advised action.

Above all, distrust the man with the simple remedy. It is not due just to psychology, just lack of fresh air, just unwise diet, just fear, lack of work, lack of balance—"giving to the ship's motion". These factors may contribute towards seasickness, but the causes of the malady are more complex and vary with the individual.

Some modern drugs can stave off the worst effects of seasickness but it is best first to try for natural immunity. The side-effects of some pills are unpleasant and may result in your being less fit for work. The long-term effects are unknown. Sometimes people reap enervating side-effects and seasickness as well. Some do not, but immunity, if given, seldom appears to compare with natural immunity.

Once most stomachs are adjusted to seagoing, the best routine is a new cook daily. This gives everybody the chance to demonstrate his culinary art and the sooner the rota can be established the better. A crew of six, like ours on *Benbow*, is a luxury that enables two persons to be on watch together. Generally I carry a smaller crew which does not run to this. I show on this page

SOME WATCHKEEPING ROUTINES FOR YACHT VOYAGING

Ship's Company: 3	1st day	2nd day	3rd day		
Midnight–0300	Skipper	3rd hand	Mate		
0300–0600	3rd hand[1]	Mate[1]	Skipper[1]		
0600–0900	Mate	Skipper	3rd hand		
0900–noon	Skipper	3rd hand	Mate		
Noon–1500	Mate	Skipper	3rd hand		
1500–1630	Skipper	3rd hand	Mate		
1630–1800	3rd hand	Mate	Skipper		
1800–2100	Mate	Skipper	3rd hand		
2100–midnight	Skipper	3rd hand	Mate		

Ship's Company: 4	1st day	2nd day	3rd day	4th day	
Midnight–0300	4th hand[1]	3rd hand[1]	Mate[1]	Skipper[1]	
0300–0600	3rd hand	Mate	Skipper	4th hand	
0600–0900	Mate	Skipper	4th hand	3rd hand	
0900–noon	Skipper	4th hand	3rd hand	Mate	
Noon–1500	3rd hand	Mate	Skipper	4th hand	
1500–1800	Mate	Skipper	4th hand	3rd hand	
1800–2100	Skipper	4th hand	3rd hand	Mate	
2100–midnight	4th hand	3rd hand	Mate	Skipper	

Ship's Company: 5	1st day	2nd day	3rd day	4th day	5th day
Cook for the day (does no watches)	5th hand	4th hand	3rd hand	Mate	Skipper
Midnight–0300	4th hand	3rd hand	Mate	Skipper	5th hand
0300–0600	3rd hand	Mate	Skipper	5th hand	4th hand
0600–0900	Mate	Skipper	5th hand	4th hand	3rd hand
0900–noon	Skipper	5th hand	4th hand	3rd hand	Mate
Noon–1500	4th hand	3rd hand	Mate	Skipper	5th hand
1500–1630	3rd hand	Mate	Skipper	5th hand	4th hand
1630–1800	Mate	Skipper	5th hand	4th hand	3rd hand
1800–2100	Skipper	5th hand	4th hand	3rd hand	Mate
2100–midnight	4th hand	3rd hand	Mate	Skipper	5th hand

my usual watchkeeping rosters for ship's companies of three, four and five people. Encourage pride, and each cook will try to out-shine his fellows and good meals are the result. The real test comes, however, when the yacht meets bad weather. Then the quality, generosity and regularity of the catering quickly degenerates. Organized meals falter and each hand tends to look after himself. Washing up lags behind dishing up; heating soup or even boiling water becomes an athletic feat, later a frantic task. The galley grows shambolic: dirty implements pile in the sink amidst the English-man's staff of life, tea leaves. Sea water, squirting through the skylight and trickling down the mast, flushes waste food to lee-ward and the listing floor becomes a morass of spilt jam, butter,

[1] Cook for the day.

sugar. In really bad weather only true hunger brings customers into this hell-hole. But the cook of the day must leave that galley as he found it in the morning.

While the shipboard routine established itself, *Benbow* was showing her paces. The fresh north-west wind persisted. Blowing directly on the beam, it drove the yacht at 10 knots for hour after hour. We were across the Channel in half a day and, passing some 60 miles west of Ushant, the outlying island on the north-west tip of France, we surged out over the Bay of Biscay. The big Atlantic seas lifted the yacht bodily and pure white crests, bursting in the way, occasionally drove across her. We were making short work of an area that can stop a yacht in her tracks and give even huge liners a severe trouncing.

Exactly 3 days out of Penzance we sighted Cape Finisterre. Biscay was behind us and the progress continued with the yacht bowling before a strong northerly wind. This is the region of the "Portuguese Trades". Not strictly a trade wind, which blows slantwise towards the equator from lower latitudes, the northerlies off north-west Spain and Portugal frequently persist for days, particularly in summer, and are of great assistance to sailing vessels southward bound from Britain. Going the other way, of course, is a different story, when a yacht may be advised to head out into the Atlantic clear of the coast until a lighter breeze or a favourable westerly wind is encountered.

Another 2 days of good sailing and we were round Cape St. Vincent, heading for the Straits of Gibraltar, 180 miles distant. It looked as if we were in for a fast passage. There are two distinctive types of weather in the Straits of Gibraltar, each taking its name from the wind that prevails. The Ponente brings fine weather with west or south-west winds, while the Levanter is the easterly, bad weather wind. Geographical features—high mountains on each side of the Straits—have a funnelling effect and act as a super-charger. Converged into the 10-mile wide channel, a vigorous Levanter will burst out into the Atlantic like a shot from a gun. In effect it sprays out: the wind blows north-east down the North African coast, south-east up the Spanish side and if you approach directly from the west you will encounter a screaming easterly gale. There is no way round and to a sailing vessel bound for the Mediterranean it amounts to an impenetrable barrier. From whichever angle she approaches, she will find a dead headwind so that tacking to the opposite coast hardly helps. The Levanter is a strong wind—really strong, fiendish in fact—and it creates a very steep, violent sea as formidable to a yacht as an anti-tank ditch to a tracked vehicle. Slightly more westerly winds prevail in the region compared to the easterly, but when a yachtsman hits a real Levanter in the approaches to Gibraltar Straits he remembers it for life.

Within hours of rounding Cape St. Vincent we met a short swell directly on the bow. The ominous message was irrefutable: 150 miles ahead the Levanter was, or had been, blowing out of the Straits of Gibraltar. Hoping for the latter possibility, we plugged on, our sails barely filling to a faint breeze, the auxiliary engine helping out.

The wind began to veer and eventually came straight from the east-south-east and dead against us. Then it freshened. At 0400 on that August morning I called all hands to double-reef the mainsail, and during the short time they took turning-to the wind increased to a moderate gale. While we lowered the sail half-way and hauled down the reef pennants, a terrific squall struck. We secured the cringles down to the boom (making them the lower corners of the reefed sail) but in the furious wind it was impossible to roll up the unwanted canvas. The yacht, lying broadside to the rapidly rising sea, was being hurled over to very steep angles of heel and the wave tops, slashed bodily from the ocean by the terrible wind, cut like huge hailstones into the crew as they struggled in the darkness. Try as they might, they could not douse the billowing mass of iron-hard canvas. The reef points, the many small lengths of ropes sewn into the sail for this purpose, could not be pulled together. The black night, the slippery, wildly bucking deck, the constant need to hang on (or hook on with safety belts) finally pronounced the task as madly impossible. The whole mainsail must be dropped. It came down easily but had to be doused and prevented from being flogged to ribbons, and it therefore engulfed the reefed portion, making the original task no easier. After 2 hrs. of exhausting ourselves without effect it was clear that the wind, now in severe gale category, was too strong for even a close-reefed mainsail and I therefore decided to continue under the two foresails.

We put about intending to make a northerly course, but during the operation, the jib came adrift and, unsupported at one corner, billowed out like a flag. A patent quick release shackle on the clew had let us down. We dived to the mast, cast off the halyard and managed to haul the sail down with only minor damage.

Next we erected the gallows type crutches on which the main boom, not now in use, must be housed. Lumbering about as the ship rolled, the huge spar must be dropped into the recess on the crutch. It was a matter of timing: the topping lift, the wire rope that supports the boom when the mainsail does not, had to be slacked at just the right instant; then hands hauled triumphantly on the mainsheet and secured it.

Only the staysail remained set and with this we scudded away north towards the Spanish coast, where I hoped there would be less wind. Dawn came, the wind easing, and under our reduced canvas progress became very slow.

After most of us had rested (and possibly slept) we double-reefed the main properly and set it. Close-hauled, we heeled over as we drove as closely as possible into the wind and, in the late afternoon, came up on the coast north of Cadiz. We were some 50 miles from the Straits of Gibraltar. We tacked down towards our goal and the wind began to strengthen again. Soon it was back to gale force. We reached Cadiz Bay where there is more sheltered water but the wind became worse, screaming off the land and laying the yacht down until about a sixth of the whole deck space was permanently under the water. Night approached again. Below decks was a shambles. Sleep was impossible.

Previous experience had convinced me that the only way to beat into the Straits against the Levanter was by hugging the coast, and this would demand careful pilotage to ensure we cleared the shoals and broken water lying off Cape Trafalgar. Even as we struggled across Cadiz Bay in short tacks the weather seemed to worsen. The nearer we approached Tarifa the more hectic would things become. My guess was that just westward of the Straits the wind would be something like a continuous explosion. Later we learned that Spanish trawlers, abandoning their attempts to cross over to North Africa, estimated it at hurricane force. To a small vessel, a bad Levanter is a barrier—impossible, hellish.

On *Benbow* I had a good crew. No dismay, no thoughts of not continuing, nobody hinted at the joy of a night in port. Had I determined to batter a path to Gibraltar they would all have been with me—to the last shred of canvas. But the sensible action was to stop this head-on collision with the elements. Were no port of refuge near, we would have stowed our sails and ridden it out under bare poles, consolidating our position, maintaining as much as possible our hard won progress. At it was, the inviting port of Cadiz lay a few miles to windward, its bright lights twinkling tantalizingly, beckoning. There we would find shelter and rest. For that goal we continued to drive our little vessel into the storm's fury and, somehow, the comparatively short distance to travel made us all the more anxious about the yacht's gear. For longer and longer periods not only the lee deck but also the whole of the lee stanchions and life-lines were thrust under the sea as *Benbow* lay over, almost on her beam ends. Luckily we were in the shelter of the Bay and therefore no big seas added to the tremendous strains. The gear held, the canvas held, the skipper busied himself with pilotage, crossing his fingers and taking each fence as it came. Then he thanked God. We put about on the last tack, the harbour downwind a little. We surged towards the entrance and, as soon as we brought the wind well behind us, dropped the sails, started the engine and ran down into the harbour. Just under $6\frac{1}{2}$ days out of Penzance, we tied up safely in Cadiz.

Two days afterwards we sailed for Gibraltar in calm weather. From there onward it was Mediterranean sailing—warm, sunny and mostly calm. Signor Paparella, our smiling, good-natured Italian guest, poked his head out at first dawn out of Gibraltar.

"Mediterranean: leetle seas . . ."

He finished with a rude sound to express contempt. Had we not sailed from Scotland over the stormy *Atlantico*? This was holiday stuff. He gave the pump a few casual turns—a job he had taken on seriously when, under the stresses of hard sailing, *Benbow* had made "a wee drop". I have to send Signor Paparella a certificate to note his meritorious conduct in having pumped *Benbow* down the Atlantic coast.

For all that, the Mediterranean can be a stormy place and after we left Palma, Majorca, and set out to cross the Gulf of Lions, famous for mistral storms, we ran into a brief violent squall that carried away our main halyard and forced us to seek shelter for repairs. It was a hectic few hours and as we closed with a bay near the north-east tip of Majorca, I gave our guest a nudge:

"Mr. Paparella. Mediterranean—leetle seas—Ugh?"

I added some advanced English, as expressive as the Continental rude noise.

Soon we were at anchor in a beauty spot, calm and sheltered, that rejoiced in the name of Cala de Pino de la Posada.

The next day, our halyard fixed up, we continued, and in 3 days the yacht arrived safely in Italy.

CHAPTER 6

Yacht Delivery Voyages in Bad Weather

ONE of the interesting aspects of yacht voyaging is performance and management in bad weather. Yachts range from the smallest seagoing vessels in the world: indeed because of their small size their essential seaworthiness frequently is not appreciated and it is fascinating to learn that even the little 'uns are capable of surviving storms that inflict casualties on shipping. To the uninitiated this borders the incredible, and non-yachtsmen appear to explain demonstrations of these superlative qualities by a belief in phenomenal luck.

The safety of a merchant ship depends to a large extent on the correct stowage of her cargo. Her stability is decided by the way this is done. If stability is insufficient, foul weather could capsize her; if it is too great, violent rolling could damage cargo and equipment. The possibility of cargo shifting is another hazard.

Yachts are free from dilemmas of this kind. Their human cargoes and modest stores have little effect on weight distribution. Stability will be established once and for all at the design stage, when suitable ballast will be specified. A sailing yacht is given tremendous stiffness but she avoids violent rolling because the wind in her sails will hold her steady. Sail can be reduced as the wind increases and, even in a storm so great that no sail can be carried, the weight of the wind in the mast and rigging will check a wild motion. This superlative stability, her ability to return to an even keel after being thrown on to her beam end, is a big factor in a yacht's seaworthiness.

Another consideration is buoyancy, that is, the ability to ride the waves instead of allowing heavy seas to break aboard. Yachts do not carry great weights of cargo. Except for the ballast, therefore, weight is associated only with the essential strength of a yacht. Plenty of space will be left below decks, meaning buoyancy to ride the seas, and reserve buoyancy to assist stability. Ballast can be fitted to give maximum effect for minimum weight by bolting it to the keel. Only a small amount of trimming ballast need be inside. A good designer will know how strong the various parts of a yacht must be and he will specify accordingly. He will know, for example, how to distribute the driving strain, imparted from the sails via the mast throughout the hull, and he will also know how to give comfortable accommodation yet keep the yacht rigid. A heavily constructed vessel is sensible if she is to receive rough treatment, carry heavy cargoes and be pushed hastily in and out of crowded docks or loading berths; but a yacht can expect more careful handling and closely spaced, massive timbers will merely add extra weight and detract from buoyancy. Adequate strength is obviously essential, as will be proper equipment and competent handling, but stability and buoyancy are the great factors that give a tiny yacht her safety in the face of severe weather.

Some enthusiasts accord a small yacht exaggerated qualities of seaworthiness, even to claiming superiority over large steamers. Once I read a description of a liner thrashing across the ocean in heavy weather, shipping enormous waves that were causing damage to boats and superstructure, while a trim little yacht was depicted passing, riding the ocean swell bodily, her decks dry. Completely inexperienced at the time, naïve Haward lapped it up. Now I consider it armchair yachtsmanship—born of a grain of truth. A point overlooked is that any vessel, large or small, will be comparatively comfortable running before wind and sea, whereas punching against a rough sea is always a tough proposition, especially if full speed is maintained. Even apart from this, however, safe though a yacht may be at sea, she remains a severe test on mariners and their stomachs!

On having my activities explained, landsmen frequently suppose that I arrange to anchor somewhere every night and that I "hug the coast". Classically, the craving for the former practice was expressed by a rich Mediterranean novice yacht owner when faced with the end of the day: "We cannot go on, we've no headlamps!" "Hugging the coast" idealism sometimes even is assumed by big ship seamen unversed in yacht practice. Denial of yacht voyaging persists in the face of particular accomplishment. After a delivery across the Atlantic I inflicted some photographs on an acquaintance. With the yacht running before a moderate gale, my camera had captured a heap of spray bursting over her quarter—to the discomfort of the helmsman. It was one of the few good snaps of the spool but did no more than justice to the prevailing conditions. Comment was that "of course, photographs always make the sea look impressive. . . . Obviously conditions were nothing like as bad as that"! In fact, anybody who has tried photography from a yacht's deck will complain that it is seldom possible to make rough seas look rough.

As with any seagoing where a living is to be earned, yacht delivery work is influenced by economic considerations. An early get away from the port of collection and minimum calls *en route* decide the prosperity of each job. A 9 to 5 working day does not enter into it and, indeed, if an anchorage is sought, whether by day or by night, the voyage will not be going according to plan. Bad weather will be delaying matters, or some fault in the yacht may cause the hitch, and because a firm quotation is nearly always given before starting, a few stops will immediately begin to knock a hole in the profit margin. The voyage is prolonged. The time required to earn less money increases. Hungry mouths have to be fed longer. The contractor experiences a two-way pinch. Added to this he practically always has a time table to stick to and the next customer will be in a hurry to have his yacht moved.

As always in this mad modern age, there is a struggle to prevent home "expenditure rising to meet income", and the delivery skipper pursues the unoriginal method of trying to enlarge the latter. But he cannot call on a boss with a well rehearsed plea for a salary increase. His solution is to pile more voyages into less time. A pressing need to carry on in all weather results. Nevertheless, I generally avoid taking a yacht to sea in strong headwinds, and a gale from any direction is a sound reason to stare poverty in the face in port. Confidence in the yacht concerned also affects the decision to move. A good craft, obviously well equipped, can be expected to weather a bad blow safely. It is when a hull is old and decrepit, perhaps without claiming a professional surveyor's recent attention, that a prudent delivery skipper proceeds with caution, cursing himself for landing a crazy commitment. He may doubt the strength of seedy looking canvas and cordage. He may know the bilge pumping arrangements will probably foul up at the first stroke of the pump. He may fear sludge in the fuel tank will permit only intermittent performance from the engine, and with plenty of attention to filter cleaning at that. He may wonder how electrical equipment could possibly have survived so long in its dank environment and provide him with 1,500 high voltage sparks per minute, the basic need of a petrol motor is to maintain cruising speed. The delivery skipper knows that rough seas and strong winds will realize these fears more quickly; thus by setting off when it is calm he will discover and rectify the more elementary troubles first, giving him a chance to know his ship more thoroughly and anticipate more complex difficulties that will surely occur if the weather deteriorates. Progressive troubles, though exasperating, he may keep pace with; everything going wrong at once, complete catastrophe, sabotages more effectively.

Beyond these matters there is another consideration to fit into the picture. It is a golden rule—*never miss a fair wind*. Whether under sail or power, a wind going your way makes seagoing in a sieve almost possible. In the most desperate excuse for a boat you will stand a chance of a speedy passage. I have met young and impecunious yachtsmen who have completed remarkable passages in vessels whose proud records properly belong to the last century. Newly exhumed from graveyards far distant from their proposed home ports, they have fortunately found, or prudently awaited, benign following breezes that have wafted their tore-outs home.

Spared the remorseless strains that contrary conditions would have imposed, they may be excused for believing yacht voyaging an easy, carefree pastime. I hope that their luck will diminish only gently and that instructional, faintly antagonistic weather will be encountered before a brisk headwind disables them or even summarily sinks them. This is the fortunate sequence of events which blessed my early days when I delivered many dealer's bargain boats at cut rates. Always my experience was one jump ahead of the current situation. It could have been the other way round, but I learned a lot fast. Without a doubt a bad yacht in rough sea teaches more in 5 min. than a millionaire's ship in a year. Do not despise the shoestring yachtsman. He is having fun and if he goes to sea he will gain much excellent experience—or take up hiking.

If bad weather develops when you are already at sea the situation differs somewhat. A port of refuge may be desirable but impossible to reach or have an entry so perilous as to rule it out. Unless shelter to windward is fairly close, a sailing yacht will find progress against a gale impractical except if she is a very capable vessel. If they cannot reach shelter, most will be forced to lie-to and consolidate their positions as much as possible until the wind eases or changes.

A gale on the beam will permit continued, even if hectic, progress provided the yacht's gear is good. The navigator must be confident of his position and of pilotage details ahead. Progress towards the port of delivery may be practical, but if a river bar has to be negotiated before gaining calm water, or if heavy overfalls exist at the entrance, he may choose to slow down, anticipating how long the bad weather will last. Alternatively he could proceed to a snug anchorage near his destination whose approach he knows is safe. If doubt prevails, however, or the coast he is approaching is a lee-shore, he would be best advised to lie-to well clear of the land until the blow abates.

Similarly, even a bad following gale should afford safe, excellent progress, but to use it a skipper must have thoroughly sound ideas on how to cope on arrival.

CHAPTER 7

With "Misha" from Ireland

WHEN Geoff Palmer and I travelled to Strangford Lough, Northern Ireland in October 1953 to collect the 9-ton auxiliary Bermudian cutter *Misha*, we were soon to consider some of the points discussed in the last chapter. Conditions were stormy but by the time all was ready aboard our sturdy, well found craft, remarkable for her large doghouse, the current gale eased. However, the local R.A.F. Meteorological Office was pessimistic and maintained that the break would be short, the weak ridge that gave the respite having another vigorous trough hot on its heels. A new rain belt was timed to arrive at midnight, by which time the wind would be strengthening, back in the south again.

Chock-full of the delight which purveyors of local knowledge can scarce conceal when they describe the more hazardous features of their coast, charming Irishmen described the entrance to Strangford Lough as a "wall of water". At the time murky drizzle hid this phenomenon alleged to be some 4 miles from Strangford village where the narrows terminate at the sea. When the visibility cleared the tide was roaring out at full bore. Then, even from our distant viewpoint, we observed a tumbling white demarcation line, and in astonishment I noted how the outflowing torrent appeared to climb upwards at the bar, boiling as it did so. I felt like Macbeth, forced to acknowledge the versatility of Birnam Wood at last. Cynicism had to go: we gave the locals full marks. The tidal stream that fills and empties the big Lough reaches a velocity of $7\frac{1}{2}$ knots in places as it careers to and fro along the pipe-line. When the ebb stream meets the sea there is a dreadful flurry of breakers, and no small craft is advised to leave in the face of it, yet a small auxiliary yacht cannot expect to punch down against the flood.

Our drill was to slip our mooring towards the end of the falling tide so as to reach the entrance at slack water. We timed it right, but were surprised at the threatening steep sea still astride the buoyed entrance. Doubtless the swell running in the Irish Sea, the left-overs from the last gale, accounted for the situation to some extent. *Misha* climbed high over waves that seemed on the verge of breaking, and doubtless had been until the tide had eased: then she gained the safety of the open sea.

I likened the place to Salcombe entrance in bad on-shore weather. Once, when a southerly blow was in full swing, I had made an ill-advised attempt to leave that Devon estuary, only to beat a hasty retreat when I encountered the inshore approach to the bar. Much of the yacht's crockery was lost, and the skipper was a more humble, wiser man. I remembered that before the war the Salcombe lifeboat had capsized attempting to put to sea in the face of that bar at its worst.

Our experience at Strangford was not dangerous—we had awaited the correct tidal conditions to avoid danger—but little imagination was needed to perceive its hazards in bad weather.

My thoughts about lifeboats at this time later struck me as strange, because before we were to reach England another R.N.L.I. craft was lost in the call of duty. The lifeboatman braves situations that every sailor, almost by instinct, seeks to avoid. Other mariners exercise the right of prudence and thereby enjoy a fair margin of safety at sea. As mentioned already, if a harbour is dangerous to enter they can elect to stay outside, where they will ride out a storm without accident and, of course, if putting out is hazardous they can remain snugly in port. Not so the R.N.L.I. crews. With their eyes open they resign prudence for the need to cross dangerous bars or leave shallow harbour mouths, no matter how bad the weather. Their appointed task demands it. Neptune the payee, the coxswain signs an open cheque for peril.

Glad to be over that hurdle, we lay for the Rockabill, where we would close with East Ireland just north of Dublin, from thence planning to work down the coast inshore of the off-lying sandbanks. But the wind backed steadily, heading us to the east until our yacht was careering towards Wales, the unfavourable side of the Irish Sea during sou'westerly weather.

At midnight we double-reefed the main, and on the opposite tack lay for Ireland once more. The rain began at 0015—full marks to the weather man—and only a racing fanatic would have dismissed thoughts of shelter. A vigorous blow was developing rapidly. We were well north of the dangerous Kish Bank and had a safe approach to Ireland. Studying the chart I noted that Skerries Bay, tucked behind St. Patrick's Island inshore of the Rockabill, was sheltered from south-east winds veering west. So long as the early morning shipping forecast did not predict an easterly in the Irish Sea, we could confidently expect a safe anchorage there, and if Skerries were open to the gale it would be a fair wind for Dublin. There were no off-lying dangers and, though the rain had closed the visibility, I was confident of establishing my position.

Just before dawn the Rockabill was sighted fine on the port bow, its light penetrating about 4 miles through the murk. We were heading straight towards our haven; 0800 found *Misha* tucked under a protective piece of Ireland, comfortably at anchor, her crew enjoying the sleep of the just. Though not "anchoring at night" our bunks were no less comfortable.

Improvement came at dusk and, as often happens, a veer brought the wind from the north-west, our signal to be off again. After a breakfast-supper, we carried this fair offshore breeze down the rest of Ireland's east coast. In the morning, glorious sunshine enhanced our way, making it as delightful a day as any in October, and the setting sun showed *Misha* standing seaward from the Tuskar Rock, departure point for Land's End. But again the high pressure ridge was a brief feature in the weather scheme. The wind backed steadily during the night, though it remained light and innocuous. The change was unfolding more slowly than on our first night out of Strangford: no rain at midnight, gale in the morning this time. Though I paid the saying scant attention, "long foretold, long last" was to be more applicable than "short notice, soon past". However, I considered the morning radio forecast seriously because a widespread blow was promised, and sea area Lundy, where *Misha* now lay close-hauled, was obviously going to receive its share. Already it was included in the preliminary gale warnings. No longer heading for Land's End, our yacht had been forced on to a south-easterly course that would bring her up on North Cornwall's inhospitable shore near Bude.

By deduced reckoning, Milford Haven lay some 25 miles to the north, but by the time we could expect to reach it, even in the existing fresh breeze that would take us there, it was likely that the visibility would have deteriorated.

Unless navigation was spot-on we could end up in the confused seas of St. Goven Shoal or sluiced into Jack Sound, rock strewn, tide enraged. Apart from the hazard it meant surrendering sea miles hewn from a headwind, progress to be guarded jealously. I determined to hold on to our gains and ride out whatever was in store.

Remaining sailing time before the gale obviously must be used for getting to the westward. Sea room, and the most favourable position for weathering the Longships after the blow, were the requisites. *Misha* was put on the port tack and lay a course west by south. Within half an hour we double-reefed the main; an hour later the jib was stowed. The ship was going great guns, her lee-rail awash, the log purposefully spinning off the westing. The sea was rising.

Early in the afternoon hove-to. Duly warned of the impending gale and therefore resigned to it balking our passage round Land's End, we gave up beating to windward fairly early, before the yacht became a shambles and her crew weary. I went to the trouble of setting the trysail to see how *Misha* would lie "a-try". We did not bother with the storm jib because we found she lay comfortably under trysail alone. We lashed the helm up, squared up on deck and went below to keep dry. The seas were approaching about seven points off the port bow, and compared with the recent close-hauled work, blessed peace reigned.

Theoretically, when a small yacht rides out bad weather, the crew relax in their bunks—presumably without a care in the world. Not being a stoic, I cannot fall in with the drill. There always seem to be things to do. Soon I was changing from dry pyjamas to wet clothes and oilskins to go on deck and restow the mainsail. Removed from the mast track to make way for the trysail, the luff had freed itself from our lashings. Then I had to turn out to haul on the trysail sheet—a brand new rope was stretching. Next the bilge needed pumping: "Your turn, Geoff!" And my crew's rest was spoilt. No sooner was my shipmate back in his bunk than I had to investigate a strange new noise—the tiller had freed itself and the yacht had paid herself off and gathered headway. This time patience had gone and I neglected to don oilskin trousers—a ridiculous way to save trouble. With spray travelling horizontally, my pyjamas stood no chance.

At 1600 it was really blowing. The leech of the trysail began to flog and no amount of hauling on the sheet was of avail, even when putting the helm down and partially luffing. At times it was as if a giant was trying to shake the mast out of the yacht and it seemed best to stow all canvas. Today I see no real advantage in setting a trysail just to lie-to; lowering everything and lying a-hull in the first place avoids much trouble. If the intention is to jog slowly to windward, that is another matter.

I thought this must be the height of the blow, but during the early part of the night the wind increased further. At 1800 the B.B.C. crackled out their ideas: the gale in operation on all coasts was expected to be severe in many areas including Fastnet and Lundy. It certainly seemed as though the wind reached Force 9 for an hour or two, and that means a real blow in any seaman's language. I had ridden out similar stuff in this area 3 years before and had come safely through by lying-to under bare poles. This time I determined to experiment with other tactics. A great length of $1\frac{3}{4}$ in. rope was dragged from the forecastle and streamed from the bow as a double length, one end being secured to the mast, the other to the winch. A third, lighter line was prepared for a canvas bag I had laboriously stitched to hold oil, but I did not intend to use this latter gear unless things became desperate. The deck work was not done under ideal conditions. Howling wind and searing spray combined to befuddle the mind; the ever present need to hang on complicated and lengthened every task. I had thought there would be a tendency to stern way, but in reality, when my work with warps was done, it was clear that *Misha* was making to windward at perhaps a quarter of a knot. The gear streamed along her windward side, just out of reach at the cockpit. Truly our doghouse was a standing storm mizen!

Some people have expressed doubt that this could happen and though reporting the fact I do not propose to explain it more fully. The only thing I can add is that, without having heard of *Misha* to my knowledge, an experienced Scottish yachtsman recently told me that he had seen a 6-metre fore-reach to windward under bare poles and manoeuvre to moorings.

Rigged from the bows, despite her doghouse, the warp was useless, as would have been a sea anchor and also my oil bag. Had further action for survival been necessary, we should have had to run dead before the wind and sea and steered to keep the stern accurately facing the oncoming waves. Streaming drags astern also might have helped.

While working on deck I had sighted, for an instant, two white lights of some other vessel. Because of the restricted visibility, she was close. Down we went into the trough again and she was out of sight for good before I could establish her course, but the next few minutes indicated that she did not require our portion of ocean. Fear of collision was hardly felt: *Misha* seemed so minute in the huge sea running, and so alone in a dim, wet hell, that it was hard to conceive of anything else solid near. However, it did help me overcome my lethargy and, as a riding light, I secured to the boom the electric inspection lamp. This done I felt the ship was properly served and that it was past my bedtime.

It was now 1900 and seemed to be blowing harder than ever. Possibly out of concern for his skipper's comfort, Geoff had taken the windward berth and, as is the case too often in yachts, the bunk board was none too high. The light was off and in the leeward one, comfortably supported by the back panelling, I was just dozing off, when suddenly a ghastly, bigger-than-ever crash dragged me back to wide-awake consciousness. Mattress, pillow, blankets and Geoff landed on top of me, complete, as despatched from the berth opposite. Luckily my shipmate was entirely unhurt, but we thought the ship must be stove in. However, an inspection found everything in order. We arranged ourselves for sleep again, Geoff taking the cabin floor this time, putting his mattress on various ropes and fend-offs to keep it clear of bilge water sluicing about to leeward.

Morale was none too good for the next hour or so. The fury of this sledge-hammer blow shook us. We were reluctant to believe that our manmade cockle-shell could survive while all nature was tearing itself apart. My pet theory was that a huge sea would crash on *Misha*, and raise her outsize doghouse from her decks, baring for its successor the huge opening which had been exposed. With the yacht heavily water-logged, subsequent seas would stand a sporting chance of claiming another victim for Neptune. Chasing the thoughts were plans to deal with the emergency and fight a rearguard action for survival. Ample sails would be available; prompt action, lashings, battens, screws and nails—and some luck also, would be required.

At 2130 the wind began to ease and at the same time we noticed a change in the yacht's motion. Soon after sounds of solid water in the cockpit summoned me from my bunk. The wind had veered perhaps four points, and though it was dark it was apparent that a cross-sea was rising over the old swell, with the result that water slopped over the decks more frequently. The bilge pump dealt comfortably with what found its way below.

Now we knew we had won through. Thankful relief surged into our minds. Since then I have weathered many gales in yachts and though I am always thankful when they are over, I am less easily frightened by the sea now; therefore, the relief of a safe conclusion is seldom so intense. It had been a wild night and, like others, this gale had claimed its victims. Away to the north-east tragedy overtook the Arbroath life-boat. Attempting the hazardous approach to her home port after investigating a distress call, she capsized and all but one of her gallant crew were lost.

At 0530 we set the mainsail and foresail but, with the jumble of seas which followed the veer, little progress was made. We felt stiff, cold and weary and kept our canvas reefed, though really this was the time to drive the yacht under full sail. The Longships was still to windward and, despite the veer, we still could not lie that course. The change of wind merely made the starboard tack the more favourable. Jogging along we took 30 hrs. to get round the corner and tie up in Penzance.

Two days later we left, spick and span again, the ship's company recovered. A light westerly helped as we romped towards the Lizard under sail and power, intent on catching the last of the flood round that headland. As I have stressed, a successful passage round the coast means catching the tide at the headlands—all the headlands if possible. Later, having rounded Britain's southernmost tip, we made some progress without the motor, but it was started again when the evening forecast promised plenty of wind to come. It looked as if we should have all the sailing we would want and there would be no need to eke out the fuel.

It began to blow in the night and there was an essential difference between this and the other winds we had experienced. This was a fair wind. Start Point was abeam at 0315, and around dawn the B.B.C. gave their "perhaps reaching gale force" hint. We were half-way across Lyme Bay, making excellent progress while a strong wind steadily heaped up a big sea on the starboard quarter. Three overtaking coasters were sighted during the forenoon and two of these were held in sight for more than 5 hrs. At 0900 the main was close-reefed as rain came with a vicious squall.

At 1230 the visibility was good enough to discern the dim blur of Portland Bill, 7 miles to the north. We altered course for Anvil Point and for an hour wind and tide carried us towards this headland at a fantastic rate, by which time I decided the Needles Channel would be very rough. In fact, I now believe a yacht may enter it in a full gale safely, providing the tide is flooding, but at that time, with the southerly wind in the Force 7 category, I preferred to weather St. Catherine's Point and enter the Solent from the east. We had to haul on our sheets, bringing the wind slightly forward of the beam and the lee shrouds dragged through the sea. I knew about St. Catherine's and determined to keep clear of its race.

It was touch and go about the tide. According to plan, we had caught the first of the flood off Portland, but I feared it would be fully spent before we rounded the southern tip of the Isle of Wight. Forty-four miles over the bottom in 6 hrs. is as much as anyone can hope for aboard a 9-tonner but actually we were a little past the headland when the west-going stream started. Quickly it gained its well-known pace, progress diminished and the battle was drawn out into the night.

There was no doubt about this Force 7 business now. But just around the corner was warmth, rest and shelter. I was glad the solid *Misha* had first-class sails and rigging: she would see us through safely. Nevertheless, this was no time to test the equipment with a gybe, nor by putting about.

When at last the Nab Tower was near the beam, Geoff crawled out to take the helm and I went forward and dragged down the mainsail. Only on the foredeck was the full fury of the screaming wind felt. It was blowing far harder than I had thought and on the other gybe we left the mainsail stowed.

An hour later we were in sheltered waters and the wind was no more than moderate; but when we reached Hamble it had settled down to blow again. But we did not care: *Misha* was in her winter quarters.

CHAPTER 8

Wensley's Wave

INDIVIDUAL scientists derive empirical formulae from research data and, having resolved the variables into an equation, are sometimes gratified if the arrived constant is endowed with their names. A doctor investigating certain characteristic, if infrequent, human ailments, obtains some satisfaction if the disability is later classified by his name. Fishermen, having trawled previously unfrequented shallows, perhaps with good results, have had the banks designated with their names on later charts. Why should Adrian J. Wensley-Walker, who may later be renowned in science, exploration or the arts, not have a wave named after him? Born as a ripple under the lee of the Biscay coast, snowballed by a vicious easterly, it became a full-sized ocean monster that rolled a rollicking path across the Atlantic, declining or dissipating heaven knows where. Probably only four people know about it. To them it is Wensley's Wave.

In April 1956, the four of us ghosted out of St. Peter Port bound for Tangier and Marseilles in the beautiful French auxiliary cutter *Janabel* (57 ft. L.O.A., 40 ft. L.W.L., 12½ ft. beam, 8 ft. draught). The vesper airs died as darkness settled; the 5-second flash of Les Roches Douvres became an integral part of the peaceful scene and it seemed unreal that the B.B.C. had just warned us of southerly gales in Finisterre.

We motored through the night, and noon the next day found us running towards the Fromvieur Passage with a Force 3 easterly breeze. This channel inside Ushant is the more direct way from the Channel Islands for the north-west tip of Spain and, provided you have a good commanding wind or full power, you can negotiate it at any state of tide. The Le Four Channel, which carries you round the corner close to the mainland of Brittany, is your choice if you plan to make port before crossing the Bay of Biscay. Both these channels are well marked. The tidal stream should be noted carefully, for it is very strong; but it is the same going outside Ushant too.

Before we closed with Ushant all hands were working, pulling down the first reef in the main. The B.B.C. was still sticking to its gale theories, but it now seemed likely that we should meet a blow from the south-east and not southerly, as was hinted first.

Two hours before midnight we pulled down the third reef and at 0025, 19th April, the log read: "Both foresails lowered and this eases the vessel considerably. Wind has slowly increased since close reefing and is now south-east Force 6 to 7. Barometer 766 and steady. Clear night."

From 1800 until the same time the next evening the yacht ran 190 miles by patent log—and after that latter reading we never saw the instrument again. A jerrycan, fixed close to it came loose and, swinging about, apparently fractured the mounting.

That was a day of surfing, surging, exhilarating speed. The sea built up and the slops over the quarter insidiously became solid water; then whole wave tops. The furious wind was a fair wind and I was loath to cry for mercy. We hung on to our treble-reefed main. Soon it was routine to bring the stern dead before the more threatening seas, but this only slightly reduced the helmsman's dousings. It was not easy to judge the potentiality of each wave. Added to his problems, the man at the wheel occasionally had a skipper nagging him, hating to see the yacht careering off course, moaning over the loss of the patent log and predicting that the sun would never reveal itself to his sextant again:

"The course is south of west. We're bound for Gib.—not Canada."

Janabel is a fine modern yacht, but her cockpit is only of the semi-watertight variety. Portions of Atlantic which settled in it pursued two different courses. Part went directly back via the cockpit drains, while the rest cascaded via the locker doors into the bilge, there to be pumped out by hand-draulics. The man on watch now became an irritating pest. Each time the yacht surfaced from a particularly good one he would blow on his hand whistle with raucous self-importance—as though those below could not

73

hear sounds like Niagara discharging into the bowels of the ship aft. At first we dutifully turned-to and cleared the bilge on each occasion, but later we grew blasé, inspecting it first before deciding whether it was worthy of our attention.

By 2100 I decided to throw in the sponge and we stowed the main and continued our course under bare poles at a speed which varied between 3 and 6 knots. Seas now came aboard less frequently but, when they did, the amount was heavy. Generally the yacht heeled over in the process and this ensured that at least half a cockpit full would spill out to leeward.

Thus went our fortunes for the next 35 hrs. At least we were proceeding in the right direction and, all in all, we probably ran some 130 miles with no canvas set. With plenty of sea room and with no landfalls to worry about it was a satisfactory state of affairs from the navigator's viewpoint. The gale, being astern, was not holding us up.

Some 3 hrs. before it eased a really large sea swept the yacht. *Janabel*'s main companionway is not situated adjacent to the cockpit under the doghouse, as is usually the case with yachts of her type, but further forward on the starboard side of the coach roof; nevertheless a torrent of water poured at full bore down this hatch which had been left slightly open for ventilation. I remember hitching my head over the bunk board and gazing at solid water surging across the saloon. Watchkeeper Wensley-Walker blew on his whistle while it slowly subsided into the deep bilge below. There was still room for a couple more good ones, I thought, as I opened the hatch and exchanged ribald comments with the helmsman about his prowess with wind instruments.

Next came Wensley's Wave. We have discussed it, embellished it in many places and over many cups and glasses, and maybe we have stretched it, before uncritical audiences, into the saltiest yarn of the year. Be that as it may, I am now your faithful reporter. Once more *Janabel*'s slumbering watch below was awakened, this time by a thunderous roar intermingled with the thrust of the sea that was squirting in through every orifice and unsuspected crack. As it died away the familiar heavy waterfall noise seemed anaemic—even though we realized it had never operated more efficiently. This time relief was my only emotion when a shrill whistle came from above. Whatever else might have carried away, Wensley was still there.

74

As this particular monster had approached, the helmsman had classified it as one of the get-it-dead-astern variety and had acted accordingly. Even so, solid sea had come aboard, completely filling the cockpit and engulfing everything in its path. Having been brought dead before wind and sea, the yacht had remained more or less on an even keel, causing the cockpit to remain brimful for a considerable time and, apart from what came in through other routes, double the usual amount went below.

All hands were galvanized into action and the pumps were manned. *Janabel's* very deep bilge was exactly full. The auxiliary engine was immersed except, because of a fortunate detail of design, the oil filler entrance. Pumping was a lengthy business because the strums to both pumps became blocked and exploratory arms were required under deep, oily waters. I was later surprised to find that none of this had found its way into the engine oil-sump because the dip-stick was well immersed. It must have been a good fit.

Soon after this the gale was over, and shortly before dawn we set a staysail. Gradually we hoisted more. The wind continued brisk the whole way to Tangier and we entered that harbour 7 days and 2 hrs. out of Guernsey.

CHAPTER 9

"Cohoe" and a Winter Gale

RIDING out a gale at sea is the straightforward, if uncomfortable, answer; yet running, or even beating into it to shelter is probably the more common way out for the coasting yachtsman. I have explained my reasons for keeping *Misha* at sea during that second blow we met. Besides wanting a more accurate landfall than I could have hoped for had I run back to Milford Haven, I hated the thought of surrendering those hard-earned miles to windward. Professional pride and the hard economics of the game will find me tacking up to shelter or even broad reaching to a port barely down to leeward, but I have never run back. Returning from a reconnaissance, a poke out of the harbour to confirm whether the blow is as bad as was expected, is not included in this comment. There is neither shame nor anything lost in a look-see.

Cohoe is an over-grown Tumlare, steeped in fame. The well-known yachtsman Adlard Coles has owned three *Cohoes*, perhaps each one an improvement on her predecessor as far as ocean racing goes, but it is his first one, this sleek Spartan little craft, enlargement of a design first aimed at giving Scandinavians a thrill in sheltered waters, which reserved him a well deserved place in the minds of British yachtsmen.

Thirty-two feet over all, $25\frac{1}{2}$ ft. on the water line, with a beam of $7\frac{1}{2}$ ft. and a draught of just over 5, she first came into the news during the 1948 Santander Race, when the whole offshore fleet ran into a vicious gale which had eluded the meteorological men's scouts and appeared out of nowhere in the English Channel approaches. *Cohoe* was reported missing but in fact every yacht weathered the blow safely and in her class *Cohoe* was second only to *Mindy*. Shipped to Bermuda in 1950, Adlard Coles from thence sailed her to America and, with three other British yachts in the vicinity—*Samuel Pepys, Mokoia* and *Vertue XXXV*—encountered a tremendous storm *en route*. Not a true hurricane, indeed well out of the tropical storm season, this depression gave strong gale to storm force winds and a bad time was had by all. Of particular interest is the fact that we have three accounts from those yachtsmen embroiled in it, and these are to be read in *North Atlantic* by Adlard Coles, *Vertue XXXV* by Humphrey Barton and *Deep Sea Sailing* by Erroll Bruce. The America-Bermuda Race put *Cohoe* on the first leg of her return voyage, and after that she entered the 3,000 mile race to Plymouth, gaining first place and the distinction as the smallest yacht ever to have won that marathon event.

At Hamble River in December 1954, her new owner required her up at Pwllheli for laying up—a mere 360 miles coast crawl to be added to her log. However, although she was to be manned by a keen crew, the weather during that winter had been so appalling that I expected a tough trip. One of November's savage gales, besides causing the usual damage all over the country, had wrecked the South Goodwin Lightship with the loss of all but one aboard her. Shipping in distress was a regular event, flooding and destroyed sea defences a daily topic. This was the background when Ted Brace and I boarded *Cohoe* and the confidence we had in her was in no way unnecessary. The gale of 4th December shifted to the west in the evening and the meteorological men expected it to ease and veer further. We planned a good night's sleep in the sheltered Hamble and an early start on Sunday.

The easing process took nearly all day and we had a tough time beating out of the Solent and forging a painful path towards Dorset. Some squalls were so prolonged and so ominous that I doubted several times whether there was going to be any real lull between the current depression and the next that was doubtless in the offing. However by nightfall the sky cleared, the wind swung right to the north-north-east and dropped into faint airs and *Cohoe* eked out her limited fuel for the auxiliary motor. We continued our steady progress, damp but otherwise in comfort. At dusk the following evening the latest of the variable airs settled in the west. We were approaching the Lizard, pleased with ourselves and looking forward to a night's rest in snug Penzance

Pool before tackling the west coast passage. Now we had to pay off to the south-west: a good board seaward, we thought, then the port tack would bring us into Mount's Bay.

At 1730 drizzle blotted out the Lizard light and the wind backed further and started to freshen. We changed the genoa for the No. 1 jib. We would thrash a path into Penzance more quickly, I thought, though feeling a tinge of annoyance in having failed to obtain a running fix on the coastline before it disappeared. Dangerous rocks extend nearly half a mile seaward from the Lizard and a navigator likes to be reassured with an accurate fix, especially if beating round this headland at night. However, morale was yet high. I was confident that a lighthouse with a light of 3 million candle-power would not remain hidden for long. After we had put about on to the port tack I sighted it again—just a pin-prick now—and it showed clearly that another board would be necessary before we could weather it.

The wind was increasing with speed and determination. At 1800 I started on the first reef; then I went straight ahead with the second. Almost every gust seemed intent on surpassing its predecessor in strength and it was not long before I had substituted Falmouth for Penzance as our next port of call. With a substantial Force 7 wind, south-west we paid off and ran northward. Once again driving rain closed the visibility but I was sure the Lizard would reappear after the squall.

At 1920 I was able to obtain a rough bearing of it again, apply this to the chart and obtain a running fix—something to go by, at any rate, but I must not forget my pinch of salt. Apparently our northerly course would bring us to Manacles Buoy as intended. The moon above the clouds was giving some light and this would help navigational problems considerably. I was confident that we should see the land in dim silhouette without getting too close—or else we should sight the Manacles flasher. Had the night been utterly black it would have been necessary to allow for considerable error and run much farther down wind for fear of striking Black Head or the jagged Manacles themselves.

Then came a screaming squall and everything was blotted out as the full gale struck in a smother of spray and lashing rain. Ted battled with the helm; *Cohoe* ran, her double-reefed main and No. 1 jib driving her through the darkness at a tremendous rate. One's senses were numbed by the fury of it but my last bearing of the Lizard (W. by N. magnetic) enabled me to be confident of my latitude—the distance of the light had been the difficulty— therefore I was able to continue this headlong rush for at least 10 min. in safety. Within that time the sky lightened a little but the wind seemed to back a point further and, if anything, increase. Soon Black Head could be seen dimly, fine on the port bow. We were too far inshore and a gybe would be necessary to clear the Manacles.

Of course to gybe the main was out of the question and our attempt to put about was carried out too quickly. The bow was blown off before the yacht even approached stays. Therefore, wishing to lay the new course as quickly as possible, the main was dragged down and the ship run off the wind with her foresail gybing across like a shot from a gun.

Now nearly south-west-by-south, the wind increased further. Having backed to this extent, the Lizard afforded no shelter and in the dim light an enormous, pure white sea could be seen building up. Were the gale to continue to back, the full fetch would run straight into Falmouth and I wondered what sort of mess would be kicked up in the entrance.

That fence could be jumped later: the urgent matter was that we were travelling too fast even without the main, yawing about behind the jib, which occasionally gybed over with a terrible report—despite the valiant efforts of the helmsman. The surf ride became hectic and one in particular seemed to go on and on, the helm hanging useless. In a detached way I thought it would continue for ever—but of course it did not, and when the end came *Cohoe* must have looked as if she were landing in the trough, having been dropped from a great height.

One striking point was that, despite the lack of control, there seemed no danger of broaching because the foresail was all the time dragging the bow forward, but, because of the frequent uncontrolled gybes, I do not think the ride could have lasted long without the canvas blowing out. We stowed the jib and continued under bare poles.

While I worked on the foredeck the clouds began to break and the moon came through. At the same time the wind veered a full four points and came screaming at us from the rugged cliffs. As if by magic the mist vanished and I could see that we were in St. Anthony's Point red sector. This lighthouse lies on the eastern side of Falmouth entrance and the red arc shines over the Manacles: although we were heading to clear these rocks they still lay to the north. It is worth noting that though the flashing buoy marking the reef was little over a mile away, the sea was so rough that it was yet some time before we sighted it.

Under bare poles there is no doubt that *Cohoe* would have run like a scalded cat, but as soon as we had located the Manacles Buoy the course towards it brought wind, now westerly, on the beam. Sail was required and I hoisted a small portion of the main, Spanish reefed. At first there was reasonably good progress but the gale continued to veer until even quite a substantial amount of canvas set this way could not be hauled sufficiently flat. The tiny storm jib was then hoisted, but it was soon apparent that we might even have to tack to reach Falmouth: therefore the third reef in the mainsail was pulled down and the sail hoisted properly.

Snugly rigged in this way, she lay right over to the north-west gale and crashed along close-hauled, making a real four points off the wind. The huge following sea had subsided with the veer but, even with a fetch of 3 miles extraordinarily big, steep waves, completely covered with foam and a brilliant white in the moon-light, gave us a very wild ride. We passed the Manacles Buoy and concentrated on sailing as close to the wind as possible without letting the sails flog. Clearly they would stand no bad treatment in this weather.

Soon came a stupendous, biggest-of-all squall. The sky went black again and the wind blew, and then blew harder. And then more yet, until it reached a fantastic crescendo, until it seemed the sails must become rags, until it seemed impossible for the mast itself to stand. But the gear held. Into the foam to starboard the lee coaming disappeared. The maximum angle of heel was reached but the wind rose higher and higher: lying over so steeply all excess wind was spilled from the sails and this was undoubtedly why we never lost the lot. The important thing was to prevent the canvas flogging—luffing would have produced ribbons in no time—and on this Ted was intent while I went forward to be ready to lower the main instantaneously at the first sign of it giving way.

Pinned securely against the dinghy by the tremendous pressure of wind, I mused on how much safer I was than Ted, who lay spread-eagled across the cockpit, mostly standing on the inside of the lee coaming. I felt a triumphant thrill because it was clear that, come the winds of all hell, our apparently frail craft was virtually unsinkable. Waves, foam and spindrift broke over her and into her cockpit, but that was watertight and canted over, a surplus was simply lost to leeward. On top of this she was going to windward. Admittedly we were in what normally would be considered sheltered water, but many a yacht of *Cohoe*'s size and larger, for reasons I shall explain later, would have been unable to continue under such conditions.

The squall passed, the sky cleared and the gale carried on. Having passed the Manacles, we were now in the white sector of St. Anthony's and it was a moot point whether we could weather the light without tacking. If we could regain the red sector it would mean that we were in fact clawing to windward of the harbour entrance; and after an age, it seemed, that occulting light slowly took on a reddish hue. Another squall came and went— again a violent increase in wind way above the gale, but it could not equal its forerunner. For a time the wind backed half a point and enabled us to lay for Falmouth Bay a while. When it eased *Cohoe* was really in the red sector and lying squarely for Falmouth entrance.

A glance at the chart confirmed that, once in the harbour, a dead beat would be necessary to make up to the anchorage off the town, and in the prevailing weather I thought frequent tacking would be too much for the canvas. Apart from this, the moorings there would be extremely exposed: the gale would be screaming straight down the reach. St. Mawes was a far better proposition. It was very sheltered, besides being an easy run from the harbour entrance.

At 2245, 40½ hrs. out of Hamble River, we clawed into Falmouth Harbour and paid off towards St. Mawes. Not knowing whether we should find a mooring, the anchor was cleared away. The sails were lowered and we drove in comfortably, under bare poles. As the little village broadened on the port bow we found the blessed shelter of the hills above. The inherent hardness of seagoing was, for a time, at an end. The engine was started—it had kept dry under the watertight cockpit—and the last few drops of petrol carried us around the next bend where we found a mooring.

I checked with British Climateology, who collect and record

all British weather reports, and was told that the highest gust reported during the evening from the Lizard had been 78 knots— i.e. 89.8 m.p.h.—and this had occurred at 1935 when, it was mentioned, the wind suddenly veered a full 40 degrees. For 5 hrs. the wind had gusted above 47 knots. I had expected to learn that the highest gust occurred during the squall I have described as "stupendous, biggest-of-all", but, it will be remembered, the veer occurred a short while before this—just after we had stowed *Cohoe's* No. 1 jib, snugging her to bare poles. However, as one who experienced them all, let me make no bones about it: that superlative squall after the veer, through which *Cohoe* sailed under treble-reefed main and storm jib, was in no way second-rate stuff.

Ted brought the matter up: how would his converted 6-metre, or indeed any other yacht, have fared in that blow? The past night was still so vivid and awful that we firmly wrote off half the yachts in Britain. We ignored the important fact that *Cohoe's* feat was remarkable only in that she had kept sailing.

Considering that our craft carried a normal mainsail, treble-reefed successfully, a critic may be forgiven for exclaiming: "What a yarn! Nothing on *Cohoe* carried away: therefore your squalls could not have gusted anywhere near the 90 m.p.h. mark." As mentioned, the gust which was thus recorded by an anemometer less than 10 miles away found the yacht temporarily under bare poles, but other squalls of similar ferocity were encountered through which we sailed windward. Clearly our craft could keep going in extremely severe conditions and the following is an explanation.

When going well to windward *Cohoe* reaches a big angle of heel. At, say, 60 degrees each additional degree will produce a loss in sail area in the vertical plane that is far greater than occurs during similar changes in degrees of heel at initial heeling angles. Resort to diagrams will explain this. Thus, during a squall, an extra gust will produce a yet greater angle of heel only to very substantially reduce the effective sail area and largely nullify its effect. A governor is coming into operation: hence the expression, not strictly accurate, "maximum angle of heel". The vessel has an automatic "luffing" device without the sails flogging. Beamier yachts, having more initial stability, would hold their sails out to the full fury of the wind to be blasted to ribbons.

Theoretically, roller reefing would make it possible for their mainsails to be reduced immediately to suit the wind—right down to handkerchief area if necessary. However, in the face of such destructive force developing in so little time, the practical course would be to stow all canvas in double-quick time. It will be realized that the dinghy sailor's technique of partial luffing, or indeed the slightest flogging of canvas, would in such a wind mean the end of any sail. A safe harbour near or not, most yachts would have to lie a-hull, or forfeit some sails, which amounts to the same thing in an unseamanlike manner with added difficulties.

Another factor in *Cohoe*'s prowess was her watertight cockpit. Her lee coamings were way under the waves during those squalls: under such conditions Ted's little *Manka* would have speedily foundered. Like so many others her action for survival would have been hulling or, if that became unsafe, running under bare poles, streaming drags.

Lack of time forced Ted to leave and he was disappointed not to see *Cohoe* at Pwllheli. My friend Tug Wilson, a very experienced yachtsman on Naval leave at the time, was on the Falmouth train like a shot from a gun.

Further gales developed during the week and gusts of over 100 m.p.h. were reported from various parts of the coast. On Friday there was a break—a flat calm in fact—and using the engine all the time we had a quiet passage to Penzance where we intended to load more fuel. Saturday however brought renewed bad weather and we stayed put.

The midday Sunday forecast spoke of fresh to strong northwest winds backing west and we thought we ought to have a go. As dusk fell we slipped out of Penzance Pool, setting a double-reefed main and a No. 1 jib. As we reached across towards St. Clement's Island, off Mousehole, I think we were both surprised at the force of the squalls that swept down over the hills. Going inside Low Lee Rock, we passed a fishing trawler towing another towards Newlyn.

Six o'clock, pitch darkness, the screaming wind a full Force 7, *Cohoe* was hard pressed despite her modest sail plan as she lay for the Runnelstone. Occasionally this light buoy winked its message when, for an instant, the waves between us solved the intervisibility problem. Now we were meeting the massive Atlantic rollers which were capped with heavy crests and our yacht battled into these. The wind gusted further as a hail squall arrived. One glance with the face exposed to it was most painful: the helmsman retreated as much as possible into his oilskin.

Conditions were such that *Cohoe* ought to have been reefed further and her storm jib flown in place of the No. 1, but to go out into a pitch-black night in the middle of winter when such a rig is essential seemed hard weather gluttony. Land's End can provide a very unpleasant time in this sort of weather and off Cape Cornwall there would be a vast area of heavy tumbling seas stretching over 12 miles to the north as well as a substantial distance westward. Chaos was developing below decks. Sleep would not be easy to come by; while on deck every wave seemed to have something hefty to send aboard and some of this was arriving in the cockpit more or less intact.

The yacht was taking punishment. I was sure that even Tug, though he relished hard weather and was silently watching the scene from the companionway, realized that to continue would be a sentence of severe hardship indeed. I thought so, anyway. Reluctantly, but convinced that it was the sensible course, we put about and ran back to Penzance.

Now local salts began to shake their heads. To return to port because of bad weather indicates inexperience and lack of judgement: you must never go out to "see what it is like". A conservative estimate of our E.T.A. Pwllheli was 3 months ahead. Another less far-sighted individual advised us to put *Cohoe* in Penzance Pool and go home for Christmas. I began to tell one bronzed fellow how we had previously struggled into Falmouth. He was quite polite but clearly his "Oh yes", was "Oh yeah"!

However bright your star, these things pick away at morale.

The point these dismal fortune-tellers omit is that if you will put to sea and remain there for a day or two it is very likely indeed that you will, if nothing better, bite a good chunk out of a coastal voyage. Even in winter, between hard blows, there are spells of moderate weather for 36 hrs. or so. Around the British Isles, at any rate, there is no "close season" as some like to imagine. Many people give the impression that, in the same way as black night descends over the Polar regions during winter, so our coasts are swept by gales that never abate.

Resisting these prophets, steadfast in the faith, *Cohoe* put to sea again at 1130 on Tuesday, 14th December. The Plymouth meteorological man had been voluble, almost dogmatic. A fresh to strong west-south-west wind would increase during the night to Force 7 and a veer west-north-west, with clearing skies, would come around 0300 next morning. No gale was expected.

This time, under the usual double-reefed main and working jib, it was a beat to the Runnelstone. My log showed the wind as fresh, but as we neared Land's End it piped up into the Force 6 category. The going was hard but nothing like on Sunday night and we were content to struggle on, taking a pride in the progress. Once the low, angry Longships reef was weathered, it was a relief to free the sheets and slowly bring the tall granite lighthouse round on the quarter. The hard, south-flowing tide made it a lengthy business. At first we steered N.N.W. to clear Cape Cornwall Bank and its lumpy seas; then we settled on N. by E.$\frac{1}{2}$E. for the Smalls, by this time less than 90 miles away.

Cohoe went well during the first part of the night but the meteorological man's veer came 7 hrs. early—at 2000 in fact— and after this the wind eased to Force 4, giving slower progress in the cross-swell.

At 1000 on Wednesday morning the Smalls, the rocky outpost 15 miles west of the Pembrokeshire coast, was abeam but soon after this the little auxiliary had to officiate in place of the wind. But the afternoon was a glorious compensation: brilliant sunshine and light south-south-east wind that gently increased until by dusk, our little yacht was broad reaching under main and genoa at a speed of 7 knots.

Before this breeze came a small Naval vessel had altered course to examine us closely and those on her bridge waved vigorously. We began to wonder whether they recognized our little craft: who knew, perhaps some of them had raced against her neck-and-neck in the R.N.S.A. yacht *Samuel Pepys*, over 3,000 miles of ocean.

With the night came the cold, raw and penetrating, but the progress remained excellent. There is little else to tell. Bardsey came up at 2020, St. Tudwals pathetic little light showed up a little later, 14 miles distant in the good visibility. At midnight we entered St. Tudwals Roads and an hour and a half later we swung round into Pwllheli Harbour, the way lighted by the moon over the clouds, and helped ourselves to a mooring.

CHAPTER 10

Hugging a Cold Coast-line

To Northumberland in *Swan of Arden*

THE presumption of "hugging the coast" necessarily assumes that the sea in the immediate vicinity of the land is less tumultuous than farther offshore. If the wind blows from the land this is true, and creeping along under its lee is a decidedly good idea—providing you wish to proceed in that direction and do not have to cross a broad sea or deep bay. Hugging the Biscay coast in order to reach Portugal from Ushant would exactly double the direct crossing. From Land's End to the Smalls Lighthouse at the entrance to the Irish Sea is 99 miles; if you follow the coast up past Padstow towards Lundy Island, and from thence out of the Bristol Channel via the St. Gowan Lightship and Milford Haven entrance, you will have to cover nearly 40 miles more before reaching the main shipping route again. Both these areas have a good proportion of on-shore winds which will transform the 5 miles or so next to the shore from a relatively safe place to one of special peril. Besides, many parts of the Biscay coast and pretty well all North Cornwall, and North Devon as far as Barnstaple Bay, are most inhospitable places, best given a wide berth. There are plenty of other coasts and shores that are also dangerous, with treacherous off-lying shoals, swift tides or overfalls, to be treated with respect by all navigators. Rather than hug them, a nice grizzly bear is recommended.

But not all the land meets the sea in such an uncouth way. There are coasts that are steep-to, i.e. having deep water near the shore, where prevailing winds blow from the land and if these follow the general direction of your route it is sensible to use any shelter they offer. Such luck seldom holds throughout a voyage. There are many gusty corners to our islands which mark the end of shelter. Also only a short fetch between you and the shielding coast is necessary before a strong breeze creates a sea rough enough to make a yacht uncomfortable. To be worth while, gaining comfort from a sheltered coast means keeping close under the land and careful pilotage to skirt off-lying shoals may be necessary.

When the wind is blowing along the general lie of the coast, projecting headlands, under whose lee calm water will be found, will be of help to a yacht beating to windward. You will do well to stand into these bays because the yacht will go faster and point higher into the wind in smooth seas. Also it will give the crew a spell of relief after the discomfort of punching big head seas. Tides are generally weaker in the bays; therefore it is good tactics to arrange beating round the exposed headland when the stream is going your way, dealing with the sheltered parts when it is contrary.

The owner of the M.F.V. type yacht looked down on us in *Swan of Arden*:

"I don't envy you at this time of the year. What will be your first port of call?"

With wide cruising experience, including a trip to the Orkney Islands in a 4-tonner, he had no illusions about our February voyage to Blyth in one of Frederick Parker's fine Class III offshore racers.

"Hope we shall make Ramsgate," I said. "But I would not be surprised to find ourselves in Newhaven tomorrow and jolly glad to settle for that."

From our berth in Lymington River the breeze appeared only a point east of north, suggesting a good weather shore to the Straits of Dover. That far we ought to find shelter by hugging the coast. However, I know how river valleys deflect a wind and feared the true breeze was more easterly, tending to blow down Channel. Probably it would be dead against us when we rounded Dungeness, making a long beat towards Dover. From Dover, you round the South Foreland and Ramsgate is some 16 miles to the north. The more I considered the matter in the light of the keen frosty morning, which spelt winter with a capital "W", when it comes to sailing open cockpit 8-ton yachts to windward at night, the less sure I was of getting so far in one hop. There would be only two of us; as usual coastal delivery work warranted skipper and one crew. Two mouths to feed, two fares per British Railways; these things have to be kept at their economic minimum, especially when tough conditions are more likely to prolong the job.

It guaranteed us at least 50 per cent of our time in the fresh air, plus the periods with all hands on deck. Despite protective clothing, such a régime beating against truly icy stuff can wear down ability to survive. Time below deck may be insufficient to sustain the off-watch crew. Time at the helm becomes a nightmare. Doubtless man is hard to kill but just as mountaineers may die of exposure if the weather goes against them, so I suspect this kind of watch-and-watch in a small yacht eventually would cause casualties. It never fails to startle me that amateur yachtsmen can be found to come as crew for such projects. Desperate desire for seagoing experience by those smitten with the "yachting-bug" is the cause and I was lucky to sail with stoic Ron Holman, telephone engineer when he pu꜀ues a non-insane occupation. An Arctic explorer could have served me no better.

We cast off and motored our 26-ft. L.W.L. auxiliary sloop out of the river, where I hoisted the mainsail and No. 2 jib; then I rolled five turns of the former round the boom with the roller reefing gear. Lymington is surprisingly sheltered and a brisk steely breeze was blowing straight down the land-locked Solent against the north-east flowing flood tide. The sun lit the crests of the short wavelets. My job being on the foredeck, I donned oilskins early, but my crew was wet before he got around to his. Wind and water are wonderful cooling agents; make the former a February nor'easter and you are hard-pressed to maintain the 98°F. we human beings are supposed to provide for ourselves. Saboteur of personal thermostats, *Swan of Arden* settled down to work in her usual dynamic way, heeling, driving to windward easily, knocking the popple into spray, ice-cold stuff that frequently came as far aft as the cockpit.

This was the start of the sheltered part. We began watches as soon as sail was set and Ron went below to keep warm. Winter's early night was with us before I had done my 3 hrs. Darkness came as we beat past Cowes; then, laying longer tacks, our route bore round towards No Man's Land Fort by Ryde. We gained more protection from the coast as it ran east-south-east towards Southsea. Beyond there, the Selsey Bill promontory would give us shelter.

Off Hayling Island the west flowing ebb began to slow us. Three hours in the cockpit left the helmsman chilled to the marrow. We yearned for a night's rest, thinking of an anchorage in Chichester Harbour and the next fair tide round Selsey. As usual, factors for and against were apparent. Unlit buoys off Selsey Bill lead to the Looe Gap inside the Owers Bank. In daylight we could follow this inshore channel and gain as much shelter from the coast as possible. The alternative route is some 7 miles offshore, round the Owers L.V., the advisable way to go at night except in perfect conditions, including a bright moon. However, though awaiting the daylight tide in Chichester is attractive, by the time you have water to cross the bar, there is barely time to catch the fair stream round Selsey. Further, the anchorage by the Hayling Island Yacht Club, the only practical one to find in Chichester Harbour at night, while snug against a sou'wester is open to the north and east, and the existing strong wind would not give us a comfortable time. Moreover, by the time we reached it, secured and made ready for sleep, we should have less than 5 hrs. if we were to catch the morning tide. I could see us missing it, awaiting the next, and then nightfall would force us outside the Owers after all.

Plenty of snags, plus the demoralizing thought of stopping barely before beginning, but the deciding consideration was that Hayling Yacht Club's bright characteristic light which normally establishes the entrance clearly was not exhibited that winter's night. We would have to rely more on the weak red flasher on the outer perch which can barely be seen before you reach the shallowest part of the bar. It all seemed difficult and because the wind had eased a little, I chose to get on with the voyage. Frozen feet were ignored and the *Swan* was headed seaward for the Owers Lightship.

The midnight weather forecast reported Force 7 at the Royal Sovereign, 40 miles to the east, and as we approached the triple flashing Owers there seemed little to choose between the wind at either lightship. Shelter from the shore had gone. The fetch from this bitter nor'easter stretched from the east of Littlehampton,

14 miles of it. A typical Channel chop and a heavy swell was careering at us. Long streaks of foam between the nearer bursting creamers were clear in the moonlight. A mile or so south was the closest we could claw to the lightvessel. We continued the port tack, holding a course E.S.E. for another 4 hrs., crossing well seaward of the coastal shipping route, and sighting larger ocean going vessels as they came in for their Dungeness landfalls. So much for hugging the coast; but *Swan of Arden* loved it. Suitably reefed, she thrashed to windward in a smother, laughing at her crew of weak, warm-blooded flesh, so distressed about those few missing degrees F. that made all the difference.

Before dawn we put about to head north for England. I hoped to see Brighton but after 5 hrs.' endurance we were rewarded with Worthing—a disappointment to the tune of 10 miles down wind. Remaining daylight was used beating onwards until, 25 hrs. out of Lymington, we crept thankfully into Newhaven.

Altogether a rugged trip; yet the wind had been mostly north-east—an offshore breeze. The Owers Bank and unlit Selsey Bill were the main reasons why we could not make short tacks close under the land. The Owers is adequately lit by the light-vessel at its south-east extremity. Nevertheless, to head for the shelter of the shore immediately after weathering it would have involved skirting to windward of shallows known as the Shoal of Lead, on which the moderate gale would have been breaking heavily. Furthermore, we should have been close to the unlit East Borough Head Buoy, a thing to avoid during darkness. Truly, offshore winds do not necessarily provide a comfortable passage, least of all if you have to tack.

After 2 days the easterly died away and we left Newhaven by permission of the auxiliary engine, carrying almost a complete calm as far as Great Yarmouth, where a breeze sprang from the east-north-east. A hunch paid off here. When on passage across the Wash approaches, that expanse of shallow water between the Lincolnshire and North Norfolk coasts, I normally take the inshore route through the sandbanks. You start by leaving Yarmouth Roads, proceeding northwards through the Cockle Gat, the narrow channel between Caister Sand near the shore and the treacherous Scroby; then, skirting Cromer, you head W.N.W. seaward to pass between Race Bank and Docking Shoal. Through this well buoyed channel, the course for the Humber Lightvessel leads you clear of the Inner Dowsing and lesser dangers. The advantage of the route lies in the possibility of gaining almost a whole tide—and the streams run swiftly. The flood round the Norfolk coast converges on the Wash ports, meeting the rising tide from the north that also helps fill Boston River and King's Lynn. Thus, if you carry the tide north through the Cockle, past Cromer, you will reach Race Bank at the start of the ebb out of the Wash proper. Of course, if your timing is unfavourable the opposite will occur: you may punch a foul tide for 12 hrs.

Though *Swan of Arden* was all set to take the start of the fair tide through the Cockle and enjoy good time towards Cromer, and though this route would bring the newly found wind on her quarter, I decided on the alternative course, that would keep us as far to windward as possible. I headed seaward of the Scroby Sands, close to the Cross Sands Lightvessel; from thence along the main coasting route past the Dudgeon and Outer Dowsing Lightships and direct for Flamborough Head. Substantiated by the shipping forecast, my fear was that as we progressed north the wind would be persistently less favourable. There might be a chance of lying the course from the Outer Dowsing to Flamborough, but from the Humber Lightvessel, where the inshore route across the Wash terminates some 17 miles nearer the coast, a strong north-north-east wind would successfully slew even a close-winded yacht to leeward of the great Yorkshire headland.

Sleet came at dawn, bringing a bleak leaden hue to the wintry daybreak. His 3 hrs. up, Ron went below thankfully to thaw after I had struggled into all available clothing, everything that would go under my roomy oilskin suit. The effect of dressing had helped the circulation, but I yearned for my sleeping bag. Close reaching, the *Swan* was looking after herself well and, with only an occasional adjustment on the helm, I was able to brew coffee. A Dutch coaster was coming up astern, rolling and pitching in the steep uneven swell for which the existing light breeze could not account. Farther to the north real wind clearly had been blowing for some time; yet it was surprising when we soon encountered the remarkably precise demarcation line between fair and foul weather. Suddenly, after the Dutchman took the lead, the *Swan* was romping along at top speed as if loath to let the coaster get away with it. Immediately she demanded proper attention from the helmsman who gulped down the last of his coffee and crawled into the bleak cockpit, now a spray-covered site, to do his duty. Next the full main was only for the racing fanatic; others would reef.

Torrential rain augmented, then replaced, sleet as the heavy squall struck and I scrambled forward to roll a substantial amount of mainsail round the boom. With the halyard let go, the change in sail area paid her off a point, setting her on a collision course with an approaching south-bound collier. The helm lashed, I continued with my job with the reefing gear at the mast, mumbling expletives that sought to establish that if ever there was a time for a wind-driven tiddler standing on her power-gives-way-to-sail rights, this was it. And credit where due, the big coaster hove round to *port*, safely bringing her *starboard* side to mine. As she passed the officer on her bridge examined *Swan of Arden* through binoculars. I gave him a wave, appreciative I hope it looked, and just in case he said "Daft yachtsman, don't you know it's winter!", I shouted in defiance, because I knew he could not hear, "Good for you, wheelhouse sailor boy!". Then returning to the cockpit, I accentuated the swagger that is natural for somebody clambering about the windward side of a heaving yacht's deck, especially when clad in two pairs of pyjamas, four jerseys, heavy, long woollen underpants, trousers, windcheater, oilies and seaboots. Yet hypocrite Haward knew right then what he would have given for a nice snug wheelhouse!

Another ship had been in sight when we had changed watches, a small, barge-like coaster, heavily laden, broad on the starboard bow. It had been overhauling us only slowly and now, with the increase in wind, the tables were turned for a while, even despite the substantial reef I had rolled down. However, the squall eased and, while the heavy pall of cloud miraculously cleared, the wind settled down to a steady Force 6.

We kept company with the slow coaster for some 40 miles, then, as I had feared, the wind backed a little to the north and slowed us up, forcing us to harden the sheets. We passed the Dowsing at 1300: 45 miles to Flamborough. With satisfaction I realized that my choice of route was paying dividends. It looked as if the starboard tack close-hauled would just see us clear of Yorkshire's rugged, easternmost headland. Then we could pay off a little and have something in hand for a further change of wind. Had we been closer to the Humber, it would have been necessary to tack.

Two days out of Newhaven, 3 hrs. on and 3 hrs. off, we were now subjected to bitter conditions and a wild sea. Below decks was a shambles, cooking an impossible feat. We fought a desperate battle against weariness and the cold, but there could be no let-up. We were spurred on by the threat of a strike, for in just 2 days British Railways were likely to come to a standstill, and I was determined to catch the last train home from Blyth. It was a winter's offshore race against the National Union of Railwaymen.

At 1800 the radio broke the good news—the strike was off. Shortly afterwards Flamborough's five flashes showed on the leeward bow, intermittently amongst the big swell. We were able to weather the headland comfortably and, no longer plagued with the problem of our return home, we put into Scarborough in the small hours.

Thirty hours later we proceeded, despite the early morning forecast talking of gales in the vicinity. The harbour officials had kindly noted the details for our sea area: "Wind south-west Force 6–8, veering north-west to north".

The rugged Yorkshire coast from Scarborough runs approximately north-west towards Tees Bay, with High Whitby Head a prominent half-way mark. While the wind remained south-west we could hug the shore, keep close in and gain real shelter under the high cliffs. However once we reached Tees Bay, although the coast line turns more to the north, it was likely that the approaching cold front would have passed, treating us to the northerly winds behind it. Then there would be no more shelter and with the dead muzzler possibly reaching gale force, tacking would soon pall. If we made Hartlepool at the far end of Tees Bay, we could consider it a satisfactory day's work.

At 0845 on the Sunday the trains nearly stopped, *Swan of Arden* was sailing free, snugly reefed before a fresh sou'wester off the land. With deep water right up to the cliffs, we were in absolutely smooth water, making excellent progress in comfort. As the wind increased we shortened sail further, taking our time at the reefing gear and rolling the main evenly round the boom. With Terylene this is particularly important because a slight defect in the set of the sail may cause exceptional leech flutter, even with battens rigged.

At 1115 Whitby Harbour was abeam—6 knots; very satisfactory for a yacht of 26 ft. waterline length. The noon (Sunday) shipping forecast was precise. A small vigorous depression would move south across our area in the afternoon, the associated cold front sweeping down the whole North Sea like a scythe of ice. Already radio programmes had been interrupted with a special warning that the south-west gale in areas Forth and Tyne would veer north-west to north. The grandeur of Yorkshire encompassing beautiful Runswick Bay and steep-to Cowbar Nab was still our sheltering coast, but clearly the hours were numbered. Once the wind swung towards the north with a gale force flurry, a heavy sea would quickly assail the rocky shore. If she were to reach the shelter of Hartlepool, our yacht must batter a path in the teeth of it.

A stop at Whitby had been an attractive but impractical thought because we passed the harbour at dead low water springs. A booming swell was pounding heavily on the bar and we saw the offshore wind blasting the tops of the breakers backwards as they crashed on to the rocks. No entry here until there was more water, by which time the entrance might be wide open to the gale and dangerous at all states of tide.

The snow began imperceptibly; it was the heavy clouds and dim light which gave the game away. The wind increased, piping up to the Force 7 mark, but still the coast gave shelter. The free ride ended off Huntcliff. As Saltburn pier came into view the wind swung round north-west with diabolical glee, quickly engineering something vicious out of the fetch across Tees Bay. With nine rolls in the main, the mainsail head half-way between the jumper struts and the spreaders, the *Swan* paid off north by east; barely north of north-east soon after.

A brief clearance; then a heavier snow squall blotted out the visibility and passing inshore of the Salt Scar Buoy, I could barely see the shore.

Happily it was short-lived, there was little substance behind the cold front. But while it lasted it was a wet, chilly business, tacking into the short sea that immediately developed. We made two boards seaward before we crossed the mouth of the Tees, by which time the skies had cleared and we had given *Swan of Arden* her full mainsail again. We entered Hartlepool Harbour in a light breeze. We made Blyth the next day after another 6 hrs.' sailing.

Harbour Launch from Londonderry

ANYBODY intending to buy a yacht should appoint his own surveyor. A good broker will offer this advice and prefer you to choose your own. He himself is prejudiced, wishing to promote a sale. A surveyor should be hard-boiled and happy to condemn as he finds. The fact that his words may drastically reduce the value of somebody's property (or rather reveal its *true value*) must not worry him at all. In the U.S.A. gangsters are said to have tame lawyers: to ask your yacht broker to recommend a surveyor is to encourage the same thing.

Nor should it be thought that a delivery skipper can replace a surveyor. If he is to have the job of moving a newly purchased yacht, a skipper's concern is that she will, at the time, be seaworthy enough to make the required voyage but it will not be his business to worry about obscure defects or hidden deterioration that may mean costly repairs later. Anyway, apart from questions of competence—a good seaman and navigator is not necessarily a good surveyor—a delivery skipper probably will not see the vessel until after the purchase has been completed; therefore he will be too late to guard the buyer against a foolish deal.

Nevertheless, before putting to sea a skipper must be confident that his vessel will make the voyage safely. Particularly if there has been no recent professional survey, he may find himself deciding that the boat is unfit for the passage—or his first encounter with contrary weather bring him to this conclusion. Then he will spend additional time, for which he did not bargain, trying to put matters right, but if he cannot exclude the possibility of disaster he will be forced, finally, to spill the unwelcome news to the owner. Inevitably this will mean a loss all round. Even if the expenses of the delivery crew and modest daily wages are met, the business will be unsatisfactory because if the craft had been in proper order she would, in all probability, have reached her destination by this time. Despite this the reputation of a delivery skipper may well suffer in the eyes of his customer who will find criticism of his wonderful bargain hard to bear. He may wonder whether the sad tidings really conceal cowardice.

A misleading fact is that his yacht may subsequently be moved by somebody else in fine weather without incident. This will gratify a bargain hunting owner but it is no proof that the decision of the first skipper was wrong. The most desperate excuses for yachts can go round the coast until it begins to blow. Only with wind and rough seas will the test come, and the distress signals, life-boat and (or) tragedy.

For a considerable time now I have accepted the fact that yacht delivery work, particularly in the older and cheaper craft, has an element of "no cure, no pay" about it. Often this has made me prefer a hazardous voyage rather than face the task of telling a customer he has bought a "pup". I have even banked on the British weather being kind and have put to sea with my eyes in blinkers.

I know of one experienced yacht delivery skipper who lost his life when an old conversion, doubtless purchased at bargain price, sank under him.

In telling the dilatory story of *Harbour Launch 42451* I confess I subsequently wondered why I had not immediately appreciated how weak and unfit for sea she was. I can only take comfort in the fact that the "obvious" escaped a number of other people also. True indeed is the saying that it is easy to be wise after an event. Let bargain hunters take note that it was the professional expert, the yacht surveyor, who drew attention to the crux of the matter. Called in all too late, when the craft was half-way to her required destination, his report stated:

> I should imagine that the craft was originally fitted with thwarts which subsequently were removed in order to give free access through the hull. The result is similar to removing the thwarts from an ordinary dinghy and expecting the sides to remain in place. This arrangement may be satis-

factory for harbour or river service but it is entirely unsuitable for the open sea.

Learning the hard way often makes a good yarn and when I proposed to record the sorry saga of *H.L. 42451* her owner said that in fairness I ought to mention that my expenses were out of all proportion to the job on hand. If by "job", he meant his boat, that is true; but always my thoughts were on economy. Very soon I was spending nights in harbour aboard his virtually open boat in mid-winter. With hotels a few minutes walk, I was bedding down under a cross between a leaking bus shelter and a tattered tent. The story could not have dragged on as long as it did without mounting expense but the owner was informed of these details as they occurred. Balanced against a vessel of value, the outlay would not have been out of the way, but *H.L. 42451* was not worth very much in the first place; thus the demands of the voyage represented a considerable percentage increase on the price that was paid for her. Altogether she levied a high cost financially and in physical hazard.

The challenge that a passage in an open boat holds for me has, on occasions, landed me in uncomfortable situations, but I had once before made a coastal voyage in an unconverted 36 ft. ex-Naval harbour launch without many delays; therefore I had more enthusiasm than qualms when my old stalwart, Noel Tringham, and I, travelled to Ireland to take this similar craft, *H.L. 42451*, to the Thames. She had a 25 h.p. diesel engine, an advantage, I considered, over the petrol/paraffin motor that was aboard the former commitment. She also had two aluminium shelters, one over the engine aft, and one amidships which I thought would serve as a cabin. The Navy had used her as a diving boat, for which purpose, apparently, it had been convenient to remove her thwarts. She had been working in the sheltered waters of Lough Foyle and now, having been sold, she lay at the Maintenance Base at Londonderry awaiting our collection.

We obtained timber and canvas and covered in the open part of the boat forward to minimize shipping spray. Gear for the voyage was ordered—compass, navigation lights, fresh water containers, paraffin cans for cooking fuel and essential extra drums with which to supplement the modest 15-gallon tank that carried fuel for the engine. Other bare necessities included a primus stove, eating and cooking utensils and timber to knock up a couple of bunks in the bare centre shelter.

Though they had sold *H.L. 42451*, the Navy accepted a praiseworthy feeling of responsibility for those charged with taking her away, and besides helping us with our preparations for sea, they wished to know details of our ports of call, estimated times of arrival and so on. This is always a difficult question to answer because, when taking a small vessel round Britain in unsettled weather, the sensible plan is to stay at sea as long as the conditions remain favourable. "Never miss a fair wind" applies to any small craft, sail or power.

My policy has always been to phone my wife as soon as I put into port. Joan keeps a watch on the prevailing weather and will have a rough idea whether I would make an intermediate port of call or whether I would continue to my final destination. Besides this, the coastguard service tracks all coasting vessels as far as the weather, particularly the visibility, permits. In the event of doubt, phone calls could be made to coast stations and harbours *en route* before thinking in terms of trouble at sea. The important duty rests with the skipper of a yacht, who always ought to report his arrival regularly, whether to a friend, relative or a business organization. If he does not do that somebody may start to worry unnecessarily.

Our first departure from Derry in *H.L. 42451* was a short-lived affair. On turning the first bend in the river I noticed that the bilge below the engine was filling rather rapidly and investigation revealed that the silencer was rusted through so that the engine cooling water was being discharged inboard instead of over the side. We returned to base and handed the craft over to the local engineering works for repairs. We were lucky to be able to fill in time by going straight on with another job.

November gave way to a stormy December before *H.L. 42451* was ready for our further attention. Noel Tringham was now unable to come with me, having arranged to join another vessel, and because the economics of this kind of work provides little more than a fair wage for the skipper I prefer to take crews who find values other than money to compensate their voyaging. The reward must be to answer the call of the sea but towards Christmas such a call is regrettably rare in the northern hemisphere. Therefore I was lucky in contacting Tim, an experienced yachtsman, who seemed keen on even the most Spartan of voyages. His one stipulation was that he must be home for the festive days, a reasonable request. We met on the Belfast Ferry, among starry-eyed Irishmen bound for the Emerald Isle.

Though fitted with electric heaters to assist, we found our diesel none too easy to start. One of the Maintenance Base mechanics advised us how he used to get over the trouble when the craft was in his care:

"Just a whiff over the air filter with a drop of ether," he said. "And she'll be away in no time!"

It worked wonders but the difficulty was to buy ether. Apparently the murder industry favours the stuff for its various techniques, and the law restricts its sale to those who have doctors' prescriptions. However, we discovered that model aircraft engine fuel is almost the same fluid and Londonderry's leading toy shop was pleased to supply a bottle.

In the rough accommodation improvised under the midships shelter we laid out our sleeping bags; Tim on the bunk built over the spare fuel drums on the starboard side, I on the wooden contrivance erected 2 in. from the floor on the centre line of the boat. We reinforced the aft end of the shelter with very ripe tarpaulin which Tim had won from a rubbish dump, but it was difficult to anchor the lower ends to the floor, and the various bits tended to flap about in the wind. That enabled light to come in, but with it would come the cold and the rain. The forward part of our hut was an aluminium bulkhead with a sliding door. We turned in that night to have fitful sleep, being unaccustomed to our wet and draughty environment. The midnight shipping forecast talked about south-west winds reaching Force 7 and veering later.

At 1100 the next morning, with seven shopping days to Christmas, we cast off from Londonderry and proceeded down the Foyle. In the Lough we began to realize the strength of the wind. Heavy squall clouds brought torrential rain and brought the westerly wind well into the full-gale bracket. The channel runs close to the north-west shore of this expanse of sheltered water but, despite the very short fetch, quite a lively sea was following us on the port quarter, and the craft could be seen to be making considerable leeway. What was going on outside the Lough held little appeal, and we tied up at Moville, 5 miles from the sea.

Lunch by primus and the weather eased a little. We set off just before dusk to obtain a compass check and, by the time the operation was complete, the wind had dropped to around Force 5. Christmas was coming and the tide was right. I knew Tim was just rearing to be off, and for my own part I wanted to have the open Northern Irish coast, with its awful rips and races, somewhere astern of us. After some contemplation I decided to have a go. We could always turn back—there is no law against that. It was not even like some harbours where a jaunt outside for a look-see and a subsequent scurry back meets with the berthing bloke demanding harbour dues again. We donned warm gear and oilies. Tim tacked down the tarpaulin flap over the bow section, left open in port to lead the mooring ropes ashore, and out we trudged.

Perhaps it was just as well that darkness shrouded the entrance because had we perceived the size of the seas before meeting them we should very likely have fled back to Moville, there to be bottled up for days. A huge Atlantic swell, the product of the persistent blow, was running along the coast and, in the many areas where overfalls and rips abound, these waves were apparently becoming unstable and their tops were tending to tumble.

The wind had veered further; thus boosting the swell round Inishtrahull Island, and sending it towards the shore south of us. Mostly we rode it well but at one particular place, when we had progressed about 5 miles on our way, some heavy slop tumbled aboard amidships and it became necessary to pump immediately. I realized that we were passing through an unstable patch and felt no cause for alarm. The general way the craft behaved was reassuring.

At 1800 the radio forecast indicated the urgency of the situation: "Wind west to north-west, Force 6 to 8, backing south-west. Good visibility, becoming moderate or poor." My log entry noted the present wind west-north-west Force 5, with good visibility. Despite the pessimism of the B.B.C., I was confident that the wind would ease further before backing. That is what generally happens as one depression comes in on the tracks of another; failure to mention the lull was due to the "lows" moving so fast that the meteorological men did not consider the pause worth bothering about.

My mind was set on Fair Head, barrier to the Atlantic swell

and shelter against sou'westerly weather. We must reach that corner quickly; Rathlin Sound would have no shelter for us tonight. In fact, we were given 3 hrs. in which to do it and, helped by the favourable tide, it was enough. The launch came under the lee of the land as the tide turned northerly to empty the North Channel, and the wind began to pipe up from the southwest.

Then all progress came to a halt because the engine packed up. Dirt in the fuel tank, debris that looked as though an oakum picker had used it as a waste basket, had been sucked into the pipe. The filter was clear of the stuff: it was so big it had not got that far—thus time was wasted in tracing the trouble. I blew the pipe through to the tank and bled the pipes to the injectors, then she started up again.

Meanwhile wind and tide had carried us well north of Fair Head and clear of its sheltering shoulder. It was quite a tussle to punch back. No sooner was it done than the engine began to labour again. It was the same trouble but this time I went to the seat of the stoppage, removing the sump plug from the fuel tank and pulling out a great lump of the offending material. Then I blew through the pipe and we were off again. I had stopped the motor before it had become completely starved of fuel and so it was unnecessary to bleed the fuel pumps.

Off Fair Head for the third time, we were able to continue down the sheltered coast. But the wind continued to strengthen and a short steep sea developed, into which the launch began to pound heavily. Spray was quick to find the weak spots in our midship shelter. It was my turn at trying to sleep, and I was glad of the waterproof cover to my sleeping bag. Even so my improvised pillow was soon wet and splashes of water on the face inhibit sleep far more effectively than do indigestion, cold feet or a guilty conscience. I was glad to give up the attempt and grapple instead with the problems of progress. The launch was being slowed by headwinds and was starting to leak.

Tim had pumped her dry earlier but, when I took over, the propeller shaft coupling was again awash and churning up the bilge water under the after floorboards. I told my mate to have a shot at sleeping, thinking I could easily pump her out myself and hold the course as well. In fact, this was an effort because the pump was out of reach of the helm and working it for only a very short time was enough for the boat to be blown badly off course. The drill was twenty-five strokes, then to the tiller to straighten her, then back to the pump again: it was a lengthy operation.

The Maidens Rocks, lit by a triple-flashing lighthouse, was on our port beam and I was heading for the Hunter Rock flasher. The wind was settling down to a hard blow and clearly would soon be up to gale force. There would be no shelter after passing Muck Island until we crossed Belfast Lough. Even a mile or so from the land, from which the wind blew slantwise, our launch was making heavy weather of it. There was only one prudent course; put into Larne, the "short sea route" channel port a few miles away.

We entered as dawn was breaking. There seemed few facilities and, after berthing in poor shelter in a dock enclosed by wooden piers, we had an uncomfortable morning. Later we learned that the best place for small craft was across the narrow entrance to the Lough, in a little stone harbour, and here we were able to secure the launch safely and take the ferry back to the town side of the water. Then we found a kind-hearted landlady who helped us dry out our gear and bedding that had been completely soaked during the latter part of the night. By evening a severe gale was blowing.

The next afternoon we were off again. The general outlook appeared stormy and certainly another vigorous depression would come in from the Atlantic, to bring the same kind of weather we had met already. However, it did seem as if there would be a pronounced lull meanwhile. Certainly we would cross Belfast Lough and make Donaghadee just beyond, but I had my eyes on Dublin Bay. To get there in one hop would require up to 24 hrs., but if we could ride out the next gale in the inner harbour at Dun Laoghaire, we should have half the Irish Sea behind us. It seemed possible that a real veer in wind might follow and, with a breeze behind us, we could start to eat up the miles. Milford Haven for Christmas would be a real possibility, and that would avoid the expense of return travel to Ireland afterwards. Though the difficult leg round Land's End would remain, a substantial part of the job would have been completed.

There was still plenty of wind in evidence when, clearing the shelter of the land, we began to feel the draught out of Belfast

Lough. Punching and pounding, the craft began to leak once more. During the night's rest in Larne she had "taken up"; the leak begun during the previous leg had stopped, but now it was clear that this modest head sea, the product of the short fetch out of Belfast Lough, was enough to grind the planking together and permit the sea water to seep in. Something must be loose somewhere.

However, progress was excellent and, though the breeze remained a vigorous Force 5 with strong gusts, the radio forecast still hinted that there would be a lull. I thought we ought to forget Donaghadee. We carried the fair tide down to the South Rock Lightship where a big swell heralded the type of weather prevailing in the Irish Sea.

Once again our attempt at an ordered routine failed to bring rest or sleep to the watch below. The ability to remain at sea for an indefinite period depends more on this factor than is generally appreciated; and it is a particularly important matter when voyaging in small craft. After we had passed the lightship and were heading across 60 miles of open sea to the approaches of Dublin Bay, I handed over to Tim and went through the motions of turning in. The launch was now pounding very heavily even though her speed had been reduced. The sensation and the noise in the midship shelter was ghastly. Sleep was quite out of the question.

She appeared to be badly designed for facing heavy contrary weather. The forward section is broad, flat bottomed and without a decent "V" section to cut into the advancing seas and carve a gentle landing ground. Most of the weight is aft, including the heavy engine, with the result that the bow tends to rise higher and slam down harder. We were now lumbering slowly along, so slowly, in fact, that it was difficult to maintain steerage way, but the hull was striking many of the advancing waves as if they were solid rocks. Such was the violence of one of these thuds that the valves in my radio were broken. This occurred just before midnight, putting us out of touch with the weather situation.

I turned out at 0200, glad to be clear of our streaming hell-hole of a "cabin". Little progress had been made over the last 3 hrs. and the South Rock Light could still be seen astern. The launch was leaking heavily and needed pumping despite Tim's efforts. This time I cleared the bilge before taking the helm, then, left to my own devices, I reviewed the situation.

The wind was Force 6, south-west and dead ahead. The lull as forecast showed no signs of materializing. The stars were out and, because there had been no substantial veer when the clearance came, I saw little hope of better conditions. Probably this *was* the "lull". Soon the wind would back south or even south-east and pipe into gale once more. If that happened, the Irish coast would provide no general weather shore although Skerries Bay, still 45 miles distant, would give shelter. Farther down, Dun Laoghaire in Dublin Bay seemed a long way off. Our vessel was progressing at less than 1½ knots. The cards seemed stacked against us. I pumped the bilge frequently and studied the chart by torchlight between spells of bringing the boat back on course. A coaster overtook us, rolling and pitching, but making enviable progress.

There was one other alternative to running back to Donaghadee: Ardglass, which now lay a little abaft the beam, just 3 miles E.N.E. of St. John's Point. I had no detailed chart of this little fishing port, but I had heard that it gives good shelter and was not dangerous to enter even during on-shore winds such as were blowing now. Thumbing through Reed's light list, I learned that the white sector of an occulting light led you into the entrance clear of all rocks. It was nearly low water, but there would be plenty of depth at the outer breakwater. At 0500 I called Tim to tell him to give up his attempt to sleep. Soon we could both try it without the banging and bumping. He turned out as we altered course.

There was nothing to the pilotage. The occulating light soon showed up, first green, until we reached the white leading sector. We ran in before wind and sea rounded the breakwater and tied up leeward of the fishmeal factory, very complete with smell. On the far side of the basin the gale cone hung dismally, faintly outlined by the first hint of dawn.

Our bilge pumping system was unsatisfactory. We had been using the small plunger pump alongside the engine. Normally I find the type efficient and reasonably fool-proof but, although I spent several hours taking this one to bits, it remained a poor device and hard to work. Clearing the bilge had been a tiring, disagreeable operation and in the future it promised to be a frequent necessity. Amidships was a No. 5 semi-rotary pump, an unusually large size for a 36-ft. boat. I do not think we were the first to while away hours pumping *H.L. 42451*.

A semi-rotary pump is efficient but will fail when the smallest piece of debris sticks in its valves, and it is therefore essential to have a good strum-box to filter the bilge water. We made one out of a gallon oil can, then we bolted the pump to a position within easy reach of the helmsman. In future, if there were pumping difficulties, it would indicate something very wrong with our vessel.

The weather outlook was poor. The next morning, 22nd December, I telephoned the local meteorological station for a forecast. The wind would remain strong, veering later northerly, and possibly increasing to gale. The forecaster agreed our best plan was to leave the boat at Ardglass and go home for Christmas. I looked at the chart. Dublin Bay was dead in the wind's eye at the moment and recent experience proved we could make only very slow progress. I studied the North Wales coast. A berth in Bangor, on the Menai Straits, would suit me for Christmas. The course from Ardglass would bring the wind on the beam and though we would roll heavily, our speed would not have to be cut down. But Tim said:

"What if the promised northerly gale comes before we make the Menai Straits?"

He was quite right. With the wind blowing straight on to the coast, the approach to the Straits has its dangers. The channel between Puffin Island and Anglesey is guarded by areas of overfalls and these must be negotiated before gaining shelter. Regretfully I said that we had better find out the times of the Belfast-Liverpool ferry, and Tim went off to make inquiries.

Then, in a bare half-hour, a remarkable change came over the weather, the sky cleared and the wind eased. It was contrary to everything the meteorological man had told me less than an hour ago, and I walked up the road to phone him again.

"I'm glad you rang. Latest reports change things considerably. It looks as if the south-west wind will die out and there should be a fine spell tonight. The northerly blow I spoke of may yet come later."

Here was a chance that must not be missed. Tim came back with the news that the Irish ferry services took a day off on Sundays; the next one would be on Monday night. I told him we would take the Dublin boat. But my shipmate had had enough. My sudden enthusiasm failed to infect him. He had come for pleasure, and knew it was gaining on him. He wanted an insurance on his Christmas pudding and was determined to rely only on British Railways, who guaranteed to get him home by Tuesday. My E.T.A.s were a myth. And I entirely sympathized. If I had been without obligations regarding *H.L. 42451*, I should already have offered unconstructive suggestions about her and withdrawn my labour a while back. But, being pledged to complete the voyage, I would not admit that it was degenerating towards madness. Possibly with unnecessary brusqueness, I said:

"O.K., but I'm off as soon as possible. So please pack your gear as quickly as you can."

Just before he left, he questioned me with some incredulity:

"Do you really think you will make Dublin tomorrow?"

I replied in the affirmative. We shook hands and Tim helped me cast off. Feeling very much alone I plodded out of Ardglass, sad at losing a good shipmate and realizing that from now on I was likely to be on a single-handed delivery.

CHAPTER 12

"Sans" Crew, "Sans" Clock

THE wind had dropped quite light by now and a sloppy swell was all that remained of the bad weather. I had to punch against this and a contrary tide to clear St. John's Point, and it was a slow old game. Just how slow, I determined to calculate, and I looked at my watch, having already noted my departure at 1205. It had stopped and was almost fully wound. Neither shaking nor swearing did it any good.

A watch or clock is a navigational instrument. Without a patent log it is secondary only to a compass. Unless you know the time you cannot know when to expect a landfall. You cannot be sure of the distance you have run, and in thick weather you could be in danger of blundering on to shoals or rocks. Thus I gave the matter some thought. There was no policeman between here and Dublin to tell me the time. However, the weather was clearing and the visibility was expected to be good; therefore I had no qualms about carrying on.

One must also know the time to calculate the state of the tide and the direction of the tidal streams. Though it did not concern me on this particular trip because I was alone, another obvious but nevertheless important use of a clock is for establishing the change of watch. Without it there can be distinct differences of opinion in the matter. The man lying warm and comfortable in his bunk will be convinced that his mate in the wet above has ridiculously extravagant ideas on the flight of time. A clock or watch is the essential referee.

The motion of the launch was nothing like so bad as it had been when we were battling towards Ardglass from the South

Rock Lightship. In a few hours it became almost calm, but it soon was clear that she was leaking worse than ever. Without a timepiece I could not check an interval with strokes at the pump, and I can give no details. However, with the big semi-rotary at hand I always kept the bilge clear, though it became tiring and I worried about the condition of the boat implied by the work. I remained perfectly confident of reaching Dun Laoghaire, but it seemed that any further bad weather would bring about a dangerous change in the vessel's seaworthiness. The gap between Ireland and Land's End, 130 miles of exposed sea completely open to the Atlantic Ocean, is an area to take seriously.

The launch plodded on. Night fell, starry and clear. Without a watch there seemed an intolerable gap between the loom of St. John's Point light going down and the Rockabill light coming up. Eventually it obliged, and when I reached the lighthouse itself the tide added its help, swilling me towards massive Howth Head and Dublin Bay in excellent time. I think I motored into Dun Laoghaire Harbour at about 0100.

Before turning in, I pumped her dry and wrapped insulating tape round the dip-stick to seal the oil sump. I was up about 5 hrs. later and found the bilge water just below this level. Two thousand double strokes with the big No. 5 semi-rotary pump were required to remove the influx. This was while lying at rest in harbour—at sea she was much worse. Clearly something had to be done, but I found that the local boat builder had too many craft on his slip even to haul the launch out. He suggested John Tyrrell of Arklow, 23 miles down the coast and, when I phoned him in the afternoon, I was told to come right away. They could haul the boat out the next day, Christmas Eve, and I would be able to go home while they fixed the trouble.

A fresh north-east wind with drizzle set in with the early dusk, by which time any hastened preparation for sea was complete. On the last 2 hrs. of the south going tide I motored out of the harbour, pumping the bilge that had accumulated during the 2 hrs. I had been ashore. As soon as I came into the rough water, caused by the brisk wind blowing into Dublin Bay, I had to stop the engine. The water-cooling pump had packed up. Drifting inshore on wind and tide toward inhospitable Dalkey Island, I discovered that seaweed was jammed tightly in the inlet pipe, and hasty efforts to clear it were unsuccessful. The engine had cooled a little by this time: I therefore restarted it and ran it dead slow, heading back for the harbour I had just left. Reaching the entrance, I cut the engine and the launch was blown into safety. If I could not fix the trouble quickly, I could now pick up a mooring or drop anchor.

One hour later, everything in working order, I left Dun Laoghaire again and, by the time I was round the south extremity of Dublin Bay, the favourable tide was finished.

The wind strengthened as I approached Wicklow Head and progress was slow against the flood tide. After bringing the headland abeam, it seemed an age of pumping and roaring before boisterous seas before I reached the Horse Shoe Bank Buoy. The night was very dark and, though close to the rugged coast, no silhouette was visible. I began to wonder what Arklow entrance would be like in such weather.

I badly missed my watch. I could not log the time of passing the red flasher of the Horse Shoe nor could I note the interval in time before bringing the No. 1 Arklow Bank Buoy abeam. Thus I could not gauge the effect the strong north flowing tide was having on my speed. When both lights had disappeared, an endless time dragged by without the lights of Arklow town coming up. I was expecting them fairly quickly.

The launch was heading down the coast, inshore of the dangerous Arklow Bank. If I went too far seaward, I would be amongst the breakers; if I wandered too far towards the coast, I would blunder into unlit Mizzen Head. The impenetrable black night created a steadfast belief in being tightly hemmed in. Arklow Bank lies 6 miles off the coast. I had that much latitude, but I felt as if I were walking down the central white line of a busy main road. Disaster from either side seemed imminent.

I could still see Wicklow Head light but now I had lost all sense of time and the rising sea was throwing the compass about. So I began to wonder whether my bearings of it were accurate; also, for no good reason, I harboured doubts about my previous calculations of compass deviation.

What must have been a brief spell of time appeared to rush haywire into eternity. The hiss of the creaming crests, the thumping of the engine and the endless pumping to be done seemed to have been with me for ever. My nerve was on the wane, I dithered between the sodden chart and the helm. I could see

Wicklow light, but a good way off now; why not Arklow Town? Was it because I was too far out to sea? The fear of diving on to the death trap of Arklow Bank surmounted the other possibilities, and I altered course to run inshore. Wicklow's triple-flashing lighthouse was now a hazy glimmer in the bitter driving rain and it was more difficult than ever to establish its bearing with any accuracy.

Then we rolled and lumbered amongst a heap of overfalls and a faint suspicion of the land showed dead ahead. Mizzen Head: I *was* close inshore.

Still no sign of Arklow, I was now confident of my position. I steered to the south-east for a while, then back on course. The contrary tide must have been taking 4 knots off my speed, but as soon as I had cleared the Mizzen, Arklow Town lights would open out. And that is what happened. It seemed as if a nightmare had passed and, like all bad dreams in retrospect, the anxiety that had been real indeed now appeared stupid.

There remained the entrance to Arklow Harbour. With the on-shore wind, now east-north-east piping into a real blow, I expected a heavy sea there, but, with her bilges mostly clear by virtue of good pumping by a hard working mariner, the buoyant launch rolled past the outer breakwater without difficulty. Soon I was safely moored in the sheltered pool. The bilge was cleared finally before turning in; then came well earned sleep.

Severe leaking is not always easy to rectify. Examination with Tyrrell appeared to establish that most of the influx was at the meeting place of the keel and the diagonal planking. There was evidence of weeping between the seams of the inner planks at the turn of the bilges, but I felt that the plank edges along the keel, the "garboards"[1] were the important things to consider. By 1000, Tyrrell had the launch hauled out and it was decided to refasten the planks where they joined the keel. We were fairly certain that this would rectify the trouble and confident that the remainder of the voyage would not see the craft deteriorating.

Now I could go for my Christmas holiday and see Joan, the smaller Hawards and their cousins in Lancashire. After stowing equipment and seagoing gear in Tyrrell's store, I just made the

---

[1] On a longitudinally planked boat, as opposed to the diagonal planking of 42451 the plank next to the keel is called the garboard strake.

station by the time the Dublin train was due to depart. A cheerful official greeted me:

"She won't be here a while. You'll be having some dinner now and be back at a quarter to two."

I obeyed the instructions, although I returned to the station 5 min. before the advised time, just to be sure. The last coach left the platform as I reached the barrier. Recriminations would have been cruel; the porter had only sought to do the best for his customers. I asked the time of the next train and whether it would catch the Liverpool ferry.

"Five thirty, but that's another company's boat you're going on."

"But what time will I arrive in Westland Row?"

"Seven forty-five maybe, and then, maybe not."

I had to have a go anyway. Failure would mean being stranded in Dublin all the next day and it is grim spending Christmas alone in a strange city.

In fact, the railway company achieved great things—as far as Dun Laoghaire, but the signals were against us from then on. Containing my frustration quietly amidst singing Irishmen, I was ready to leave Westland Row like a shot from a gun. Outside was a taxi driver who was on my side. Whatever the record to the B. & I. dock used to be, he broke it and I was the last passenger up the gangway.

A surprising number of delivery jobs at the start of 1958 found me returning to Arklow early in January determined to bring *H.L. 42451* at least to Milford Haven or round the Land's End corner before having to join another vessel on 9th January. Unfortunately, the weather man was not on my side. Tyrrell had refastened all the plank edges to the keel but, on relaunching, the craft was still leaking substantially. The water could be seen welling between the inside planking at a number of places at the turn of the bilges on both sides. Fastenings around these places also were weak, and rectifying such trouble in a boat of this construction is a difficult proposition. Tyrrell, with two new boats building with precise delivery dates, could undertake to give no further help for at least 3 weeks.

I was very disappointed. I had been fairly certain that the main trouble had been where the planks joined the keel, but it now seemed as if many other fastenings in the double skin were loose also, making the hull rather like a rotten orange.

Morale dropped. Hoping to buy my way out of the project, I even obtained a quotation for shipping the hulk as freight from Dublin, and learned it would cost the kind of money I would normally cheerfully undercut. Then I thought of mechanical bilge pumps, and an excursion into Dublin brought to light a delightful Lee-Howe horizontal piston pump that could easily be belt-driven from the main shaft.

Because the costs involved in this desperate voyage have been criticized and also because I, personally, felt touched at the gesture, I would add that Tyrrell's engineers efficiently installed this outfit into the launch and, with typical Irish hospitality, particularly remembered to forget to add the cost to their account.

With this fixed up, I felt I had done all I could for the boat's future safety and, seeing no let-up in the bad weather, I left her securely moored in Arklow Pool to join my next commitment. Before returning to Ireland I attended to my own safety and borrowed a self-inflating survival raft—a modern and most practical life saving device for all small vessel seamen.

CHAPTER 13

End of a Misfire Bargain

ON Tuesday morning, 11th March, Dubliners still appeared dishevelled by the Sunday blizzard and continuing bitter north wind. Even the traditionally pretty girls of the Fair City obviously were not looking their best. Spring flowers were being snuffed out by a malicious return to deep winter. Land of mild, "soft" days, this might have been the granite city of north-east Scotland, and I must have been the only person there to pray that the forecasters were right in expecting the cold spell to continue. That would mean a north wind and was just what I needed to take me and *Harbour Launch 42451* down past the Tuskar Rock and round Land's End.

I was going single-handed, partly out of economy. A frightening outlay of cash had accompanied my various efforts to date, and now I must draw in my horns. But I also felt it was wrong to inveigle an amateur crew into such a voyage. I had now admitted to myself that there were more than normal hazards in this adventure.

With satisfaction I noted that the wind still blew from the north as the diesel train sped down the beautiful coastline of Bray. Dismay did not come until I arrived at Arklow Harbour just before the 1340 radio forecast. The breeze had backed eight points. The meteorological men confirmed the matter and the southerly gale arrived during the night.

At dawn, Thursday, 13th March, a fresh breeze blowing from the west-south-west, I motored out of the harbour hoping that the veer would bring a further improvement and that I would be able to make Milford Haven. I looked upon that as a fair passage for a lone seaman. The early morning forecast, which I picked up as I began the run down the coast past Arklow Rock, hinted at strengthening winds backing south during the night. I would be off Pembrokeshire by then and could run into the Haven.

The sun rose into a clear sky and, apart from a few squally showers, the worst chill was taken from the wind. I settled to a pleasant morning's coasting close inshore across Courtown Bay and inside Blackwater and Moneyweight Banks. Then I steered east of Long Bank for the Tuskar Rock, my departure point from Ireland.

The water-cooling pump now began to give trouble. It was a gear type and was hard put to deal with air occasionally sucked in when rolling brought the sea water inlet towards the water line. The answer was to loosen the delivery union and let the air locks go free. In heavy weather, a weak gear pump often will only function if this union bleeds continually.

The wind had been dropping and had veered north-west. The crisp morning had all the qualities of spring, and I felt on top of the world. Her cooling trouble solved, the Dorman diesel was thumping away contentedly, pushing the launch forward at nearly 7 knots. A feeling of well-being forced me to consider the idea of heading straight down to the Longships and round South-west England. It would break the back of the voyage, whereas halting at Milford Haven for a rest meant adding 40 extra miles to the job. In this boat I felt in no mood to do extra miles just for the hell of it. However, it is 130 miles from the Tuskar Rock to Land's End, and I could not expect to reach the vital corner before dawn on Friday. The meteorological men would have to modify their ideas on the night's weather, but it was not just optimism that made me think that the further veer to the north-north-west hinted at a longer fair spell than had been forecast.

During her stay in Arklow Pool the launch had taken up but now, motoring even in almost perfect weather, her weakness was manifest again, and she had to be pumped out every $1\frac{1}{2}$ hrs. to prevent the coupling on the main shaft from being immersed and kicking bilge water about. Clearly an encounter with rough contrary weather would open her up more, and I had no wish to experiment with her leaking potential. After considering all aspects of the matter, I decided to set a course from Tuskar Rock to the Longships, and later review the situation on receipt of the 1340 weather report. I could alter course for Milford at any time during the next 40 miles.

The meteorological men confirmed my ideas. That afternoon they put less emphasis on the depression in mid-Atlantic that would initiate the next crop of gales and talked about the low over Manchester moving away east-north-east. Then they became precise: "Lundy: wind west Force 2 to 4, becoming south-west Force 3 to 5. Good visibility". In fact, the general synopsis did have its warnings, but the detailed forecast for my sea area predicted nothing really vicious for the next 24 hrs. and that was by now more than enough time to reach Penzance. I jumped at the chance of turning the corner and ungrudgingly dedicated myself to another 22 hrs. or so of unrelieved steering.

Variable light winds in the afternoon changed to complete calm at nightfall. Tell-tale streaks from the west hinted that the front in sea area Sole was on the move again, now an associate of the depression in the Atlantic. *H.L. 42451* thumped along her course, across the big gap between Ireland and the Longships. Still the sea was glassy. The forecasts for the sea areas broadcast at 1758 (no general synopsis is given on this occasion) confirmed the stove-fire lit, the brew prepared. "Lundy: wind south-east, Force 3 to 4, increasing to Force 5 to 6 (and 6 to 8 in area Shannon). Moderate visibility, becoming poor."

At 2300 I went through my drill to take the edge off a sleepless night—cat-naps of from 2 to 5 min. intervals between checking the course and keeping a look-out. A gentle breeze had sprung from the east, enabling the boat to steer herself for modest periods. It worked well and was a pleasant change. I turned out from the bench alongside the engine regularly every few minutes —until 2355, when I dropped into a snooze lasting 10 min. I awoke cursing—I had missed the midnight shipping forecast.

I must have been a little over 40 miles from Pendeen Point, the north-west extremity of the Cornish peninsula. This would put me beyond the half-way mark from South Wales and therefore it did not really matter what the meteorological men thought. There could be no point in turning back now. The easterly breeze had hardened a little. Clearly the doldrums had passed. A few minutes later, surveying the darkness ahead, I sighted the loom of Pendeen's bright four flashes every 15 sec. There was the corner, clearly seen, a comforting sight, although I knew I was still a long way off. The loom of a powerful light is sometimes visible as far away as 60 miles.

The R.A.F. grid compass, set on the aft bench only a few feet away from the heavy diesel engine, had given me deviation problems, therefore it was good to have the course confirmed irrefutably.

During the last part of the night the wind began to rise. At 0330 the loom of the guiding light ahead disappeared in the rain. The vessel's motion increased and heavy rolling brought an additional compass difficulty. I was steering by an instrument that must now be treated with reserve. The card would be thrown against the compass bowl or its glass cover and stick, thus being unserviceable except as a very rough guide. Reference to a couple of ships, a few miles on the starboard beam and overhauling me only slowly, was necessary to keep the boat on course. After they had disappeared the wind direction was a useful check and later a group of fishing vessels helped when they showed up on the port bow in hazy glow.

The wind veered a little but remained broad on the bow, and although conditions became very wet, with spray driving over the boat, the speed hardly diminished. At 0445, Pendeen was sighted again, this time a vigorous light above the horizon. The shelter of the north Cornish coast was appreciable, but a vicious short sea continued to develop.

Although it was now the easiest and nearest port of refuge, I did not favour St. Ives because it is a bad place when strong winds veer beyond south-west—as generally happens before the end of a gale. A heavy scend runs into the harbour and craft permanently stationed there moor both fore and aft to strong cables. Without these proper arrangements for bad weather a vessel like *H.L. 42451* would encounter difficulties. On the other hand, it was clear that the last few miles from the Longships to Mount's Bay would be a very rough ride.

Harbour Launch 42451 ploughed on towards Pendeen and the Land's End corner in a smother. Leaking increased as the motion shook the weakened structure. Previously it had been necessary to pump out every 1½ hrs., but now the mainshaft coupling would begin to throw water about only 25 min. after the bilge was cleared. Before we began to round the Land this situation deteriorated further and I left the mechanical pump working all the time. Then the rate of influx could only be gauged by looking at the discharge pipe, and it spared me the kind of stress suffered by hypochondriacs. I could no longer watch the water creep higher round the engine, anxiously comparing its progress with the previous occasion.

Dawn found me a few miles from Pendeen, the light still clear through the rain-charged aura. The hills inland could not be seen, only a brief sector of hazy coastline was discernible. I headed off to clear the yet invisible Brisons, and, even though I was well under the lee of the land, the steep sea was sending spray continuously over my boat. I was still tempted to settle for St. Ives but the real safety and shelter of Penzance Pool or crowded Newlyn hardened my heart and spurred me onward.

The Brisons came into view and I made heavy weather of the well-known popple off Cape Cornwall. Hindered by these steep seas, it was surprising how the furious wind blasted me bodily to leeward out to sea. I found myself making a very wide detour. A big allowance was applied to the course before I clawed back, heading for Land's End and the channel close inshore. Here I would find shelter from the east wind and would avoid the hard battle involved by going outside the Longships Rocks.

Close under the rugged cliffs, even the turbulent gusts could do no more than scrape the surface of the water, and in blessed comfort the launch thumped past the Armed Knight and skirted the rocky coast beyond, before standing seaward for the Runnelstone. It was calm before the storm, peace before battle. Soon I would meet the full fetch out of the Channel.

It was surprising how quickly conditions changed. By now the wind was at gale force and suddenly my little vessel was struggling into the teeth of horrible seas—great wild brutes, irregular, distorted and of immense size. While the launch sometimes forged a reasonable path over them, she reared upward into thin air with increasing frequency to crash into the trough beyond, her whole frame shaking and bending, the forward shelter jerking back bodily as if it were completely independent of the hull. It was like riding an outsize concertina, not like steering a boat.

Hanging on to the tiller and the engine shelter, watching carefully for the best way of guiding the frail craft over the seas in order to eliminate as much pounding as possible, the spray driven by the full force of the wind directly at my face felt like blocks of ice. My eyes fought for the right to see and suffered torment in the process. It was as if dry salt was being rubbed into them. It was particularly hard to raise them high enough and long enough to scan the wild horizon for the Runnelstone Buoy which must at times have been lifting above the waves ahead.

The tide was running to the west and progress seemed painfully slow. The first sight of the buoy was a heartening event, but I knew that only substantial progress beyond into Mount's Bay would bring relief. Only then would I be round the corner and no longer testing my craft to the limit by bucking straight into the terrible seas. Astern I sighted a fishing boat, wildly tossing and only occasionally in view, struggling toward me from the west. I looked upon her as a fellow sufferer and, almost at the limit of my visibility, she certainly seemed a helpless orphan of the storm. In fact she was an able, powerful vessel, in full command of the situation. She was not of the same class as my weak, leaky boat, whose survival now depended on a mechanical bilge pump.

Slowly the Runnelstone was brought abaft the beam and I altered course a little to head along the coast. The battle remained the same. The violence of every wave filled me with concern for the deteriorating hull, manifest by the steady increase in the output of the mechanical bilge pump, now discharging almost at full bore. The working planks might suddenly break away at a weak spot, but I was disinclined to reduce speed because, in the face of the gale, I had bare steerage way as it was. These were critical moments. The pump must not choke, the hull must not let me down, on no account must the engine pack up. The Runnelstone Rock was now down wind, an area of tumultuous foam; soon the rocky coast on the port side would be a treacherous lee-shore. The huge seas thundering along those sheer cliffs were like hungry, wide open mouths awaiting their prey.

A great big wave sent its creaming top clean over the boat, searing my face and eyes as I hung on tight awaiting the inevitable crash as we tumbled into the abyss beyond. It came as a sickening blow, then the convulsions ended as the gallant boat struggled forward again. I shook myself into action and made an inspection. The pump seemed to be at full bore and sure enough the strum-box in the bilge was completely immersed, whereas previously it had always been sucking at least a small amount of air. I looked at the limber hole in the bulkhead forward of the engine and noted the water running aft as fast as possible. Forward she had been and perhaps still was, filling up too quickly for this hole to clear the forward compartments. Perhaps it was also too fast for the pump's capacity. Speed seemed essential. I ran the flexible hose of the No. 5 semi-rotary pump forward to the midship bilge and began to pump hard by hand, at the same time bringing the boat back to course to clear the land and regain sea room.

While I worked I noted with satisfaction that the M.F.V. *Jacqueline*, now nearly abeam to starboard, had altered course to close with me and was flashing her Aldis at me. Her skipper realized I could be in difficulty and was standing by.

It was not long before I felt the hand pump sucking. The situation was still under control, and most of the additional influx had been due to solid water coming over the bow. The patchwork of weak canvas rigged forward could not put up much defence against green stuff, and during the continuing struggle to make port it was now necessary to help out the hard working mechanical pump with the big semi-rotary. *Jacqueline* kept station with me now and I was most grateful for the escort.

Gradually we drew past Lamorna Cove and clawed into Penzance Bay. Twenty-eight hours out of Arklow, in sole charge of a poor tired boat, I thankfully rounded Low Lee Buoy and ran down to Newlyn.

The gale lasted 3 days, then it continued to blow from the east but not so hard. Four days later I brought the launch into Falmouth. On arrival I had to keep the engine driving the mechanical bilge pump while I slept. Eventually she recovered and "took-up" so that you could leave her for 12 hrs. without the dip-stick hole becoming immersed.

I frown at jumping from one delivery job to another before completing the first, but *Harbour Launch 42451* was a special case, and I had vowed not to put to sea in her again without good weather or a fair wind. A boat called *Misty Law* was ready to be brought down Channel and round to South Wales, and this easterly was just what she wanted. The Plymouth meteorological office confirmed no change for some time and I therefore left

H.L. 42451 in the care of R. J. Burt on one of his moorings in Falmouth Harbour.

Bear with me as far as the next chapter, and you will learn that *Misty Law* arrived in a West Country port at the end of this same week with a spot of trouble in hand. The next Monday a terse telegram added its worry:

"Phone Burt—Love Joan."

H.L. 42451 at it again!

"We just saved her in time but my Sunday suit is ruined!" was Ron Burt's brief explanation.

It had blown so hard on the Saturday that Burt's men had been unable to reach her and they had decided to let her be until Sunday. By then the sou'easter was a solid Force 9, screaming over the exposed moorings and *H.L. 42451* seemed badly water-logged. In fact, the water was up to the side benches when Ron hired a powerful motor boat and towed her to the shelter of the Customs Quay. The engine was flooded and had to be stripped down.

Fully informed at all times, this last news prompted the owner to appoint a surveyor to give an opinion on his purchase. I have already quoted from this report. Investigation showed *H.L. 42451* not worth the cost of repairs.

So it was all for nothing. The hectic struggle down the Irish Sea and round Land's End was to no purpose. Nobody gained anything. Even Burt lost out to the tune of his church-going suit which he was wearing when immediate action was seen to be necessary.

The lesson is as old as the hills. Never buy a boat without first having it professionally surveyed. And anybody, even a too clever yacht delivery man, who involves himself with a misfire bargain boat does so at his own peril.

CHAPTER 14

Sea Law—"Misty Law"

SHE was just my idea of a fast cruiser. A large open cockpit, comfortable accommodation, plenty of power and, in these days of ex-this and converted that, she was spared that conventional requirement of the speedy power craft, hard chine. Her sleek rounded hull, with a decent "V" section forward would give progress in a seaway without the desperate pounding characteristic of so many of the flat-bottomed brigade. With a length overall of 40 ft., her layout was of the cabin cruiser type, though her size provided for more room below decks than is usual.

Built in 1935; before that era when an enclosed wheelhouse became a "must" for power craft of over 30 ft., the helmsman stands on the port engine box, his head just above the windscreen but, theoretically, in the doldrums created by its concave design. In fact, the position was rather exposed for a coastal voyage in March and the easterly wind that had halted the drawn out saga of *Harbour Launch 42451*, seemed likely to persist and provide a fair but bitter wind for our passage as far as Land's End. However, with the power at our disposal, we could resolve a following Force 4 on Beaufort's scale into a complete calm.

"She's a bit reluctant to start when cold," said the yard engineer when handing over. "However, once the motors are warmed up you shouldn't have much trouble—except perhaps from dirty fuel tanks. I would keep an eye on the filters if I were you."

I have spent many hours in cramped quarters and in athletic contortions, stripping down fuel filters and blowing back through blocked pipes, and his words caused me neither surprise nor dismay. I did not expect to be caught out on that score—perhaps the commonest cause of engine failure at sea in small boats. A boat that has just been sold may have lain idle for many months while her previous owner advertised her and neglected her, hoping for a speedy sale. Little maintenance will be lavished when somebody else may take over the responsibility at any moment. Deterioration at amazing speed results. Apart from other items, corrosion and muck in fuel tanks will happen out of nowhere and when the vessel does eventually put to sea in rough weather, this is efficiently swilled along the pipe line until the filter is overwhelmed. The finest way to clean a fuel tank is to take the boat to sea in a gale.

All was ready by Friday and we left early in the afternoon in glorious sunshine and a light south-easterly breeze. I was not alone on this trip, having been blessed with a pierhead jump by Maurice Durman who had travelled from Oswestry on immediate receipt of my invitation.

We were delighted with the power packed under our feet in the shape of the two Kermath six-cylinder, twin-ignition petrol motors. Their economical speed, if that is the right word for such thirsty contrivances, gave *Misty Law* about 10 knots and she could probably attain 12 or 13 knots at full throttle.

Delight suffered its first pinprick immediately we left. Speeding over sheltered waters, I noticed water spraying from the starboard engine and investigation revealed its water pump leaking badly. A worn driving shaft was the trouble. Packing the gland in a makeshift way helped but still some water was being flung over the distributor and so I rigged an old oil tin to shield the electrics.

Later this engine stopped. Fuel appeared to be reaching the carburettor and I assumed a slightly choked jet was the trouble. The engine ran again for another half-hour, after which I had to take the carburettor down in my search for dirt. All seemed clear, the fuel apparently in abundance, and though the engine restarted when priming petrol was injected through a vent, it refused to continue as soon as this fuel supply was used up.

Throughout yachting there is a happy explanation for badly running motors that otherwise applies only to badly behaved film stars. No real action is taken when an engine is said to be temperamental; it is an expression that permits a boat owner to stagnate in self-pity. He may even boast of his bad luck to his friends, convinced he is powerless to rectify the trouble, and all the while the machinery of his yacht will deteriorate further. He is back in the Dark Ages; he may well think a sorcerer has made a model of his vessel and stuck pins in the power plant. The hard fact is that machinery fails only when something is mechanically wrong, and it should never be beyond man's ingenuity to discover the faults. Except where irreplaceable parts fracture, the yacht's owner or engineer must bear full responsibility for a breakdown at sea. There is always a reason and his job is to establish and rectify the fault. Hoodoos and Jonahs do not come into it. Such creatures live with the fairies at the bottom of the garden.

Man is not infallible but we are wise if we admit our failures, crush temptations to create a scapegoat, and, if possible, learn from mistakes. Thus I learnt from *Misty Law*'s starboard engine.

(When later investigation established causes, the engine was thought to have stopped because of restricted fuel, and refused to start again because the carburettor was taken down, examined and reassembled with a gasket back-to-front, restricting the tiny air vent that enables the bowl to fill up with petrol.)

By the time I was completely baffled by this engine, we were beginning to cross a wide bay, and the strong tide running off the easternmost headland was soon to be in our favour. To punch back to the nearest shelter would be a lengthy job. Apart from a minor fault that had easily been rectified, our other engine had given no trouble, and there was no reason to doubt its reliability. Even if breakdown had been suspected, I should have been chary of retracing our steps to what was the nearest port because that would have involved bringing dangerous overfalls, with a strong tidal set towards them, close under our lee. To be set into these rips would be hazardous for a small craft under full command in good weather. Now the following breeze was freshening steadily and it seemed a better proposition to continue before it towards the next safe harbour.

The port engine packed up suddenly just after midnight. The cruiser fell off into the trough and rode the rising seas comfortably. The white horses kept a steady background noise on which the hardening wind in the meagre rigging played its mournful tune. The first check revealed a squirt of fuel from the pipe adjacent to the carburettor when the starter motor turned the engine, actuating the mechanical fuel pump. I did not continue this test for long because it was difficult to prevent the escaping petrol from running into the bilge and, besides, I wanted to conserve battery power. Here, as in the other engine, I was deceived because in fact the mechanical fuel pump, though operating to a degree, was not drawing sufficient fuel through the partially blocked fuel pipes to feed the engine under load.

I say deceived because from the start the water pump on this engine had tended to shower spray on the distributor and latterly the increasing sea had occasionally soaked everything in *Misty Law*'s cockpit, including the h.t. cables and ignition equipment. The cables were covered with braided cotton and proofed with shellac, but the shellac coating was cracked in many places and salt water had got in to weaken the insulation. I suspected that the breakdown was caused by this obvious fault.

After taking down the carburettor—a very awkward job on the port engine—we thought that the fuel supply was adequate; therefore we concentrated on the electrical side. Before each attempt to start, the coils, distributor, leads and plug insulators all had to be carefully dried—a frustrating business when a sea often slopped aboard to undo everything just as it was nearing completion.

We worked throughout the night without success. We changed the coils with those of the other engine in case these were not up to scratch. We cleaned all the electrical contacts, including distributor, coils and plug electrodes. We removed the carburettor again and ensured all the jets were clear. All by torchlight, the yacht steadily taking a wilder motion as the weather worsened, the crests slopping into the cockpit when one would meet up with us at breaking point. At times we managed to make the motor fire, but it never picked up enough to put into gear. By dawn our efforts had flattened the starting batteries, and we turned our attention to the auxiliary generator. This latter equipment was truly 100 per cent duff.

The south-east wind had increased to Force 6—confirmed by the coastal station reports on the 0645 shipping forecast, when we were also informed it would probably increase to a gale. Despite the difficulties caused by her motion, *Misty Law* rode the seas buoyantly, demonstrating excellent stability. She was drifting down wind at about 1 knot. A light was sighted just before dawn which I identified and reckoned to be 15 miles off. After half an hour on the auxiliary generator we turned our attention to jury rig, hoisting my sleeping bag as a sail. Of heavy canvas, it gave an area of some 30 sq. ft., but was not large enough to provide steerage way. By this means alone we could not bring the wind round on the other quarter, as was necessary were we to sail into port. More make-shift canvas must be set and for the moment I preferred to continue our efforts with the engines. I had not given up hope of restarting them; therefore, leaving our single "sail" billowing proudly before the mast, we again put our heads down amongst the generating equipment. Once working, the engine would see us in port in under 3 hrs.; improvised sail was feasible—I was confident of that—but it would take very much longer and we might be forced to anchor in only partial shelter on arrival. It was comforting to know we had excellent ground tackle.

On that stormy winter morning, however, I was prepared to pay quite a few shillings to avoid another day's discomfort aboard the broken down *Misty Law*. This kind of thing did not happen often and I was going to go "splash", but I did not consider either myself, my crew or my ship in dire peril. It would not have been the first time I have brought a yacht to safety under jury rig. I hailed a homebound trawler and inquired her price to tow us. Her skipper's guarded reply came via a deckhand on the fo'c'sle head:

"How much is it worth?"

"Twenty pounds."

Immediately the men on the trawler began to prepare a tow line. After a while the fishing vessel came round to hailing distance once more, and I shouted again.

"Is that price satisfactory?"

A man in a red smock standing on deck below the wheelhouse raised his arm deliberately in acknowledgement.

A Force 6 wind over a lumpy sea provides a stupid place for prolonged negotiations, particularly when they have to be shouted between two vessels, not all the time within hailing distance; thus I accepted a quick verbal contract.

The tow wire was sent across via a heaving line, and I secured it to the winch on *Misty Law*'s foredeck. Then the trawler towed us carefully at about 4 knots to the harbour. From then on things went sour.

With twenty pounds in cash and a prepared receipt, I went to find the skipper of the fishing boat. He had already gone ashore and, on being summoned to the Customs Office, I found him with the Customs Officer and another man. I outlined the facts to the Customs Officer, but found that these were immediately disputed—chiefly by somebody who had not been there at the time. In effect, it was denied that any agreement had been reached concerning the price of the tow. Heavy salvage claims were made.

I was tired. Had been without sleep for over 26 hrs. I viewed these events as unworthy even of anger. I felt that I had done my duty. Had the trawler skipper disputed the price he asked me to mention, I should not have taken his tow line. I felt amused when concern was expressed over whether or not *Misty Law* was insured. I said that I did not know, and perceived that squeezing blood from a stone was known to be an unprofitable pastime.

This is not to deny that there are times when salvage claims are fully justified, but in those cases there will be no agreement for towage.

The local yacht yard was humming with fitting out work, and they could do little to help us. However, the owner's agents at a nearby port made arrangements to fix us up and an obvious step was to tow *Misty Law* there.

Two cheerful fishermen bowled in and plucked us out of the harbour. Proceeding at nearly full speed in their powerful fishing boat, the bar-taut tow line could not withstand snatching as the vessels rolled independently on the swell. It parted twice, our end drifting under us and fouling the propellers. When we finally arrived, my wounded assertion that, had these speed maniacs not tried to out-do Sir Malcolm Campbell, their tow line would still be as good as ever brought the rejoinder that, if I had thought to put my engines into gear in time, the parted rope would not have snarled round the propellers. Both remarks carried truth, but my chief objection was that our tugmaster had such a disarming smile that it was impossible to get annoyed.

Then the overhaul was started. The tiny cracks in the shellac coating of the braided cotton h.t. cables had caused permanent moisture. Water had passed through these cracks and soaked along the whole length of the wires like a lamp wick. By bending the wires, water would squirt through tiny holes all the way along. All the electric wiring was renewed, new coils supplied and the distributors overhauled. The starboard engine carburettor was reassembled with its crucial gasket the right way round and, using a fully charged battery, the engines were finally started up.

After a brief trial the old, old fault was established—dirty fuel. One-third full, the fuel tanks no longer gravitated petrol to the first filters; therefore, the quality of the flow could only be gauged by the output of the mechanical fuel pumps when each engine was turned over with its starter motor. Fuel squirted out all right but it was now clear that this was insufficient to run the engines under load. Despite the fact that the pipes were blown back until a healthy bubbling occurred in the tanks, it was also necessary to ream the exit from each fuel tank. This dislodged hard grit caked there. Then both motors ran satisfactorily on a 2-hr. trial in rough water.

Considering that the maximum fuel consumption of each engine could exceed 5 gallons per hour, it struck me that the exits from the tanks and the gauge of piping for conveying the fuel to them were too small and allowed little latitude for the inevitable debris that must at times restrict the flow. All dirt in a fuel tank has to be swilled along the piping until it is separated from the fuel at the filter. However, having cleared everything out, this plumbing was now as perfect as could be and *Misty Law* was ready to continue her voyage.

Owing to the delay Maurice ran out of time and I felt blessed with luck in meeting Neville, who was eager to take his place. Exactly a week after our ignominious tow into port, *Misty Law* roared proudly out to sea in weather that might have been dreamed up by the local information bureau. Surrounded by a complete pall of heavy cloud, a strange clearance of blue permitted a wide shaft of sunlight to bathe the seaside resort we had left. We who remembered the recent days of continuous rain were not deceived, but clearly our host town was seeing the light a little before the general clearance spread in.

Wind south-west Force 4, the sun now lighting the whole sea in blue and brilliant white, our fast cruiser showed just what a thoroughbred she was. Buoyant and graceful, she rode the seas without any pounding, without losing speed and without heavy seas coming aboard. Her clean forward lines and rounded bilges were a delight. No hard-chine soap box, this honey. That she had two very greedy petrol motors to drive her was, in this age of high speed compression ignition, a drawback that could be rectified.

What did appear hopeless of remedy was my new crew's personal plumbing. Poor Neville found his digestive processes going in reverse, his whole being weakened to the core. After his two heroic hours at the helm, while I rested, I became single-handed. However, with the speed at our command the rest of the voyage down Channel was quick.

We were crossing Mount's Bay when the starboard engine suffered a fuel stoppage. Just beside the first filter was the starter for the auxiliary generator. This was "live": if it were connected by a spanner to the rest of the ship, fireworks resulted. Previously I had told myself that I ought to disconnect the battery, but I had overlooked the matter. Working to take down the filter I was sitting on a fused bomb. Petrol trickled about as I tested the flow, cleaned the filter and hauled myself upside down to blow back through the pipe to the tank. On reassembly my spanner became the firing lever. There was a stupefying flash, then a flame licked the petrol filter, luckily now partially screwed home. I turned off at the fuel tap and, initial shock over, thankfully saw nothing serious develop. A bucket of water doused the half-hearted fire. Then I *did* disconnect those leads!

On course N.N.W. we were round the southernmost tip of England and making for Penzance, where the tanks aft would have to be replenished. My two dypsos did not drink mere pints! We tied up just before midnight.

Not even the world's best cure for seasickness—reaching port—was working rapidly. Next morning my crew said he would have to leave.

By midday the sun was clearing the fog that had come in during the latter part of the night and a gentle breeze was coming from the south-south-west. A glorious Sunday afternoon was bringing a hint of summer to our rain-weary land. Such a day could not be wasted. I must do the last 110 miles across the mouth of the Bristol Channel to Milford Haven alone. Ruberry's Garage were delighted to supply 95 gallons of petrol, and I was ready to leave at 1330.

A brief compass check for northerly courses, and *Misty Law* sped out of Penzance Bay, past Mousehole and offlying St. Clement's Island, past beautiful Lamorna Cove and along the rugged coastline towards Land's End. The sun had broken through but the high land was still shrouded in haze. Visibility was mostly a bare 3 miles. The air was warm yet crisp. I felt alone and grateful for it. I would not have to spoil things by telling a shipmate how glorious it all was.

Inside Lee Ore close under the cliff edge, went *Misty Law*, herself a man-made thing of beauty, a joy in her own right, my means of viewing nature from this fascinating angle. Strictly, of course, I was not alone. I passed under the granite of Gwennap Head on which stood the coastguard station, doubtless manned by the duty look-out. From the sea it was a small but impressive outpost; clean and solid in the sunlight, the white flagstaff contrasting with its colourful Union Jack. Farther on there were more signs of life; people walking along the cliffs, also enjoying the spring-like weather. Small black dots they seemed, and I felt proud as I realized that the distance to Land's End, where we all seemed to be heading, would represent a couple of hours' rough walking for them while *Misty Law* and I would be rounding the Armed Knight in a fraction of that time without effort. Although I was 200 ft. below them, I felt like a man on horseback—superior to the pedestrian.

Though only a mile offshore, the Longships remained covered in haze until I reached the channel inshore of the outlying reefs. Then the mist swirled clear to reveal the tall lighthouse, gaunt and resembling the background in smuggler films where actions are so often played out before drifting vapour.

The cruiser hauled round to starboard and, as I went through the channel, I was able to obtain another compass check. With ship's head N. 19 degrees E. by compass and lying for the next coastguard station on Cape Cornwall, I noted 3 degrees E. deviation. Then we ploughed through the popple that fusses around there even during calm weather and punched the tide towards the Brisons.

At 1523 Pendeen Point was abeam, the course N.N.E. for St. Ann's Head, 92 miles distant over a calm blue sea. Nine hours more and I should be in Milford Haven. I looked forward to dropping the hook in Dale Road and earning a night's rest.

We sped away from the Cornish coast; the evening gave way to darkness and the summer-like warmth had gone. I remained intent on steering a good course because I knew that the mist that had vanished completely in the late afternoon would return soon.

The weather forecast warned that it might be even more than mist. "Lundy: wind south to south-west, Force 2 to 4 becoming south to south-east Force 3 to 5. Moderate visibility becoming poor with fog patches."

At 2200 the low cloud line to the north-east, dark against the moonlight scene, began to deepen. Then it covered the whole sky. Haze turned to fog and the moon disappeared. The arcs of visibility of the navigation lights became clearly defined where the moisture particles were illuminated in a red and green glow to port and starboard. I put on oilskins: fog sinks slowly and insidiously into unprotected clothing. One moment all feels well: then all of a sudden you are soaked.

Misty Law sped on until midnight when I stopped the engines and their unsuppressed dynamos to listen to the shipping forecast. Freshening winds from the south-east would possibly become strong. There would be fog in Lundy, Fastnet and Irish Sea. Taking into consideration a brief period at slow speed because of a particularly dense patch, I had reckoned my distance would be run by 0045, but now, at the slower speed at which I proceeded on restarting, I calculated an extension to 0100. After that time great caution would be warranted, and possibly a complete review of the situation. We hummed on into the murk, the starboard motor back firing occasionally in protest at the slow revs. These Yankee Kermaths like to hot it up.

Study the chart and you will see that my landfall was to be a rocky coast with deep water right up to steep cliffs. All possible approaches should be safe because the moon above the fog cloud was giving reasonable light. There was one snag: Crow Rock and the north-west Toe, an isolated shoal with an unlit beacon some 3 cables seaward of Linney Head, itself 4 miles to the south-east of Milford Haven entrance. I did not want to blunder on to that. Therefore, over the last 2 hrs., I had purposely steered a little to the west of the course. This might bring me into Jack Sound entrance, where a rip-roaring tide would create difficulties, but in that case I was confident that I should hear St. Ann's siren, which would then be up-wind of me, before reaching the coast. In the event of a bad landfall to the westward, I should see Skokholm Island light or hear its fog reed.

One o'clock, visibility poor and nothing by which to gauge it accurately, except that I seemed to see all my wake, I reduced revs and peered anxiously over the windscreen. The wind had already backed south-east, and was on the starboard quarter. It was freshening, too, and a lumpy little sea was throwing *Misty Law* about a bit.

Five minutes later I heard a fog reed, clearly dead ahead and coming from heaven, it seemed. A second after, briefly, I saw a faint red tinge in a portion of the sky at something like an elevation of 45 degrees. Skokholm Lighthouse on its high cliff. Hard about Haward—before you are hard aground!

Heading straight back towards Cornwall, *Misty Law* roared away at full throttle. The spray that ripped over the boat as she thrashed into the head-sea washed the sweat from my brow. Then I slowed down, glanced at the chart and headed E. by S. for St. Ann's Head. My position had been pinpointed. I was surprised how far you could not see.

It should be added that if the steering position were enclosed by a wheelhouse, both visibility and audibility would have been further restricted. Were such a craft to have run her distance as I had done, a man on the foredeck as look-out would have been essential. Thought: open steering positions are advisable for single-handers.

Five miles to go and I gloried in the full cruising speed of 10 knots. Soon I would hear the siren at the entrance to Milford Haven. Even so, I realized that my problems were not all solved. Finding St. Ann's Head was one thing but Skokholm's light had been virtually invisible except to the lighthouse keeper, and I wondered about creeping into Dale Road. Easy in theory, not so good in practice when you are all alone, can see nothing and have to be helmsman and pilot at the same time. The final difficulty to be considered was that there is no navigational lit buoy to help in the Roadstead itself.

Just after hearing St. Ann's siren the port engine became starved of fuel. I wanted the two motors for things like "full astern aboth", and anyway each tank was probably equally dirty, meaning that the other's days and minutes were numbered. I went through the usual drill on both fuel filters while the cruiser wallowed in the trough and when I had finished I was delighted to note a sudden clearance in the visibility. St. Ann's Head light was shining brightly. The joy was short-lived, however, for within 2 min. the fog rolled in again and blotted out everything.

A mile to go, still keeping the siren on the port bow, I detected another noise, an anguished wailing sound from the siren of a steam trawler, soon to be found hanging about off the Haven. Probably she intended to stay there until dawn or until the fog cleared. After altering course to go round her, not quite sure which way she was heading, I began to wend my way into the black entrance.

The occulting glimmer that normally lights the whole scene brilliantly was snuffed out by the fog before I entered what would have been its red sector. I was in pea-souper darkness until I picked up the first lit buoy, a double-flasher, which I left to port. Then I sighted a single-flashing light and, obeying the buoyage rules, headed to bring this on my starboard side, but having to head north seemed all wrong. My chart was an old one and I remembered that a new light had been established on the first headland inside St. Ann's. This was probably the one, not a buoy at all, in which case I was heading for the rocks. Sure enough a dim line of foam appeared close ahead. Full astern the lot and, steering stern foremost into the channel, it was good to feel the boat being dragged backwards as if by the scruff of the neck.

Out in the channel once more, I lost sight of everything and edged farther into the Haven. Then being single-handed with plenty to think about and look out for, I neglected methodical pilotage and could not decide whether the next headland in sight was Dale Point or the one before. The solution was to follow the land and I found myself cautiously making a voyage round the little bay that is seaward of Dale Point. My position thus established, I reached the Roadstead. Those who have been lost in a London fog to the extent of not knowing which side of the road they are on will appreciate the situation. Finally clear of Dale Point, and sheltered from the south-easterly swell running into the Haven entrance, I dropped the hook and turned in.

Eight hours later *Misty Law* sped up the Haven in sunshine to pick up her mooring at the Lawrenny Yacht Station.

A few months later solicitors to *Misty Law*'s insurance company wrote to me:

"You will by now have gathered that the other side finally gave in and accepted the £20 arranged for towing. . . . I am sure you will also be delighted that your word has finally been accepted."

CHAPTER 15

Tragedy

THE mate poked his head from the quarter-berth and shouted to the watchkeeper:

"You're all right!"

Gruffly spoken for a youngster of 20 years, the remark punched out reassurance tinged with contempt. The third hand was fussing as the ex-German 22-ton auxiliary sloop *Marianna* lay over to the rising wind. Spray over the cockpit was becoming more and more frequent. Raw to the business of yacht voyaging, he felt his plight was unfairly remote from the delightful photographs of sparkling seas and pretty yachts which had led him from the magazines to this wild night in the Wash.

I was delivering *Marianna* from Southampton in the south of England to Sunderland on the north-east coast. The yacht was in need of a refit but, after restitching the mainsail and awaiting a break in the foul weather, we had made a good passage along the English Channel and round past Suffolk. Then it was light airs and power to head across the Wash—that aptly named area of shoals stretching north from the chilly Norfolk coast. Good motoring weather had been wasted while the magneto was overhauled and, by the time our auxiliary was earning its keep again, the wind had veered west by north and was freshening.

I had worked all the afternoon on the engine and wanted an hour or so in my bunk before relieving the third hand. Before turning in I rolled a stiff reef into the main. We were snugly rigged: even so, the man on watch had the jitters and continuously resorted to calling the skipper—just for the companionship. It provided only jaundiced company but he settled even for that. I was most grateful for the mate's stolid support.

The snow came as I finally gave up all ideas of sleep. I began to don as much out of my seabag as would fit on at once. Then I sent the third hand below. The wind was still veering. The north-east Docking Shoal Buoy was astern and, close-hauled, we could only just lie for the Humber Lightvessel. The remainder of the passage was going to be tough: a true December voyage.

Snow can create that worst of all situations: strong winds coupled with foul visibility. Sitting in an open cockpit, it seemed as if the flakes against the eyes and face were blocks of ice. It was impossible to look where we were going for more than an instant and no amount of vision could penetrate much beyond the forestay. The vicious steep sea, typical of the tide-charged Wash, was rising steadily and the yacht crashed into it like a thoroughbred. *Marianna* has two interesting characteristics. Her low freeboard has stipulated a shallow cockpit, the self-draining variety being the requisite, and her helm kicks violently as she dives over the waves. Two sizes of tiller were provided and even the larger, which we had now shipped, was sometimes hard to hold. A tiller lashing was a sensible idea but it had to be adjusted continuously and this sometimes required both hands. I discarded the idea because, precariously astride the cockpit, I preferred to hang on to a coaming cleat with one hand, allocating only the other to the helm. On several occasions during the next wild 3 hours, when the yacht reared up and over extra big ones, I let the helm go to vent its mule-like kick on thin air.

Just before 2300 the snow cleared and the flash of the Humber Lightvessel was sighted some 5 miles ahead. The wind remained strong and it was a relief to have our position confirmed. I handed over to the mate, mentioning the trials and hazards of the prevailing weather, and, after rolling down three more turns of mainsail, dived thankfully into the comparative warmth below.

Cloudbanks, storm-brewed and bulbous, hinted only a brief respite from snow. I knew the north-west wind would be blowing on shore beyond Flamborough Head, 40 miles distant. As it was, the short fetch out of the Humber Estuary was giving *Marianna* a wild ride. Studying the chart, the tidal harbour of Bridlington, tucked under the shelter of Flamborough, looked good. As a port of refuge it satisfied all my honourable senses. I reckoned we had earned a day's rest: the last 70 miles from there could be polished off later, possibly after the dead muzzler had shifted, yet giving us time to be home for Christmas.

As I prepared to turn in, the yacht struck a big one. You knew just how deep the hole by the way she reared upwards before until, levelling out, the thrust against gravity gradually diminished to leave a feeling of suspended animation. Then she crashed down into the hollow and I was hurled against the leeward settee. I shouted to the mate.

"I'm all right!" the reply came back.

Calm, stolid, the best that Yorkshire breeds, he and I had been shipmates in yachts for over a 1,000 sea miles. A keen novice had changed into a competent, self-reliant sailor. I could not have wanted a better man in charge of our little vessel as she thrashed into the teeth of the wintry weather. Equally strong had grown our bond of comradeship.

Three minutes later he was gone.

Again *Marianna* crashed into the trough, doubtless her tiller tugging viciously at the helmsman. His cry of surprise and annoyance came clearly above the wild conglomeration of noise as the broken sea drove over the yacht. Then silence.

I hurled myself on deck.

Never did a cockpit seem so empty.

Ten years have done nothing to fade the memory of that tiller swinging idly, naked; horrified, it seemed, at the terrible part it must have played.

Without time to find oilies, I pushed the helm up and yelled to the third hand. We were in irons now and the stock "man overboard drill" of gybing would not fill the bill. I gathered way on the other tack, the runners a shambles, the jib aback; then freeing the sheets to run down the reciprocal course. Suddenly in the darkness came an unflurried shout.

"Here I am!"

We were doing 7 knots on a broad reach and he was out of reach on the beam. A lifebuoy was thrown but the self-igniting calcium flare failed to burn. Now: gybe. Helm up, we took ages to come round, far too long I thought, to bring up at the crucial point. Therefore, having travelled what I considered was the proper distance, I swung her round into the wind. Everything a-shake she came to a halt.

We shouted into the darkness and out of the pitch-black the reply showed him way beyond the starboard bow. I got way on again but it was impossible, in the black night, to know how our relative positions were changing. His next shout, weaker, came from the other quarter. Unable to see, relying on a position inaccurately estimated by a single sound, rendered the problems of manoeuvring under sail guess work. The water was bitterly cold and the man in it was heavily clothed including seaboots and oilskins. Speed was essential and this dissuaded me from starting the engine—a lengthy business of reaching a barely accessible fuel tap and flooding the carburettor under the floorboards.

We turned too soon after the next run back. He was dead astern when he shouted again. This time a gybe was the answer. She swung off the strong wind, both runners cast off. Then the boom slammed over and the mainsail split from leech to luff.

Now no shout came from the sea. We dragged in a mess of canvas, yelling again and again. The tragedy was sealed.

We lay in the trough and worked at the engine routine. It always took some time to start. When it came to life we cruised the area for the best part of an hour, seeing nothing. Finally all hope was abandoned, but it was difficult to comprehend that we two left must take *Marianna* away from this awful place. The mate was gone: snatched away as quickly as happens in a nightmare. We had parted company: the unimportant, wretched story of two survivors was all that could be known from that point.

I suddenly realized I was soaked, frozen and with hardly any clothes.

The beat under foresail and power towards the Humber Estuary halted after the first tack. The engine seized because a rope that had been placed on deck during the emergency was trailing astern and fouled the propeller.

Brand new and unpacked, the heavy trysail was dragged from the eyes of the ship. Trysail sheets of hard hemp were rigged and finally this canvas was set. More snow and bitter weather slowed our sail drill. Then started a hellish struggle into the teeth of the rising gale. At dawn we entered Grimsby in blizzard conditions.

My vow never to go to sea again quickly changed to a promise to learn from this tragic accident. Never again would a crew of mine be on deck or in the cockpit in bad weather or at night without a safety belt. I set about designing a suitable one for yachtsmen and the development from it, which has now been in general use for 8 yrs. Five years ago the R.O.R.C. recommended that safety belts be carried aboard all yachts entering offshore events and in 1957 the Cruising Club of America stipulated a safety belt for each crew member in the Bermuda race.

CHAPTER 16

Yacht Handling in Severe Weather

CHAPTERS 6 to 9 emphasize that yachts will safely weather bad gales. Many yachtsmen demonstrate the fact convincingly year after year. However, whenever I mention safe arrival to a landsman during a spell of foul weather, I sense an assumption that somehow I have dodged the prevailing conditions. Opinion prevails that a small yacht need only be at sea in a gale to be unceremoniously put out of business. Because gales are a common event off our coasts, yachtsmen would indeed be truly mad if this were the case, but that is either never considered or, possibly, it is accepted. In their search for sensationalism newspapers echo the view or promote it. Before a yacht is in the news it is invariably in trouble and "mountainous seas" play a leading part in most incidents. Thus the unsung yachtsman is a rather artful dodger, always able to avoid the stormy stuff or to pass through it by gambler's luck.

Once I delivered a 5-ton Vertue class sloop to Ireland and, during the crossing from Penzance, I was stopped for 18 hrs. by a vicious gale that gusted to 80 m.p.h. at adjacent coastal weather stations. At the height of the blow the owner, who knew I was on my way across and was naturally concerned for my welfare, obtained an opinion from a harbour official—a seaman, but obviously of the big ship variety. It was pronounced that no small yacht would have a hope in hell of surviving such a gale. Dismay having been caused successfully, a crumb of hope was tossed after: probably I had run back to the Scilly Isles for shelter.

In fact I had stayed where I was, half-way along the 140-mile hop to Cork. Any other action would have been more hazardous. Once bad weather is established, the poor visibility of gale-driven drizzle makes running for shelter on a rocky lee-shore the council of despair. Two days later the yacht lay undamaged in her new home port, her skipper pleased at having confounded what went for expert comment.

Naturally those yachtsmen who have not yet encountered severe weather will view the subject with some apprehension. They will be excused for wondering whether their vessels have been properly fitted out and whether their seamanship will triumph. After all, most yachtsmen, however experienced, look upon foul weather as a trial of nerve and endurance. Hardbitten old hands will think little of the novices' first blow, but there must be few who are not heartily glad when a gale at sea passes.

It is difficult to visualize how a yacht behaves in a gale and what the human element has to put up with. Still more difficult it is for the novice to decide accurately just how bad conditions are: whether his Force 7 is truly Admiral Beaufort's "near gale". Witnessing the sea from a cliff top or even from the deck of a large liner is different from the spectacle presented to the crew of a 10-ton yacht. Observers should estimate wind force by noting the look of the sea, therefore such records made at night will be of least value. The most reliable way is by using an anemometer. Having read the wind speed scale, you should subtract or add the resultant effect of the vessel's speed and its heading relative to the wind's direction. Further allowance should be made for possible turbulence or the sheltering effect of superstructure. Also, it is probable that wind speeds at the low level of a yacht's deck will be less than, say, 33 ft. clear of the sea. I mention this figure after seeing in *Reed's Nautical Almanac* that this is the correct height for Beaufort Scale measurements. An anemometer will accurately give you the *apparent* wind. Deduce the *true* wind from it with reference to the above remarks, note what the sea actually looks like, and you will begin to be a judge of those wind force numbers which you more frequently experience. It is a pity that many experienced yachtsmen who have brought small vessels through very bad weather have not been able to state accurately the kind of wind encountered. For my own part, without a proper instrument I would hesitate to be dogmatic about any wind exceeding

Force 8. Severe gales seem to blot out the memory of previous experiences and it is even difficult to conclude the details later. A human failing operates—a defensive mechanism of the mind, I call it: while in a storm you tend to think it the worst ever; afterwards it was "not so bad"! Anemometers, unfortunately, are not inexpensive. Cup type instruments only are efficient. The cheap, ball-up-a-narrow-cone gadgets do not seem to operate satisfactorily as moisture enters the instrument and gums up the works.

Until foul weather has been encountered, the environment of a tiny vessel in a storm cannot be appreciated; but the tactics to adopt are advisedly considered in advance. Ideas on proper seamanship clarified, skipper and crew can face the occasion with confidence.

Once a Force 6 headwind is encountered it will soon be realized that progress close-hauled rapidly becomes a strain on the ship's company. In small yachts the matter becomes an endurance test from the start. Provided you do not have to persist for very long it is reasonable to thrash on. Assuming that sail is reduced prudently, and given a strong craft with first-rate gear, progress may still be made into the teeth of a Force 8 gale but in doing so you will produce a shambles below deck, wear out the crew and play havoc with their sleep and their routine. Personally, unless I am too close to a dangerous lee-shore or tempted to battle towards a sheltering headland or safe harbour that is less than 6 hrs.' sailing away, I prefer to spare the ship's company and the vessel and heave-to.

Having decided to stop, the easier procedure is to stow all sail, lash the helm "down" and let the yacht lie a-hull. She will adopt a heading according to her hull shape and superstructure. The average modern cruising yacht with a cut-away fore-foot and deeper draught aft, despite forereaching with the helm to leeward, will lie beam on to the seas or even with her quarter a little towards the wind. It is far from presenting her bows to the oncoming seas, hankered after as the ideal by some yachtsmen, ancient and modern, but it is presenting her greatest buoyancy to the advancing waves and a yacht's stability can hardly be in question. Despite argument against it, by adopting this method a properly found 4-tonner (or 18-ft. L.W.L. length and upwards) can confidently expect to ride out gales of Force 8 or even Force 9. Of course, good sea room, clear of races, overfalls and similar dangers, is assumed as is a good bilge pump with proper plumbing. A watertight or self-draining cockpit is an advantage but not essential and in a very small boat will be rather unsuitable in other ways.

Alternative tactics are to lie a-try, that is, to carry storm trysail and jib, the latter sail being sheeted a-weather to counter the luffing tendency of the former. In a Force 7 blow this method of heaving-to will probably give you an easier ride compared with hulling because the sails will steady the yacht more than will the bare mast and rigging. However, if the wind increases further, you may find the yacht becomes restless, shearing about, the trysail leech flogging at times. It will mean that too much canvas is set. In a Force 9, strong gale, all riding sail is best stowed. Then the inconvenience of the task will leave you wondering why you went to all the bother of bending storm canvas at all. At this stage the windage of the mast and rigging will adequately steady your yacht and she will keep a very healthy angle of heel. I see no reason to play about with storm sails unless you intend actually to sail with very reduced canvas. Most certainly a strong trysail may be useful in clawing off a lee-shore in desperate conditions but, if the yacht has efficient roller reefing enabling you to shorten sail to handkerchief size, you will be justified in doing without storm sails—especially if your main and No. 3 jib are of Terylene and thus probably quite as strong as heavier canvas. It is sometimes of advantage to have the boom tapering from leech to luff ends to ensure that sail can be reduced with roller gear without the boom sagging so much that it fouls the dinghy or doghouse. Building up the leech end with four battens will suit admirably. Thus Terylene and roller reefing make storm trysails obsolete— except for the flat boom fanatics. A word of warning will not be amiss. The stitching on Terylene sails stands proud, not bedding down in these hard man-made fibres as happens with cotton or flax; thus it is more vulnerable to chafe. Lee runners or even standing shrouds will hack through the seaming like a scythe in a cornfield. Loose wires must be secured and all must be covered with anti-chafe gear. Plastic piping is an excellent material.

Just before the First World War Captain Voss started something. As described in his classic *Venturesome Voyages*, he completed some remarkable ocean passages in very small craft. His procedure during stormy weather was to lie-to, stream a sea anchor from the bow and set a mizen or a small storm sail aft. This enabled the yachts he handled to face the wind, and many seamen still consider it the ideal way to ride out a storm in small craft. Because the bows of a boat are designed to lead her through the water, it is assumed that this part had best meet the oncoming seas when she is almost stopped and riding out a blow. It would also be good if a yacht could spread wings and take off. There is always drift when lying to and, if the bow heads the seas, the steering gear bears the brunt. Stanley Smith and Charles Violet suffered damage in this way while riding out a bad storm to a sea anchor in *Nova Espero*. However, in normal gales rudders appear to put up with this unfair stress. This is how Sinclair described helm difficulties aboard the 20-ft *Joan* when riding to a sea anchor:

> We had lashed the tiller up and we had lashed it down, we had lashed it amidships and we had removed the lashing altogether so that the rudder was left free to swing about as it liked. Whatever we did seemed bad.

It should be realized that a sea anchor is attempting to hold a yacht in a position completely unnatural to her and, in so far as it achieves its task, it pits its strength against the storm. Experience indicates that finally the gear parts, which is probably best for the yacht and her mariners. But if a sea anchor is the weakest link in the chain—if it ought to part first—it is difficult to see any real use for it.

Voss was not the inventor of the sea anchor but he has done more than anybody to make it part of a small vessel's equipment. Sea anchors remain standard equipment in ship's life-boats. There are moments when a sea anchor will be useful for a small sailing craft: while riding out a storm when it is necessary to reduce the rate of drift towards a dangerous lee-shore. Eric Hiscock mentions using a drogue for this purpose during his world circumnavigation in *Wanderer III*.

This is entirely different from the value accorded to the gadget by Voss, who hailed it as the miraculous panacea for survival in dangerous storm-reared seas. And besides safety, amazing comfort was promised.

> The *Xora* at once swung head to wind and rode as comfortably to her sea anchor as a vessel rides to her mud hook in a land locked harbour. . . .

Or another example:

> As the gale showed signs of still increasing we hove-to under a sea
> anchor. . . . No sooner was the little mizen hoisted and the sheet hauled
> flat, than the vessel swung head to sea and rode every sea that came along
> so beautifully that in the cabin one would not have imagined that the vessel
> was really at sea, so steady was her motion. . . . We passed the evening
> smoking, chatting and listening to our gramophone. . . .

If that does not sell sea anchors, I reckon nothing will, but it
must be remembered that comfort is an abstract quality, measur-
able in terms of comparison. Sitting in the saloon of an 8-ton
sloop in harbour, I consider to be comfortable; yet considerably
more comfort could be experienced in my favourite armchair at
home before a big fire with dry bedroom slippers on my feet
replacing damp, salt-caked shoes. But the saloon of a small yacht
in harbour is more comfortable than when she is lying at sea in
a gale. Less comfortable still does life become in the same saloon
if the yacht is being *sailed* in a gale and, if the course is to windward, you would be a little out of touch with civilization if you
were to credit your environment with any comfort whatsoever.
An elderly person, used to a good living standard, who has had
the easy life for years, would be inclined to describe a small
yacht's saloon as uncomfortable in any circumstances. The
remarks by Voss would be, for him, misleading. On the other
hand, somebody used to a more rugged life would be less
exacting in his creature comforts. And immediate experiences
have a real influence over his appreciation of comfort. Anybody
who has endured thrashing to windward in a sea that eventually
forces him to heave-to will see only blessed peace, balm for his
soul, when he stops his battle against Neptune's anger. Without
claiming credit for any sea anchor—I did not have one aboard—
I wrote as follows in the *Yachting Monthly*, July 1951, when
describing a trip across the Bristol Channel approaches in a 32-ft.
motor sailer, a stiff vessel that carried good steadying canvas:

> Punching against increasing seas, the ship's speed gradually grew less
> and by five o'clock, though on full power, she was down to about one knot.
> Obviously we could not afford progress at a gallon a mile, and we paid
> off to port, hoisted the jib a-back and mizen and stopped the engine.
> Immediate results were wonderful: perfect peace, though only com-
> parative, was to us absolute. The urgent roar of the engine vanished and the
> wild motion changed to a gentle swing. It seemed as though we were
> safely in harbour again. . . .

I flatter myself that I pointed out that the comfort experienced was a matter of comparison.

Lying under bare poles will, by itself, appear agreeably comfortable compared to thrashing into the storm. I do not think a sea anchor will improve matters further. Will it contribute towards the safety of the ship? I do not think so. In my opinion if the weather is too bad for safe lying under bare poles—and the wind probably must reach Force 10 before this is so—a sea anchor will add slightly to the hazard. In making this statement I am referring to a seaworthy yacht not to an open ship's life-boat which, with much less stability, expecially if heavily laden, may gain from streaming a sea anchor in a gale for this will haul her head to wind and lessen the danger of a capsize. However, it is unlikely that an open boat of this type will survive as bad a storm as a yacht.

Thus Voss subordinated his bad weather tactics to the sea anchor. His enthusiasm for this apparatus runs right through his book, and considering his achievements it is hardly surprising that his dogma has made an impact on the public. Unlike those of many modern yacht voyagers, the ventures of Voss were almost unique in their day. Now we have the testimony of many mariners who have wandered the oceans in tiny vessels, and the sea anchor enthusiasm of Voss no longer stands up to serious investigation. As an instrument for ensuring safety at sea, except for certain specialized uses, the sea anchor is a myth. There is no sound evidence for believing that it contributes to safety when a yacht is lying-to in a storm. I write this after considerable study, discussion and thought, as well as voyaging myself in over 300 different small vessels for more than 125,000 sea miles, much of which has been around latitude 50 degrees N. on the leeward Atlantic coast where the sort of bad weather Voss experienced occurs. It is likely, for example, that weather off Cape Flattery on the northwest coast of the U.S.A. will be similar to that found in Biscay and the English Channel approaches. By lying a-hull or running under bare poles, well found seaworthy small yachts will survive gales in the open sea reaching Force 9. This has been demonstrated time and time again; yet perusal of Voss leads one to conclude that a sea anchor is a "must" for every yacht and that none should ever run before a gale:

I may say that even a large ship when deeply laden is liable to be smashed up by a single pooping sea. Consequently, to be on the safe side, she should heave to at the beginning of a gale.

That I have personally disproved, or at least shown excessively cautious. My opinion is that a yacht will be safer longer while running in worsening weather than she will be lying a-hull. She must of course be under very reduced canvas or bare poles and may be advised to stream warps aft to slow her down further. Yet even today the author of those quoted lines commands attention on the subject of sea anchors. Misunderstanding persists to some extent because many small yachts have safely come through gales with a sea anchor streamed. They survived in spite of, not because of the gadget. Hulling, or lying with meagre sail set, was responsible for their safety. If these gales had reached proportions rarely experienced or unknown round the British coast, a less pleasant outcome would more frequently result and the sea anchor fallacy would die less hard.

Some modern yachts, unsuited to lie head to wind because of their cut-away lines forward, as well as not carrying mizen masts, have streamed sea anchors from the quarter. While riding a heavy storm that reached hurricane force, *Vertue XXXV* was severely damaged some 200 miles north of Bermuda during her transatlantic voyage of 1950. Doghouse smashed and cabin coaming fractured, only the magnificent endurance of Humphrey Barton and his crew Kevin O'Riordan saved her. As soon as the accident occurred, they put the yacht dead before the seas, one of them steering while the other worked desperately to repair the seriously handicapped craft. These tactics triumphed.

It is remarkable that as many as four small British yachts were involved in that storm. While *Vertue* was approaching the end of her great voyage, three entrants for the bi-annual Newport-Bermuda race had been shipped to Bermuda, fitted out in Hamilton and were on their way under sail to America. *Cohoe* and *Mokoia* lay safely a-hull under bare poles and the R.N.S.A. sloop, 7-tonner *Samuel Pepys* ran before the gale and like *Vertue XXXV* reported very severe conditions. Commander Erroll Bruce, skipper of *Samuel Pepys*, resorted to running under bare poles streaming warps and the yacht survived undamaged. A highly experienced seaman, he has described the encounter graphically in his book *Deep Sea Sailing*.

From yet another source comes rejection of the sea anchor

myth. Dan Mulville, experienced ocean yacht voyager and delivery skipper who has transatlantic crossings and many runs to the Mediterranean to his credit, tells of a hectic passage to the Canaries in the fast, 48-ton slender gaff yawl, *Princes Waimai* (ex-*Celia*) in December 1953. While lying a-hull in this 74-ft. yacht in a Biscay gale, he found that her long overhanging counter stern was pounding on to the seas so badly that damage threatened. Thinking it might be better if he could bring the yacht out of the trough, he streamed a sea anchor from the bow. He avoided chafe at the stemhead fairlead by shackling the warp to his anchor cable but within half an hour the wooden frame of the drogue collapsed under stress of weather. At no time was the device effective in altering the broadside position of the yacht. When the gale eased, some of the planking at the counter was sprung. A second blow was met soon after and this time a mizen was set and a stronger sea anchor with an iron frame was streamed; yet because of her pronounced cut-away fore-foot and deep draught aft even this arrangement failed to bring the yacht head to sea. The sea anchor lasted longer but eventually the frame was buckled and further, more extensive damage was inflicted on the vulnerable counter stern. Dan Mulville concludes that most sea anchors, if they are large enough to fulfil their role of holding a yacht in an unnatural position, will seldom stand up to the storm conditions for which they are thought necessary; but if they possess the intended strength a bad gale will confer additional and probably dangerous strains on the vessel.

Yachts with long counter sterns pose a difficult problem in bad weather. While delivering the 8-metre *Severn II* to Cork from the Solent in February 1956, I encountered a gale on the beam while crossing from Land's End to Ireland. Mainly because my crew was *hors de combat* from seasickness combined with exposure to the elements because he joined the yacht without adequate storm clothing, I decided to lie a-hull for a spell of sleep. A couple of hours was enough, an agonizing period in my bunk. Each terrible thud, as the typical metre class counter stern crashed down on a lifting sea, seemed to be a direct sledge hammer blow on my soul. Fearful for the vessel's safety, I finally continued sailing until my destination was safely reached.

These considerations may not apply to yachts built of steel. Remember *Endeavour*'s return from America in 1937 after the unsuccessful America's Cup challenge by her successor *Endeavour II*. Towed by the motor yacht *Viva*, the tow-line parted in a hurricane, contact between tug and tow was lost, and after several weeks the huge "J", sleek racing yacht of the fabulous days (130 ft. overall in length against 83 ft. on the waterline—much of the difference being due to her great overhanging counter stern) was feared lost. However, despite the heaving tow-line hanging from her bows, which were therefore awash and impossible to work on and clear it away in the prevailing weather, the yacht rode out the storm and sailed home safely.

Despite the claim of Captain Evans, redoubtable ocean yacht skipper of the old school, who wryly asserts, perhaps with his tongue in a weather beaten cheek, that none but yachts of the 12-Metre class reach real seaworthiness today—modern high costs having rendered the "Js" extinct—it does seem likely that vessels with long overhanging counters, if of wooden construction at any rate, will be in peril if they heave-to in bad gales. They will be better advised to keep sailing and it is likely that their buoyant hulls will soar high over the waves, keeping out of trouble longer than many of their heavier, more robust cousins. Len Evans has made many lengthy voyages in the class and says that with a strong trysail they will maintain safe progress in severe conditions. Doubtless final resort to running under bare poles with drag warps will enable them to weather extremely bad weather.

I think this latter technique represents the final course available to the mariner in the average modern yacht.

For ocean sailing Captain Evans firmly believes that more attention should be given to trysail arrangements. Rejecting the "points" system whereby the storm canvas is fed from a "siding" track into the mainmast track of a Bermuda rigged yacht, rejecting even a separate track for the trysail only, he likes to rig three standing wires, one from each mainmast spreader leading down just clear of the mainsail track. Hardened by rigging screws, these wires should have properly strengthened anchorages on deck or should be fixed to a mast band near deck level. The head part of the trysail luff is shackled to the topmost wire, the mid part to the next wire and so on. Shackles rather than spring hanks should be used as the latter will tend to hook on to an extra wire while hoisting and cause a snarl-up. This will make the trysail independent of normal Bermuda mast fittings and changing from one to the other will be simplified. With an extra halyard you can even hoist your trysail before lowering the main. On those larger yachts, where it is necessary to clamber on to the boom and scale a heaving heap of doused mainsail, piled to the extent of the luff slides set in the track, in order to reach the main halyard shackle, it will be a relief simply to pass a rope through it to bowse it taut rather than change it over to the trysail head. I always think unshackling that wire and not losing it warrants a man with three hands when the weather is rough.

I write having recently encountered a contrary gale in a 65-ft. Bermuda ketch. On changing to trysail during the height of the blow, four lower track slides on it carried away during the struggle to hoist what, in normal weather, would have been a very modest area of sail. We sheeted home but, despite doing our best with the tack downhaul, unfair strain was borne by the two lowest slides now taking the load. After a short period of cogitation, hating to write off a heap of hard work and intent on jogging to windward rather than drift backwards a-hull, I reluctantly lowered away. Later we found that the mast track screws were started at the relevant point and the track was bent. Before we could set the mainsail again it was necessary to drill new holes and harden with additional screws—an awkward job at sea.

Another example of sea anchor failure is given by Eric Hiscock in his book *Wandering Under Sail*. He was lying-to in a gale in his $4\frac{1}{2}$-ton gaff cutter *Wanderer II* some 30 miles north of the Cornish coast. He had streamed a sea anchor and had set a small riding sail aft, which soon carried away. Then he was smitten by a large sea and the sea anchor broke up, one of the oak bars having snapped:

> The boat was thrown bodily to leeward with a sickening lurch and I was hurled so hard against the cabin panelling that I smashed the whole lot in and damaged my hip and elbow. For a moment the daylight was obscured as the deck became submerged and a torrent of water poured down the companionway, extinguishing the cooking stove.

However the little yacht rode out the gale quite safely after this and it is not unreasonable to suppose that if that breaker had not parted the anchor warp Hiscock's little yacht might have suffered serious damage. Voss lost a sea anchor similarly when caught in a typhoon in a little vessel called the *Sea Queen* and blamed subsequent troubles on being deprived his favourite gadget, alleging that he later capsized because his sea anchor had carried away. He reckoned a heavier sea anchor with stronger gear would have seen him through, but there is no evidence that this would have solved the problem. As already indicated, if that little yacht had remained attached to a sea anchor strong enough not to carry away, the huge breaker was likely to have smashed her to smithereens. Under conditions such as these, the greater hope of survival lies in giving way to the terrible power let loose by exploding water. Interfere with it as little as possible. You will only get hurt.

Failure of a sea anchor to bring a yacht through a storm and final disaster is instanced by Sinclair in his *Cruises of the Joan*. After a number of successful voyages, including the circumnavigation of Britain, a cruise to Madeira and another to the Baltic, he decided to sail his 20-ft. yacht to America via Iceland, hoping that by going unusually far north he would carry a good proportion of easterly winds, the northern sectors of advancing depressions. In fact he met many contrary gales which his deep-draughted tiny vessel weathered safely, lying-to streaming a sea anchor. Finally, however, some 600 miles south of Cape Farewell, Greenland, he was severely damaged in what was obviously an extremely heavy storm, the sea anchor "plainly doing its work well".

So much for sea anchor safety. Yet a modern staunch supporter of the gadget, when taken to task on this disaster wrote:

> Prior to the gale when Sinclair lost *Joan*, he complained: "The periods of lying to the drogue were never so restful as they had been in former years, and as I had become used to thinking they always would be, the change in this respect was to say the least, unwelcome." This remark has always puzzled me; what happened to *Joan* (or Sinclair) which would account for this change? And was it because of this "something" that she lost her mast when riding to a sea anchor? . . . I would most earnestly recommend any yachtsman who is contemplating a deep sea voyage to read *The Venturesome Voyages of Captain Voss* from cover to cover before making any decisions. . . .

Which comment, to me, is like seeing the writing on the wall but stubbornly refusing to read it. I reckon that puzzling "something" was simply that in the northern climes where the *Joan* ended her days it was sometimes too rough to lie a-hull. Streaming a sea anchor not only held the yacht fairly rigidly in the face of desperately fierce advancing seas and huge tumbling crests, but also exerted a partial downward drag on the bows and thus made matters even worse. Had the *Joan* been of shallow draught, as opposed to drawing 6 ft. of water for only 20 ft. waterline length, she might have fared better lying a-hull without sea anchor. The huge destructive crest that burst on her would have had less opportunity to cause damage. The little yacht would have been inclined to slide down wind, retreating before the explosive energy that threatened to engulf her. Shallow draught confers a quality similar to that of a paper boat skating lightly away from man-made waves in a bath tub; also the lack of a deep keel gripping the relatively stationary water beneath the thundering wave crest will spare a yacht from being tripped to her beam ends. That is the start of trouble, and the mast, if permitted to get a grip of the water because of a roll beyond 90 degrees, will exploit matters further. The yacht will be turned right over and, if lucky, will come up the other side, probably missing several useful items of equipment—things like the mast, for example.

Such are the snags of yacht navigation during really serious storms. Quoting a conservative upper limit and bearing in mind differences in yacht design common today, I would say that things become dangerous when the wind in the open sea exceeds Force 9. Beyond that hulling is suspect, sea anchors dangerous toys. A yacht designed for frequent bad weather will acquit herself satisfactorily during worse winds, an additional Beaufort number, perhaps; but to say more would be to give misleading advice. However, good freeboard, powerful quarters and buoyant bow are desirable factors. Strong superstructure or a minimum of coach roofing and a small watertight, self-draining cockpit are other considerations to bear in mind for really stern stuff. Some of these factors will cause conflict. Extra strength means more weight, less buoyancy. Distinguish between a self-draining cockpit and a completely watertight one that has no lockers through which a boarding sea will gain access to the bilge. That is how Wensley's wave arrived in *Janabel*'s bilge. Take note that survival may depend not only on your bad weather tactics but also on the efficiency of your bilge pump. The last few feet of the bilge piping should be flexible, easy to withdraw from a debris-strewn bilge, enabling the strum-box suction point to be cleared frequently. Avoid relying on Sinclair's crude method on the *Joan*, after he had lost the pump handle overboard during the knock-down:

> Since the yacht was putting the whole of this below the water about twice a minute there was a great deal of Atlantic Ocean making a circular tour, in through the stern and out by the pail.

An interesting insight into the use of a sea anchor in the pre-Voss era is given in Humphrey Barton's book *Atlantic Adventurers*. Thomas Crappo made the crossing in a 19-ft. boat in 1877 and on one occasion, when riding to a sea anchor "was kept busy hauling in on the drogue line when I saw a very large sea coming and eased it off when it passed which was tedious work".

It is difficult to see why people should think they must do that rather than lie a-hull. Truly, as they say, it must have been exhausting and an exhausted crew can be a reason for disaster.

If you are fortunate enough to be going the same way as a storm, it will probably be unnecessary for you to be delayed. The navigator will wish to have a good idea of his position and will ensure that all shoals, tidal overfalls and lee-shores are avoided, but within these limitations, progress is possible under very reduced canvas or even bare poles. The helmsman will have a wet trick, but I always think personal discomfort at sea is easier to endure if the reward is real progress. What so taxes morale in slogging to windward are the poor results for all the hardship.

CHAPTER 17

The Ultimate Storm

Some Thoughts on Top Grade Foul Weather

AMERICANS have said that we in the British Isles do our yachting in conditions more rugged than they—though this does not mean they cannot nip over here now and again and win the Fastnet. My own limited experience of the U.S.A. brings memories of light to moderate breezes and glorious sunshine in Long Island Sound. Obviously that is not the whole story but without a doubt the leeward end of the North Atlantic, on whose fringes the British yachtsman tries his skill, is prone to a turmoil of gales with driving rain and poor visibility. However, there is a limit. A severe gale, Force 9, is the exception rather than the rule and the wind round Britain reaches Force 10 only occasionally and briefly. Often a depression or its associated front will pass with no more than a near Force 7 gale or just a strong wind.

Ideas on what constitutes a seagoing yacht in Britain is naturally influenced by the weather we experience. Designers have a fairly clear idea of the strength necessary to enable a yacht to come through these kinds of storms safely—even if some, perhaps trying to establish themselves in the racing field, may fall for the temptation to sacrifice essential strength for lightness and speed.

Already I have outlined the tactics used to guide a tiny sailing yacht safely through a gale. You may lie a-hull, lie a-try or run; and you can even stream a sea anchor without harm befalling you—and afterwards tell your friends it was vital. Having come through a gale, even a severe one, in the English Channel or exposed to the Atlantic on a crossing from Land's End to Ireland, you may look at your yacht with pride and congratulate yourself: "There: she's brought me safely through. She could go anywhere!"

She probably could not. She is not fit to sail the Southern Ocean with its round-the-world fetch—where Miles Smeeton said that once was enough, his wife emphasizing that twice was altogether too much; nor, for example, would you be advised to follow the routes the wartime convoys took to Russia; nor sail in winter the fast steamer route to Canada and New York, where, Erroll Bruce cites in a letter published in *Yachting Monthly*, November 1958, gales occupy 30 per cent of the mid-winter weather. Nor north where Sinclair tried to carry depression top easterlies to the New World and lost his *Joan*, 600 desolate sea miles from Greenland. For that matter you would sensibly be urged to avoid courting hurricanes and typhoons, even minor off-season disturbances, such as swallowed up the brand new American 43-ft. yawl *Renovec* on New Year's Day, 1958.

We are in fact now thinking about top-grade foul weather, aptly described by William Robinson as the Ultimate Storm.

I am inclined to think that despite their phenomenal wind velocities, tropical storms are less lethal to a yacht than the grey beards of the high latitudes. Possibly this is because of the shorter fetch of the former and despite the cross-seas produced in the centres of these storm areas.

In winter 1951, the Giles designed 14-ton yacht *Coimbra*, newly built in Scotland and bound for her home port of Cape Town, was on the last leg of her maiden voyage. Leaving Rio de Janeiro she set a course that would leave Tristan da Cunha a little to the south. Overtaken by very severe weather, with wind estimated in excess of Force 10, she continued to run with a boom staysail sheeted amidships until by cruel misfortune the steering broke down. She broached-to, lost her staysail and lay a-hull, soon to be rolled over twice in a succession of monstrous tumbling seas. A crew member was lost overboard turning disaster to tragedy. The ship was partly water-logged and only a completely tight bulkhead between the after accommodation saved the vessel from foundering immediately. From there on the ship's company's survivors worked valiantly, first rigging the emergency tiller enabling them to run dead before the storm. The main bilge was cleared; then, jettisoning all gear aft they were able to bail dry the after section which had been completely awash. Strangely, the mast was still standing, though much other gear was wrecked and eventually the yacht was able to reach Tristan da Cunha under trysail and headsails.

The accident appeared to have seriously strained the hull, as she began to creak in a frightening manner and had to be pumped constantly. No repair facilities were available on the lonely South Atlantic island; indeed, there was not even a harbour or safe mooring and shortly after reaching Tristan a further gale drove the vessel ashore.

Salient points for the heavy weather student indicate that even with a staysail up the *Coimbra* appeared to run safely before a wind estimated at Force 10. Disaster followed the misfortune of steerage breakdown. Very soon after falling off into the trough, lying a-hull in fact, she was overwhelmed by the huge seas. Watertight bulkheads prevented immediate foundering and, once run off under bare poles, she survived the rest of the storm even with hardly any buoyancy aft. The great strength of her aluminium construction and a watertight main hatch were tremendous safety factors. Apparently no coach coamings fractured as I suspect would have occurred in a wooden vessel. Being wise after the event, it is clear that had the crew more promptly rigged the emergency tiller the whole disaster could have been averted. Before she was rolled over, they feared to open the after accommodation to reach this tiller lest she take heavy water below. When this section was flooded, their worst fears were realized anyway and they belatedly rigged up the jury steering. Noel Redfern's faith in light alloy construction, reaffirmed at the conclusion of his report, is most convincing.

The subject moves naturally to Smeeton. It is typical that Smeeton should call the book of his yacht voyaging *Once is Enough*. Clearly, a common-sense title for the normal man, not for one minute do I believe that he himself accepts it. Did he not throw his challenge twice to one of Neptune's strongholds? And towards the end of the book he has a page headed "If I did it again". At the moment he is halted. The mighty sea has trumped his second card and left him baffled facing, temporarily at least, the fact that there is no known sure technique for the 20-ton

Cape Horner yachtsman. I suspect that if he sees an acceptable answer to those problems so vividly revealed to him (and so charmingly described to us in his book) he will be once more into the breach.

If you have read of his adventures in his 22-ton auxiliary ketch *Tzu Hang*, you will know how he challenged samples of the world's worst maritime weather by attempting the voyage from Australia to England via Cape Horn. How his yacht was pitch-poled—turned stern over bow—by a tremendous following sea, desperately damaged, heavily water-logged. How his wife at the helm was flung overboard 90 ft. clear but, despite an injured arm, swam back to the stricken vessel and galvanized them into action for survival: "I know where the buckets are. I'll get them." How from there, some 900 miles west of South America, dismasted, rudderless, everything a shambles, with skill and endurance they fought a successful battle and reached Chile.

Then, convinced wrong tactics had been the cause of the accident, they put to sea again in the repaired *Tzu Hang*:

> It may seem a little foolhardy that (this time) the two of us should have undertaken this trip alone, after our previous warning, but then before Clio was old enough to be a useful hand, the two of us had sailed *Tzu Hang* a long way. We were also *certain* (my italics) that the accident we had met with was because we were running before a heavy gale and that if we had followed our usual custom of lying a-hull it would never have happened, or at least in not such a violent manner, and we believed also that we had met with an exceptional wave. . . .

Despite the sentiment in the title of his book, he was having a second go, fired with the courage of a knight trying an older, yet trusted suit of armour, but which was to be of no avail. For a second time he demonstrated how tough is the ultimate storm on the 20-ton yacht. Lying a-hull this time, *Tzu Hang* was thrown on her beam ends by another monster whose crumbling top alone was as big as a whole gale-reared breaker bursting on a British shore. Yacht keels perform the function of stopping drift. Hurled beyond 90 degrees, *Tzu Hang*'s mast plunged into the water and took over that task, completing her 360 degrees turn and breaking in the process. Hulling or running, the mighty Southern Ocean held the trumps.

William Albert Robinson demonstrated that building bigger

and higher brings better results and tells us about it in his book *To the Great Southern Sea*. One of the outstanding personalities in ocean yacht voyaging, he circumnavigated the world in a small ketch called the *Svaap*, arriving home in 1931. After the war he built his dream ship, the magnificent brigantine *Varuna*, truly a yacht to "go anywhere", and in his book he describes his voyage round the Pacific which took him within the limits of Antarctic icebergs, higher than latitude 50 degrees S. In this region he encountered an example of what he calls the ultimate storm.

Having lain a-hull, with oil bags streamed, until things became dangerous, he was "awakened half an hour later by a jarring crash as if we had been struck by a pile driver. . . ." Thus began his encounter with his worst weather, so vividly described:

> It was obvious that *Varuna* was in trouble now and needed help. . . . This was final, dangerous proof of what I had always feared: that letting a ship take her natural drift would not work when conditions produced a disproportionately high, steep sea.

He shows himself a scientist, a seeker of truth:

> To satisfy my curiosity once and for all, I left her in this way (lying a-hull) a little longer to find out if it were true that "a good ship left alone always takes care of herself". The seas were so huge and concave that the whole upper third seemed to collapse and roar vertically down on us. Our oil had little or no effect now, as the surface of the water was all being blown to leeward. After feeling the shock of two or three more moderate seas crashing down on us I felt I had carried my investigation far enough. I unlashed the wheel and with no effort at all ran her off down wind before one of the real monsters chanced to break on us.

In this way, running dead before, streaming warps to slow her, with all-sail furled, the *Varuna* survived her worst storm. Robinson wrote:

> I have experienced several recorded hurricanes in my life, both on land and at sea, but this was worse than any of them. . . . When I spoke of the culminating experience of a life of voyaging this is what I have in mind. When a 50-ton seventy-foot vessel surfboards shudderingly down the face of a great sea on its breaking crest you have experienced something.

Because of the amount of work and thought that went into the creation of his lovely yacht, I feel that Robinson over-emphasizes the importance of hull design in questions of seaworthiness, and

Varuna's large size (for a yacht) is rather left out of the picture. I doubt whether a scaled down *Varuna* to *Tzu Hang*'s 46-ft. overall would have helped Smeeton. There is no doubt that Robinson experienced weather beyond the limits in which a 70-ft. yacht will safely lie a-hull; perhaps less obviously he found conditions *approaching the severity* when running with warps would be dangerous for a yacht of even *Varuna*'s dimensions. Although he uses the expression "ultimate storm"—and with good reason—to describe the adventure, he did not prove that even worse weather, which might have tipped the scales in Neptune's favour, cannot occur. Connor O'Brien made a safe voyage round Cape Horn in his specially designed ocean cruiser, the 40-ft. *Saiorse*. So did Argentinian yachtsman Vito Dumas, single handed—incidentally an avowed disbeliever in sea anchors. Did they encounter *Tzu Hang* weather or a true Robinson Ultimate Storm? That is a difficult question but to me, logically, they did not. Nevertheless I think *Tzu Hang* could have been better designed for the conditions she encountered—less heavily constructed, greater buoyancy aft, less of a pointed bow to bury itself like a crash-diving submarine—yet I feel that it is size rather than exceptionally clever hull shape that is the telling factor between the Smeeton and Robinson sagas. Remember that *Coimbra* survived running dead before, her emergency tiller at last rigged, *her whole after section and engine room flooded*.

Of the sea anchor Robinson writes:

> Voss, the leading exponent of sea anchors, unwittingly gives innumerable arguments *against* them.

Smeeton is not so sure:

> On the first occasion (when *Tzu Hang* was pitch-poled) if we had a sea anchor out on the end of our rope, a really good sea anchor, with wire strops to a thimble and shackles to a swivel fastened to another thimble at the end of a rope and if we had used oil at the same time—a constant flow from a special tank—to smooth the sea in our wake, we might have avoided the somersault which I am quite certain we made.

He puts the suggestion tentatively, however, because he concludes by saying:

> There are gales and seas particularly in the higher latitudes which a

ship may sometimes meet with, which she will be lucky to survive whatever she does.

As matters stand today, I think this final comment sums up the situation. Despite sensible design and all the techniques mentioned which are open to the seaman, a yacht, or at any rate one of up to 40 ft. overall length, will have to rely too much on luck if voyaging in our roughest ocean regions. There, ultimate type storms, superlatively bad weather, can overwhelm them. It has to be admitted regretfully that huge seas are, now and every day, being manufactured by the elements in the Southern Ocean and elsewhere and are rolling their ways across thousands of miles of desolate sea. Calling such waves "freak seas" is wrong. In their proper environment they are not unorthodox. They exist just as there is ice at the Poles, heat at the Equator, fog in London. The voyage of a yachtsman who sails his tiny ship through their reserves scot-free of damage, yet with no effective tactics for avoiding the dangers of collision with them, should be considered in the light of these facts and possibilities.

As just mentioned, some yachtsmen have safely rounded Cape Horn; yet there is no proof that their techniques entirely accounted for their success. Their courage equals their feats but I suggest that Lady Luck was with them just a little more than she was with, say, Smeeton. My feeling is that, so far, the 20-ton yacht has no proven method of surviving the ultimate storm.

Let us look a last time at that which remains unconquered by the small yacht mariner and take a glance through Beryl Smeeton's eyes as she steered *Tzu Hang*:

> Close behind her a great wall of water was towering above her, so wide that she knew *Tzu Hang* could not ride over it. It didn't seem to be breaking as the other waves had broken, but water was cascading down its front like a waterfall. She thought "I can't do anything, I'm absolutely straight. . . ."

That is the set-up that laughs at small yachts, scorns their sea anchors, their hulling, their running and their drag warps. Scorns, I think to some extent, their special hull shapes, fancy sterns or bold bows. Can anything be done other than build a larger ship? Until recently I thought not—any more than a man can clear a forest with a lawn mower. The thing was too big for him. But one thing made me think that the pessimists had no complete, 100 per cent cast-iron case. There was a chink in their armour, a thing that would not seem to add up. Why had so many yacts, disabled, water-logged and seriously damaged such as Humphrey Barton's *Vertue XXXV*, Voss's *Sea Queen*, Sinclair's *Joan*, Redfern's *Coimbra* and *Tzu Hang* twice not speedily foundered subsequently? Surely, logically, a second, even less furious sea would have quickly finished them off before their crews managed to repair the gaping holes, bail them to proper buoyancy. *Vertue XXXV*'s survival can be explained in that she no longer lay with a sea anchor on the quarter but was immediately put before the seas. Similarly *Coimbra*, apart from demonstrating the very great virtue of light alloy construction and watertight bulkheads, found safety in running dead before under bare poles. They had not encountered true pitch-poling weather. Of the others, probably in more serious bad weather trouble, taking into account wooden construction and no watertight bulkheads, there is one common explanation: after their "knock-downs" *none had masts*. Of my examples, *Coimbra* and *Vertue XXXV* only were not dismasted.

Strangely, despite my disagreement with the writings of Voss, he contributes a point, though not quite in context: ". . . don't hesitate to cut away the foremast. . . . However, be careful not to lose the mast."

When running under bare poles it is chiefly the mast and rigging that causes the undesirable speed that is the great factor in broaching or pitch-poling. A super sea anchor, if successful in checking this speed, will also hold the yacht rigid, and that will ensure that the roaring breaker, which sooner or later will strike her, has the best chance of inflicting maximum damage. The good brought about by the speed inhibiting role of a sea anchor is thus made null. On the other hand, if the yacht has no mast standing there will be no excessive speed, no point in a sea anchor, no sea anchor hazards to worry about.

Thus I suggest tactics beyond running under bare poles: lower your mast. Anybody who has efficiently shot Acle Bridge in a Norfolk Broads sloop knows that it is easy in a yacht properly designed for the purpose. Would it be possible in foul weather at sea? I see no reason why three hands could not do the job on a 20-tonner, given proper arrangements. It is said that storm fury itself, let alone the wild motion of the seaway, can make work on deck next to impossible. There is truth in the comment—I have experienced the stupefying effect of bad gales myself—yet it can be overcome by single-minded adherence to *drill*. Practise lowering the mast in moderate conditions until you know the routine thoroughly. That is how armies fight battles in the face of appalling confusion and stark terror.

Tripod tension must be maintained during the lowering operation otherwise the yacht's violent motion will take charge. The tabernacle could be mounted on the keel and projected above the deck, as in Broads yachts, but it must be insulated and water-tight from the rest of the yacht. A closing drain into the bilge would, of course, be admissible. Balancing the heel with ballast will ensure easy lowering but such pigs should be portable and in manageable sections, removable for stowage after the lowering operation. They can be shipped again after the storm, when the mast requires raising once more. Adequately strong standing gallows, preferably angle iron or alloy, should secure the mast when lowered, if possible in three places. The gaff and boom (high aspect ratio is not considered suitable for this adventure) should stow on deck in properly designed housings. The mast should be no longer than the yacht and not project overboard when lowered. There should be a means of lowering a topmast at sea if this is carried. The bowsprit should reef.

Thus you could ride an ultimate storm snugged to bare hull. A modern yacht with a cut-away fore-foot should still present her stern to the seas, a helmsman remaining on the wheel. You will now have controlled broaching, capsizing and pitch-poling dangers but the battle is not necessarily won. Those great grey-beards with their breaking crests that dwarf your little ship may yet strike you and inflict damage. Thus your yacht must be really strong, like a girder, with minimum doghousing, coach roofing. I should favour light alloy construction. The helmsman must not do a Beryl Smeeton and must be provided with a suitable shelter, at deck level or almost so, a suitable funk-hole to dive for in an instant. It will, of course, have its entrance at its fore end, the reverse of a normal doghouse, and thus afford real protection as a sea comes thundering over. If drains to this cockpit are impractical, it must be completely watertight and provided with a big hand-clearing pump.

I have recorded some differences of opinion in this chapter and

I have tried to give my reasons for my own standpoint. In some cases I have disputed matters only because I feel they are wrong in emphasis. For example, I questioned the *value* placed on features of good heavy-weather design. To keep the account straight, I must make clear that, of course, good design is important: to think otherwise is to say one approves of sin. But hull design alone cannot by itself provide yacht safety in the ultimate storm. Other factors play their part. With Robinson I suggest it was the well designed *Varuna*'s size. That casts aspersions on nobody.

Regarding design, an interesting consideration is the question of shallow draught as a safety feature when lying a-hull. In the past shallow draught has sometimes been synonymous with poor stability and deplored for really severe weather. In fact a shoal-draught yacht can be a stiff and seaworthy craft: indeed, for lying a-hull, a centreboard yacht with her plate up may be the safer vessel.

CHAPTER 18

Moving a Big Class Yacht

I'M in on that one!

A staunch shipmate of times past and skipper on a number of our delivery contracts, Denis Hoolahan is now a busy yacht broker at Birdham Pool, his seagoing time strictly limited, but he could not miss this.

Ernie Barker also surprised me. Summer was with us, meaning that the Barkers of Croydon should be anywhere in the country, possibly by the seaside *but not at sea*, providing vast areas of tent space for shows and exhibitions. Rigger of 100 marquees, Ernie was going to play hookey.

Maurice Durman was thankful that the date was May and not June 1959, because a fortnight later a huge trans-world radio communications aerial was due to be lowered from its 700-ft. mast for overhaul and his presence at that operation was essential. He could just fit in this sea voyage beforehand.

Bill King mumbled something about a house to be repaired, but I was not wrong in guessing that he could not resist adding this trip to his great fund of yachting experience. Above all Bill likes to go places and he saw that if ever this were possible without help from mechanical devices, gliders or horses, it would be so aboard the first 12-Metre built in Britain for 19 yrs. We had to take *Sceptre* from Southampton to the Clyde.

If this book is your first excursion into the world of yachting and if, for some reason, you read no newspaper or heard no radio commentaries around September 1958, you may deduce that, with only one yacht of this class built over such a long period, it means the type is no good and we now have better yachts to sail.

Nothing could be further from reality. People nowadays demand such standards of comfort, self-indulgence, silver-spoon feeding and endowed welfare, which appropriates so much of their wealth, that many fail to provide themselves with a yacht of any calibre. A pathetic solace in dinghies and models has resulted, and the term "yachtsman" has been corrupted to include their operators. Blaze the truth whenever you can: *Twelves are the only yachts!*

Designed by David Boyd for a Royal Yacht Squadron syndicate, *Sceptre* was the seventeenth unsuccessful challenger for the America's Cup. Back in this country after the races, she was soon sold and her new buyers required her back at her builder's yard on the Clyde. Moving her there was my first voyage in a Twelve. Later I sailed another, older one, *Flica I*, on a winter delivery from Cork to Southampton. I have no racing experience with them.

Her designer, who was connected with the attempt from the drawing board stage, believes that the exercise has been invaluable if we are soon to lift the trophy. The lessons learned by that sporting syndicate must be accurately evaluated and applied to future contests.

Unless yachts are seen racing against each other, it is impossible properly to decide their relative merits. After completing our delivery of *Sceptre* many people wanted me to confirm their own pet ideas and tell them that she was a slow old crate and a disgrace to British yachting. Instead I would confess that she was the fastest yacht I have ever sailed and sheer delight to handle. Then I would explain that I had never seen her in contest with any other Twelve. This did little to balk the growing opinion that *Sceptre* was the worst 12-Metre of all time; but the following season put the score right. In 1960 David Boyd's yacht swept the 12-Metre board at Cowes and elsewhere. Many a critic must have been confounded; others will have plenty of food for thought.

I thought the layout of *Sceptre*'s gear was of the highest order. In yacht delivery work, safety of sails and gear is the prior consideration; thus I have always viewed spinnaker work, particularly as practised by racing crews, with awe, but things were so well planned on *Sceptre* that losses in the sail wardrobe would be at a minimum. Accustomed to grappling with and cursing about makeshift lash-ups that are frequently tolerated as the means of hoisting and trimming sails, my crew and I were greatly impressed by the wonderful array of blocks, snatch-blocks, fairlead tracks, halyards, sheets, winches, the way they were positioned for easy use, their design and efficiency. To the problem of wind propulsion of ships we were approaching the supreme answer. This was so clear that I thought an auxiliary engine aboard a Twelve would amount to vandalism. On the wind, *Sceptre* moves fast in a breeze so barely perceptible that its direction is in doubt. She will nearly always be manoeuvrable: only in a complete atmospheric standstill, when smoke goes directly upwards, when sound travels far enough to make careless talk embarrassing, will she be motionless.

Anti-cyclones had been wandering about our part of the world some time before we joined the yacht at Camper & Nicholsons and during our preparation for sea a typical fresh north-easterly breeze covered Southern England and the North Sea. It seemed prudent to bend the trysail, borrowed from *Evaine*, her trial horse Twelve of the previous summer. Wire life-lines were rigged from the stemhead to a thigh-high level at the shrouds and down to the deck beside the big working cockpit. Being without stanchions, this provided a modicum of safety on the foredeck and enabled sail changers to hook on with safety belts while working there.

A new compass was fitted, stores loaded, the dinghy stowed in the big cockpit (still leaving room to work the ship) and each of us busied himself with his personal gear, hoping to keep it dry. The skipper commandeered the only berth with a wooden bunk board, but I brought canvas leeboards for all hands. These were fitted only with difficulty because the berths underneath the mattresses were of a hardboard composition—doubtless weight saving compared to wood.

Except for the w.c. and galley, which is a unique feature underneath her big working cockpit, *Sceptre's* accommodation is under the foredeck. She resembles a huge half-decker and some may doubt her seaworthiness on this score. However, she is equipped with an efficient hand bilge pump, very easy to work by either one or two persons, and capable of dealing with a great influx of water. I have often said that spray and slop in a cockpit is not infrequently exaggerated as "shipping heavy seas" and assumed to be the cause of the bilge filling, when in fact the influx is due to the vessel working badly.

Because of the amount of sail we carried, we met oilskin weather on *Sceptre*, but pumping was never more than an offhand doodle. However, before starting, we made sure that the pump was in good condition and we stripped and greased all screw threads to ensure that, in the event of a blockage at sea, it could be easily dismantled—despite yard assertions that it would never go wrong.

When acquired by her owners, *Sceptre* possessed twenty-two sails—quite an outfit for a sloop-rigged yacht—but fortunately we were not asked to take all these with us and a good deal of the racing gear was sent up to Scotland by road. We carried a main-sail, a low-cut genoa and another beside, two spinnakers, a trysail and a No. 3 jib. We were well equipped for passage making and the limited accommodation for five was not too badly cluttered up. We would be able to fare a little better than hard-bitten Stanley Bishop, professional skipper on the Cup races, predicted: "Sleep? You'll be doing that in a blooming great heap!"

Stan gave us plenty of very useful advice and by the evening of 21st May the shambles that had seemed to be gaining on us was under control. The three hatches over the bunks were sealed by canvas covers and battens—a most necessary precaution against slop in the sleeping bags. All the gear was properly stowed. The yacht was ready for sea.

The wind eased in the night, and next morning, when we were towed down the Itchen towards Southampton Water with a Scottish B.B.C. man shooting at us with his cine camera, the breeze came only in faint wafts from the east-north-east. To persist with my original plan to set the trysail that we had bent the day before was unambitious, but that is how *Sceptre* ghosted towards the Solent in thundery weather and poor visibility.

A thunder squall off Hamble Spit interfered with compass checking and the wind veered six points, dying soon after. Once clear of the Brambles, we pulled the trysail off and bent the main; then we continued slow progress, mostly by permission of the fair tide, and brought up to a mooring buoy off Yarmouth, thus consolidating our position before the flood turned the glassy Solent against us.

An interesting gadget, christened the Sputnik because of its projectile-like shape and claw mechanism, stands at the head of the mainsail shackled to the main halyard. This hooks to the masthead when the main is fully hoisted. By hauling 2 in. further on the halyard prior to lowering, the hooks are automatically cast off. It enables the mainsail to be hoisted on one of the very efficient genoa sheet winches because, once up, it takes the tension normally left on the halyard, which can therefore be easily carried back to its own low-powered winch.

An excellent idea, and quite fool-proof I should think but pessimistic Haward and his cynical crew, reared in delivery jobs that make all gadgets suspect, decided to forgo the convenience and ensure that the main was never hoisted those last 4 in. that actuated the claws. The tack down-haul tackle could provide a taut luff without it. I am ashamed to say that we looked upon this delightful Sputnik as just another hazard, an unusual one because our concern was to ensure that it was not allowed to function. Our fear, entirely unjustifiable, I think, was that it might refuse to *un-function*, presenting us with a full mainsail set for ever in a rising gale.

Supper and calls by some interested inhabitants ashore; then zephyrs from the north-east seemed to steady into a 3-knot breeze. The tide was still against us when we slipped our mooring and continued our way. The genoa was not much good, being blanketed by the main, but we made excellent progress through Hurst Narrows where the spring flood was still sluicing to the north-east. At midnight we reached the Bridge, the end of the Needles Channel, and bore round on a broad reach to head down Channel. With amazing suddenness the yacht leapt into high-performance stuff. From a modest $5\frac{1}{2}$ knots, *Sceptre* broke into a hissing canter, Maurice Durman at the wheel shouting in delight.

"She's going like a bomb! What happens if there's wind?"

The great spread of Terylene grasped hungrily at the Force 3 breeze, processing it into motive power with superb efficiency. Quickly the Needles became an occulting light far astern. The ship on course, I busied myself with a few jobs until Anvil light came up on the correct bearing, confirming a rather hasty compass check; then I turned in, to be lulled into sleep by high-powered sailing noises.

The relieving watch rigged the main boom guy as Anvil approached the beam. The wind had veered a little, but the genoa still pulled to leeward. Then it was Ernie Barker's turn to steer, and with his accustomed ease and minimum wheel he instilled more discipline into our thoroughbred. The short little seas on the quarter, that set her on a surf-board surge as they passed, were now quite unable to affect that straight white line of spume astern. At first others of us controlled her less well, allowing her to yaw—then saying "She yaws!"—overlooking that old, old error, too much wheel winding.

Around 0215 I awakened to hear Bill's casual voice beside the companionway giving a detached commentary to Ernie on the stresses exerted by the fastest progress to date. I turned out for a look-see. The full main was billowing, the canvas thrust into the cross-trees. The Shambles Lightvessel was nearly abeam already and, though several miles away, was doing its best to emulate a telegraph pole passing the Royal Scot. We hardened the boom guy, which we had led through a block near the stemhead to the spinnaker halyard winch. Then we hauled on the mainsheet to clinch matters. *Sceptre* has a kicking strap with a heavy shock cord attachment, but I avoid using these, belonging to the S.P.C.M. (Society for the Prevention of Cruelty to Mainbooms). In fact, the boom was broken on the last of the Cup races, with a subsequent display of brilliant seamanship rectifying the accident by securing a splint to it. A well-set-up boom guy in some respects fulfils the role of a kicking strap.

Just before 0300 the bright four flashes of Portland Bill were abeam—35 miles in 3 hrs. Though the tide had been with us, we had cleared the Needles Channel at the slack. My guess is that we averaged nearly 10 knots through the water and at times *Sceptre* must have been thundering along at more than 11 knots.

The watches went wonderfully quickly because our ship was such a delight. I have sometimes described a helmsman's job as a chore, but really it has its moments. *Sceptre* gave plenty. Equally she would thrill the artist, the mathematician or the plain romantic. At 0500 I went to bed throughly satisfied. Everything was under control and the progress was stupendous—exactly as armchair theories had predicted.

Hot porridge off Start Point and glorious sunshine; turbulence was pushing the breeze to the limits of Force 4 as it blew slantwise off the coast. The yacht was making nonsense of the contrary spring flood now sluicing strongly against her round the bold Devon promontory. We passed Prawle, its coastguard hut lit brilliantly by the sunshine; then creamed on to clear Bolt Head, with the enticing Salcombe entrance tucked snugly under its rugged wing. As we cleared the land, however, the breeze began to die and it also veered until it was almost dead aft.

The genoa slumped into a sullen heap. It was time to play spinnaker poles. The rig included topping-lift, outhaul gear, and fore and after guys. With the genoa set a-weather on this, it began to pull again. Later in the day, when the wind cunningly settled on a point favourable neither for orthodox nor goose-winged genoa work, we changed to the flat reaching spinnaker that could be trimmed for all quartering breezes—and even for a close reach with the spinnaker pole acting as a short bowsprit.

Progress across West Bay did not equal the night's run, but the sunshine was most pleasant and all hands enjoyed the sail drill. We passed the Lizard just after 1900, again finding a foul tide off a headland. After this our average was further knocked about. Pole in—pole out again. Spinnaker down—genoa up, first to leeward then a-weather again. Then repeat the drill in a different sequence. I wanted to reach the Longships at 2345 to make it a 24 hrs. run from the Needles and we had to make use of every fickle draught.

The day's run ended 2 miles short of the corner—166 miles, much of it in light airs and therefore a most satisfactory average. Now we came on the wind. Clearing the rocky outpost stretching from Land's End, we found a breeze from the north-east. At first we thought *Sceptre* could just lie full-and-by for the Tuskar, 130 miles across the sea to Ireland. However, a check with the Pole Star revealed 5 degrees W. deviation on the compass, so the course was not as good as we hoped.

The yacht's splendid windward ability was now to be revealed —and also the stamina of the crew, snatching their beauty sleep in the eyes of the sleek vessel. A short sea speedily developed and the occupants forward found the 25-degree heel disagreeable and the 45-degree heel, not infrequently shown on the clinometer, a hazard to health in a windward berth. The canvas leeboards, tacked to the hardboard under the mattresses, came adrift and two sleepers, luckily without injury, suddenly became nonplussed non-sleepers. Warm in a leeward bunk, careful not to admit being a witness lest I receive an appeal for help, I watched first Ernie, then Bill, scrape together bits and pieces and bed down on the bucking cabin floor.

168

Towards dawn I went on deck to see the yacht in action and check how the genoa and full main fared. *Sceptre* was crashing through the Force 4 slop, eating up the miles to Ireland. In finger-tip control at the big sensitive wheel, a key to the whole exhilarating scene, the helmsman guided her tightly to windward—a genuine four points off the true wind.

I watched the gear and worried for that great flat spread of Terylene, the low-cut genoa. With the yacht heeling hard, its foot was at sea-level and waves regularly broke into it with such force that the water rebounded back into the working cockpit. I have seen ordinary canvas burst under lesser treatment and the problem was to decide how much this stronger material could be expected to stand. We were going great guns and I was loath to let up, but safety of the gear was of primary importance. As early light broke over the sea, all hands were turned out and, with the yacht paid off to afford greater safety on the foredeck, we stowed the genoa and set the No. 3 staysail.

The sun rose and brought warmth. Some of the crew found comfortable billets under the windward deck around the working cockpit. Clear of the spray flying over their heads, they reclined in a suntrap. Despite the sail reduction, progress appeared about the same. At 0745 my log observed: "Wind north-east by east, Force 4, and occasional fresh puffs. Good visibility. Vessel heeling to 45 degrees at times and doing about 10 knots close-hauled."

It was an exhilarating day, the sort Maurice calls an F. 16, but going below for my camera I encountered typical obstructionism from the expert.

"Too much spray flying. Mustn't get my camera wet."

"But spray's what we want," I said. "It'll give a tang of salt to the scene."

He would not budge.

"I'm not as bad as some. A true gen-man does no actual photography at all. Even in perfect conditions he only carries out tests."

I left him in his bunk and tried to capture the seascape. Spray is no excuse for time off for my camera, but on this occasion I aimed it from such fancy angles that judder and shudder spoilt results.

Towards noon the breeze eased and after a scratch lunch we set the genoa again. At 1630, as if sprinting for the check-point, we were up to the Barrels Buoy, a little to the west of the Tuskar, and this made an average speed of 7.8 knots from the Longships. Not bad going, tightly to windward with a crew completely new to Twelves.

Except for one short burst after we put about to tack up the St. George's Channel, and a brief spell 2 days later, that was the end to real sailing. By nightfall, north of the Blackwater Light-vessel but on a board that headed us at the middle of Wales, the breeze had fallen away. Progress became dignified, though compared to the average yacht's performance in light airs, it was phenomenal. However, on the following afternoon *Sceptre* lay absolutely motionless, the sea like a mirror, a heat haze hiding the Rockabill a few miles to the south-west. We bathed, lazed, cooked supper; then ghosting a few miles through the night we saw the massive mountains of Mourne at dawn.

A light breeze came and *Sceptre* continued at a most agreeable pace, still having to tack. We lay a board to the east, opening the North Channel while the last of the flood tide filled the Irish Sea; then putting about with the timing just right we sailed past the South Rock Lightvessel at the start of the northgoing ebb. In the evening a sudden brisk breeze came from the north-west and with sheets slightly free *Sceptre* leaped joyfully forward to give us one last glimpse of her high performance. Corsewell Point to Sanda Isle in 4 hrs.

After that the wind vanished as quickly as it came, leaving us astride the shipping lane without steerage way. Using a white flare-up light to reveal our presence to a tanker with more impact than our side lights seemed to give, we enjoyed the electrifying effect. When the blinding brilliance subsided we saw that the huge approaching vessel had executed a 90-degree turn. These fireworks are the yachtsman's trump card in the collision game. From stark helplessness you suddenly find despotic power over every maritime nation. Remember, they must be white: red (distress) flares will have an opposite effect.

Needles to Sanda Isle in 4 days dead, but the last miles up the Clyde took a further 12 hrs. Around noon we ghosted round Hunter's Quay and lay becalmed until plucked to our mooring by Robertson's launch.

CHAPTER 19

A Good Weather Year

TRUE cruising yarns of our coasts depend on real British weather to make them spicy. A good yachting story requires some or all of the following:

1. A difficult yacht, not necessarily conforming to particular opinions on seaworthiness.

2. A crew of limited experience up against a new experience, preferably staggering.

3. Really nasty weather.

Except for one or two short poofs, 1959 abolished factor number three, thereby robbing the story-teller of 33 per cent of his thunder. There was a desperate shortage of rain, gales, floods, tidal waves and ice-floes. Yacht clubs threatened never to be the same again. Stories at the bar lost their punch or relied on imagination. The magazines that publish true yachting yarns struggled bravely. As a yacht delivery man I was provided mostly with work as is envisaged by land-lubbers who have had the activity explained to them for the first time—"*Simply lovely!*"

"No wrecks, nor nobody drowned—'fact nought to laff at at a'!"

As one who eggs his customers on with "nothing extra is charged for delays due to bad weather", I began to feel ashamed to take the money. However, my pessimism prevailed, sure in the knowledge that the law of averages would take its toll of prosperous times, but I wondered whether the time-table accuracy I was achieving would lull many people into a complete disbelief in bad weather. A number of jobs come my way because yacht owners cannot afford to run out of time at a half-way port of call, but the gales, that are the chief cause of these hitch-ups, were just losing interest. I became fearful lest we mortals lose our respect for the omnipotent sea.

Profiteer from a dream summer or not, I cut costs for the owner of the first yacht I delivered in 1959. *Ocelot*, a 48-ft. T.S. motor yacht, at that time was powered by rather elderly petrol engines. She was required on the Clyde and, in quoting "plus fuel costs" as usual, I reflected that the petrol bill would be heavy.

The strong easterly that chilled our bones and held the yacht in the wind on the fast running River Crouch as we secured the awkward winter cover frames on deck, died away before we left Burnham. Thus in crisp winter sunshine with a hint of fog, *Ocelot* bade good-bye to Essex. Immediately her navigator was faced with the problem of an unadjusted compass too close to machinery. It was correct only with the ship's head N. by E.; bearing away to the east or the west produced deviations of over 20 degrees. Change of deviation at times exceeded change of course, meaning the card was then slopping about in an ambiguous sector.

However, the weather was calm and without difficulty we picked our way past the Gunfleet, past the Roughs Tower and up the Shipway, cribbing the course from other ships or noting the panorama of navigational aids and sea marks. Round Orford-ness, course N. by E., mist cut the visibility and obscured the coast, but it was a thin blanket and the Pole Star was mostly in view. The Corton Lightvessel came up as expected, by which time I had decided that the remainder of the voyage warranted the attention of a compass adjuster. The Wash, the long haul to Flamborough, the Farne Islands and St. Ann's Head are best negotiated with reliable navigational instruments. Considering the many wonderful devices available to mariners today—radar, Decca, patent logs echo-sounders, direction finding radio, and the rest I felt that two magnets properly positioned beside *Ocelot*'s existing compass would be a modest enough settlement. The motor yacht was turned into Yarmouth Roads and we were soon tied up near the Town Bridge.

The old engines—they would have been "veteran" in a motor car—received their maintenance. New heavy-duty sparking plugs were located ashore—after considerable search because they were of the old-fashioned variety—and the port gearbox clutch was adjusted. I suspected the starboard toggles required a quarter-turn also, but the clutch would engage at slow speed and I postponed that job. The compass adjuster came from Lowestoft and when his job was done, we were ready to proceed.

Early night was with us when we approached Cromer. I noticed that the lighthouse on the cliff had recently changed its flash from the unsatisfactory single every minute to Group fl. (5) every 15 sec. With approval I reflected how much easier it would now be to take a bearing here.

Ocelot lunged into the fresh northerly breeze, the sloppy old Wash living up to its reputation. Carrying the tide to the north-east Docking, we would have the ebb out of Lynn Deep to help us towards the Humber Lightship. A scream from the starboard machinery upset the tactics. "Clutch plate slipped," I thought and, not wishing to disturb my crew in his beauty sleep, I stopped that engine, put the port motor into neutral, and set to work to remove the cover plate.

A quarter-turn on the toggle nuts had no effect: the clutch still seemed to be slipping. I gave another quarter-turn and a hard shove on the lever was required to engage the clutch, yet no power was transmitted to the propeller—which was reasonable because it was at the bottom of the sea.

Obvious trepidations buzzed through my brain. Should both screws be the same age it was likely that my remaining means of propulsion would vanish also—before we reached the Humber, possibly. On the other hand, if our starboard propeller had been improperly secured, or if shafts were of different ages, there would be little to worry about. Should we be fated to play around with a jury rig I felt it might as well be a good sail as a short one; therefore I determined to jump my hurdles as and if I met them. *Ocelot* resumed her course under port engine only. Speed was cut by a third; thus giving us a more comfortable ride over the lumpy head sea. We continued our way uneventfully and entered Scarborough the following afternoon, exactly 24 hrs. out of Yarmouth.

She dried out in the small hours and, climbing down the icy quayside, I noted with satisfaction that the missing propeller had vanished from an old shaft, wasted to a point at the "A" bracket. The port shaft and screw were in good condition. I was able to ring the owner and agree to proceed on one engine. He was buying new diesels and would have new stern gear to go with them. A replacement now would be purely an extra expense for the delivery voyage and I was glad to be able to avoid it. In fact I was able to reduce the owner's petrol bill by a third and he in return was kind enough to accept delivery at Grangemouth where passage through the Forth and Clyde Canal was delayed 3 weeks because of ice.

Several jobs later, the days now truly full of spring, Maurice Durman and I were back on the Clyde handing over *Careema* at Shandon in the Gareloch, having completed a brisk trip up from Falmouth. A 38-ft. express crusier, capable of $11\frac{1}{2}$ knots at economical crusing speed was just the job for the west coast in March 1959. Any other March would have been different.

We were half-way with a delivery man's dream arrangement: a trip up and another back. On this occasion good fortune was carried to an extreme. We even tied up to the vessel we had to take away. Instead of packing up and lugging our gear to the other end of the Clyde we tipped it from the luxury cruiser to Government disposal *A.M. Boat No. 122*, a 40-ft. fast seaplane tender.

Her twin 100 h.p. high-speed diesels were similar, if more elderly, versions of the power that had brought us up from Falmouth; but the hull they had to drive was rather different, being narrow gutted, the wheelhouse terminating a very short foredeck and conspicuously lacking in forward buoyancy which is of great importance to seagoing express craft. When careering downwind, lack of forward buoyancy may cause a yacht to impale herself inextricably into the base of a wave and a dangerous broach-to could result.

Shandon is poorly endowed with shops—we located none—therefore a check-over and help from Peter Boyle's men sent us quickly on our way to Rothesay for stores. Here engine trouble necessitated a trial run out of the Bay when an encounter with a short steep head sea—wind east Force 6, fetch 3 miles—stove in one of the wheelhouse windows. Maurice Durman almost swallowed the Kent Clearview screen. At the time we were moving slowly on one engine only, the starboard motor having stopped because of a fault we hoped had been remedied.

Morale was not enhanced. If this could happen in the sheltered

Clyde, what would happen when the Irish Sea whipped up some slop? To say that more speed would have averted the trouble is unimaginative because, even if true for that occasion, it would be a dangerous error in the open sea. Eventually an oversized sea would be encountered and speed would be a hollow mockery, the damage fifty times worse.

Back in harbour we enlisted the help of Peter MacIntyre's yard who covered the wheelhouse windows with plywood deadlights, each with an 8 in. diameter hole for vision. Our engine trouble was traced to a faulty fuel pump; additional spare fuel was loaded and we were ready for sea.

We set off on a wet Sunday morning with a forecast that made us feel a call at Girvan would be prudent, but by the time we were milling about off that Ayrshire fishing port, awaiting sufficient water to cross the bar, a clearance from the west tempted us onwards. Eight hours' economic cruising ought to see us to Dublin, and the back of the voyage would be broken. It took somewhat longer. Ten hours later my log read:

"0200. Bilge forward very full again after recently being bailed. In overfalls near Lambay Island. Throttle back. Water coming aboard forward and forepeak bilge (which includes the wheelhouse) is full to bulkhead, overflowing to saloon bilge. Hard bailing with saucepan and bucket is difficult because space restricts work but this gets it under control. Pumping arrangements are useless. Examine forepeak and note water gushing in via the covering boards at each plunge. After turning off the wind while clearing bilge, course is again set to clear Howth Head at slow speed."

We tied up in the River Liffey just before dawn. Later in the day, Maurice came panting aboard and threw himself down in our narrow cabin.

"That's better," he said. "Just went ashore for a Guinness but the whole pub was pounding to windward. A bad case of hard-chinitis!"

We dealt with the leaking forward by tacking canvas over the covering boards and along the topsides. Our vessel was also leaking elsewhere and while the existing pump would slowly clear the bilges in harbour a different situation prevailed at sea. At cruising speed the bow would lift, all the water in the big open cockpit running aft to the transom, away from the fixed suction point. Experiments with the self-bailers had not been successful and a new, really efficient hand bilge pump was a necessity. I obtained a vortex type capable of shifting a great quantity of water but only if the operator put his heart and soul into the job. A weakling at hand-draulics could achieve nothing.

Fuelled up once more, we left before noon on the following day, carrying the fair tide inside the banks almost to Rosslare. The headwind dropped light as it veered westerly; nevertheless our vessel had leaked somewhat during the day and clearing the after bilge now became a regular, messy and somewhat lengthy performance. The cruiser roared down the South Shear Channel past the Tuskar Rock and left friendly Ireland. By midnight we were round the Smalls; then we bore away before the westerly swell while having yet another go with the efficient but back-breaking pump. The tide was on the turn and spurred by her two gnarled but trusty Perkins, Boat *A.M. 122* roared on the crest of the flood as it filled the Bristol Channel. Surfing on the long swell was exhilarating. We entered Barry at 0700, 19 hrs. out of Dublin.

Amazingly, the next job was just around the corner—again an ex-R.A.F. high-speed boat, this time a Range Safety Launch to be collected from nearby Cardiff. As I boarded her, I saw at once that, though she was almost the same length as the seaplane tender, she was a far more seaworthy craft. The wheelhouse, similarly far forward, was more securely sunk into a really beamy hull. Most of this breadth was forward, where it was needed. From a bird's eye view she was pear-shaped and with a bold flare to her bows and a decent "V" section to her forepeak that would take some of the sting from punching to windward. It was clear that I was taking on an altogether different proposition.

Not that I was tempted to try her out in the Easter gale that sprang up. Maurice had to go home and being single-handed scotched any thoughts of giving this craft a true testing. I know from experience that it is best thoroughly to know a yacht before facing really nasty stuff—particularly when you rely on machinery that may have had little maintenance recently. In fact, when I left on Easter Tuesday, the blow having died away, I had two breakdowns before getting off Barry. Including the time to fix these and in spite of a headwind that piped into Force 4—which had really made life rugged aboard Boat *A.M. 122*—the ride to

Pembroke Dock took only 6½ hrs. Without a doubt these craft are a tremendous improvement on the narrow seaplane tenders.

As the year wore on it seemed as if a time schedule could be drawn up for the various voyages that yachts make round the coast. So kind was the weather that, using auxiliary motors when wind was non-existent, bogey times were achieved trip after trip. Of all these prosperous voyages, good fortune ran highest in the delivery of the 9-ton Harrison Butler sloop *Chincharu* from Bangor, North Wales, to Newhaven.

The gale of 26th April died by the time we had adjusted the engine timing, rigged temporary life-lines to supplement the dangerous toe-rail and renewed some of the cordage proved rotten by pulling on it and crashing on one's beam-ends.

The extraordinary feature was that all these ropes appeared in perfect condition. So did the sails, but beating out of the Menai Straits against a vigorous Force 4 breeze it was clear that these also were bad. *Chincharu* had been shipped home from the tropics recently and I think this accounts for the deterioration of her gear without the usual signs. As I rolled down a reef in the main a split started at the lower part of the leech. Hastily I lowered away further until the damage was safely round the boom. By then we were over the bar, paying off towards the Caernarvonshire peninsula, dismayed by the prospect of the 400 mile voyage in so badly equipped a yacht. Apart from the weak canvas, a brief period in the cabin while the engine took us down the Straits told of a leaking exhaust pipe, the gases discharging into the bilge. If the wind were strong we should lose our sails; if there was none we should be poisoned. The westerly wind, fine on the bow for the course to South Wales, would test our gear to the fullest. It seemed as if we ought to return to the Straits or make for Pwllheli and acquaint the owner with the sad tidings.

Two hours later a light breeze came out of the north-west and quickly veered north, Force 3—ideal safe propulsion for our handicapped vessel. It could not be missed. With a quartering wind the sails stood a chance. Perhaps we could make Milford Haven.

We carried it to the Longships. During the run prudent reefing preserved the main in a following Force 4. Everything was arranged; the breeze followed us round Land's End, dutifully backing westerly: then it went west-south-west as we left the

Lizard on the port quarter. A more serious wind caught us up off Anvil Point, but this was 1959, the passing front appropriately feeble. A classic veer came through as the rain cleared but the wind which heralded it only reached Beaufort's number 5. Reefed for serious stuff, husbanding our canvas carefully, no damage was sustained. We entered Newhaven the next day, exactly 4 days out of Bangor. A fast, lengthy coastal run, it reflects how easy passage making is when the weather is favourable. Stern comment must question a mariner's ability to deal with sudden contrary conditions in a badly equipped craft. On that voyage we were always assured of sea room and with the engine (that could be run just as long as all hands remained on deck) and the good foresail we would have been able to look after ourselves—even if not able to make to windward.

April and May were wonderful months for voyaging round the British coast and in June I completed an excellent voyage to Gibraltar in a fine seaworthy yacht that took no real notice of some of the most vigorous weather achieved during summer 1959. Then came another project for the Mediterranean.

The owner of this 43-ton auxiliary cutter, a sturdy ex-Colin Archer life-boat, had his vessel all ready for sea when the crew joined. Recently hauled out and anti-fouled, comment had been volunteered about her excellent condition. Her thick planking, trunnel fastened to the heavy timbers, certainly appeared "all ship" and ready for navigation anywhere.

All aboard—the owner, his wife, Noel Tringham, Conrad Lee and myself—it was a beat to clear the Straits of Dover. Midnight 26th–27th June found us off Boulogne, the engine driven mechanical pump taking an hour to clear the bilge. I was gratified to note the owner taking the matter seriously—some people imitate ostriches when it comes to leaking—in fact because of his concern, I paid scant attention to the matter. He was a tireless man, experienced, practical, quite undeterred by the less pleasant jobs on a yacht. With a slight jolt to my conscience I busied myself with navigation while he addressed himself to the bilges, muttering disbelief in his findings. Leaking in elderly yachts is not unusual and I was pleased with the efficient pumping arrangements. I welcomed faults at this stage of the voyage in preference to encountering something serious half-way across the Bay of Biscay in foul weather. We lay for Bognor on the port tack, a board that took 17 hrs., and the next night was approaching when we beat south to weather the Owers.

As we clawed towards the lightship, the fresh wind strengthening, we stowed the jib. Leaking now increased and we had been running the mechanical pump almost all the afternoon. A call at a Solent yard to fix the trouble was obviously a necessity. We thrashed past the Owers in heavy seas. The sturdy old ship was in her element, giving a remarkably comfortable ride considering the conditions, but now she really began to let the water in. Before the Nab Tower was abeam a milestone in our fortunes had passed: the bilge was filling despite our mechanical pump.

"Man the hand pumps!"

Conrad was the Trojan on the big semi-rotary in the lavatory and others of us worked the two deck pumps. These eventually became blocked and finally defied efforts to dismantle and clear them. An immovable out-of-reach choked strum fixed one: the other was cleared twice but finally died on us also—a poor seal somewhere along the suction line. We reached No Man's Land Fort under the lee of the Isle of Wight but calm water now did nothing to ease our predicament. Even with the big semi-rotary helping the engine driven pump it was not clear whether the water sloshing at cabin floor level was under control. Abandoning our intention of reaching the Hamble River, prudence dictated that we settle for Portsmouth Harbour. We tied up to a mooring buoy off Hardway at 2200, thankful to be there.

Extra high speed semi-rotary work now slowly helped the trusty mechanical pump to lower the bilge level, enabling us to replace the galley floorboards which had burst their moorings. Then we sat back to a welcome supper, leaving the motor to cope, but the galley was soon awash again. A pumping watch was set, a reconnaissance in the dinghy established the best place to run the vessel ashore should the water circulation arrangements break down; then came some welcome sleep. By morning that unmentionable stuff was out of view, the cabin floor drying. The engine was still running hard and each of us during his pumping watch had determined not to be beaten by the situation. Personal peril had ended with our entry into harbour; we still owed it to the ship. After breakfast we motored to a mooring off Camper & Nicholsons, where the bilge was completely cleared by their big motor pump. The leak was located at the garboard, just forward of the mainmast and was temporarily repaired from the inside. Later the yacht was hauled out for a thorough examination, the voyage to the Mediterranean abandoned for the time being. The verdict was that the hull and fastenings were completely sound but recaulking throughout was necessary.

At first I was sceptical, thinking there must be a fundamental weakness in a vessel that springs caulking like that. Frequently I have met yachts that leak badly when punching to windward but characteristically "take up" as soon as they reach port. That is a sign of wasted fastenings. No such thing happened in this case: leaking was established in one place only and, as recounted, entry into port brought no relief for the men at the pumps. A private word with one of Camper's shipwrights convinced me that withered caulking was the only scapegoat. While he hammered in new cotton with unerring skill his comments were emphatic:

"If you only have a trace of it in, quite likely what is there will spew out. She'll be properly caulked soon: then she'll never sink you."

Well ordered plans going without a hitch are of little interest save to those enjoying them or profiting from them; therefore I have omitted to mention many yacht voyages which were completed easily, or sedately, in this year of fabulous weather—though often assisted by an auxiliary motor. However, 1959 brought its share of good sailing—for example when I sailed back from Holland in *Malwen*. My associate Alex Brims delivered her to Amsterdam to ensure that her owner commenced his holiday over there; I made the return journey.

Stanley Hills himself built this comfortable 14-tonner. Thirty-eight feet overall, 29 ft. waterline, a Maurice Griffiths designed stemhead sloop, I like the type: beamy, good accommodation, sea kindly yet capable of a surprising turn of speed. I was also impressed with the standard of workmanship. Although a "back yard" job she was the work of a professional builder and looked it.

Ray Pearson and I joined at Flushing to find that the owner and his crew John Dinin, a Dartmouth cadet on leave, had everything prepared for the voyage to West Mersea. Thus the ship's company totalled four. A chat with the crew of the trim 5½-ton sloop lying alongside us; then we were off, to carry a moderate quartering breeze out of the Scheldt Estuary. It was a glorious day—sunny, warm, the sea smooth, a joy to be afloat. The forecast had told of sterner stuff coming in from the west but, basking in the sunshine or attending to odd jobs around the ship, it seemed remote from the immediate agenda. We had set off prepared for a blow but very soon after leaving we shook out the cautionary reef and hoisted the biggest foresail.

The 5½-tonner left Flushing at the same time, also bound for West Mersea and at first did very well heeling to 35 degrees at times, very loath to let us pull ahead. However, as we cleared the coast, tonnage told and our comfortable vessel romped far ahead. Later I was surprised to note the small yacht pay off W.N.W. apparently for the Galloper Lightvessel, the direct course for rounding the Gunfleet Sand. We had both heard the shipping forecast in Flushing. A typical low was coming up Channel and there was little doubt that our pleasant south-easterly would increase during the night, then veer—almost certainly before we could hope to be home. A strong south-west to west breeze would present a dead header to a yacht trying to reach Mersea via the Sunk. The obvious tactics were to make to windward towards Tongue Sand Tower on the south side of the Thames Estuary. Then a veer would cause little worry because we would pay off and hold a free wind through the Edinburgh Channel and across to Barrow Deep, thence to the Wallet Spitway—where I reckoned there would be water enough by the time we came to cross. After that a close reach ought to see us to Mersea. No tacking at all.

The rest of the day was glorious and we made steady progress in comfort. At dusk the breeze dropped light and the summer night was heralded by the West Hinder's four solid flashes, now abeam. We carried the jib topsail for a while but brought it in with the arrival of a more business-like breeze. Visibility yet remained good and the navigator noted the loom of the Kentish Knock with satisfaction. The voyage was going according to plan.

The rain came at midnight while we double-reefed the main; but soon afterwards I was able to fix our position with bearings by North Foreland and the Kentish Knock. Then the visibility closed in and the southerly piped into a full Force 6. *Malwen* thrust powerfully on, joyfully it seemed as if she were as glad as any of us to know where she was. These were her home waters: things would have to be really bad to shake her now.

I was exceptionally impressed at the way we foamed into the Estuary. No lagging in the same hole for *Malwen*; she made short work of the steep seas that had quickly developed.

Soon we gained the shelter of Margate Sands, and, as we paid off through the South Edinburgh, the sky cleared. Continuous rain turned to squally showers, the wind jumped south-south-west and continued to veer slowly. There was a nip in the air. It was lucky timing and textbook stuff. We held the port tack the whole way home and crossed the spitway at dawn, 2 hrs. before high water Brightlingsea. Then it was a thrash to windward in a brisk wind and sheltered but sparkling seas. The sun, the crisp start to a new summer's day were all the more wonderful after the dirty night. Twenty hours out of Flushing, Stanley Hills sailed his yacht down crowded Thornfleet Channel to her moorings.

I was told that the $5\frac{1}{2}$-tonner struggled into Harwich 36 hrs. later, having come to a full stop for a while somewhere off the Galloper, the veering wind becoming a disagreeable barrier. She continued to West Mersea after a rest. It seemed a case of a straight line not being the shortest distance between two points.

CHAPTER 20

New York to Greece in a Big Ketch

IT was a 13-hr. trip, uneventful and about as comfortable as a bus journey to Scotland. The engines droned happily; through the port holes could be seen, serenely peaceful, the clear night that surrounded us. Finally a powerful American voice behind aroused his companion:

"Waal, son, you're in America!"

B.O.A.C. flight 511 touched perfectly on Idlewild Airfield, New York.

Thence Bill King and I took a taxi to City Island where we saw the *Chauve Souris* for the first time, picking out this 90-ft. auxiliary Bermudian ketch from the smaller vessels lying in the Roads at the head of Long Island Sound. An October Atlantic crossing to Greece was the project and I noted with satisfaction her steel construction, high topsides and generous beam of 18 ft. Built in Holland in 1930, she had recently been overhauled and given a new suit of Dacron sails. Auxiliary power was by a 6-cylinder General Motors diesel, an efficient if thirsty monster. Some preparation for the voyage was complete: deadlights for skylights and windows as well as canvas covers, which had also been fixed over the hatches. The compass adjuster attended his job the day we arrived and various replacements to running and standing gear were in hand. We organized other essentials: boom guy gear, reefing pennants. For the latter 2 in. Dacron rope was used instead of wire, being double the strength of ordinary rope, easier to handle than wire and less likely to chafe the sail.

When the cringle has been hauled down, reeving a preventer through it is advisable; the pennant can then be eased while the reefing tackle is cast off, the additional rope thus taking its share of the strain. Using this arrangement, we found reefing surprisingly easy. Our voyage was remarkable in that, with only one exception, reefing was always done at night. The job was carried out fairly frequently, a single reef in the mainsail usually being the first reduction in our working canvas.

Anti-chafe arrangements were essential. We secured some 400 ft. of plastics hose piping round the shrouds, where the mainsail and mizen would press against them. This is particularly important with Dacron or Terylene sails because, as mentioned earlier, the stitching stands proud on these tough synthetics, just waiting to be hacked off by brushing standing wires or by sloppy runners. A topping lift inhibitor was devised to ensure that this heavy wire was held clear of the mainsail. A length of shock cord was rove through a block secured by a strop half-way up one of the standing back stays and shackled to the topping lift. The shock cord was adjusted by a rope fall. It worked perfectly.

I was surprised to note that there was no hand bilge pump. The main system relied on an electrically driven pump, fixed plumbing and out-of-reach strums at the suction points.

Since *Chauve Souris* was a steel yacht, I anticipated little leaking and settled for hacksaws, rubber hose and clips: also the largest semi-rotary pump locally available with adequate rubber piping to clear all bilges. During the Atlantic crossing the rudder gland leaked substantially because of poor packing and the mechanical pump broke down because of two rusted bolts, thus justifying this insistence on a hand pump.

With a tinge of sour grapes a disturbing comment was reported:

"Never mind the Atlantic! I wouldn't like to take her up Long Island Sound. Her mainmast is rotten!"

That sent me up the pole—literally—with a spike, but the stick seemed in perfect shape. In fact it was only 3 yrs. old but, tracked down, the rumour-monger stuck to his guns.

"The mizen was renewed but not the main."

The facts were just the opposite.

During our 2 weeks' preparation for sea hurricane "Gracie" struck the North Carolina coast, causing widespread damage.

Well to the south, her strength was dissipated before reaching us and in New York the wind gusted to 45 m.p.h. The next hurricane of the season, code name "Hannah", took a different course, finally striking the Azores around the time we left the U.S.A. After that our weather information was meagre because forecasts seaward of the immediate coastal seaboard of America are in Morse and I was disappointed because radio engineer Maurice Durman, who has often crewed with me on delivery voyages and can dream in Morse, could not make the trip. I re-read *Rules for avoiding tropical storms* with interest. *Chauve Souris* is a fine, able vessel, well found and obviously powerful. Eyebrows were raised when I mentioned she had no storm canvas. With all Dacron working sails and two very deep reefs in the mainsail, I did not consider this a necessity. Actually, I noted a spiritual blank from the owners of the above mentioned eyebrows when I mentioned our bilge pumping arrangements. If Dacron cannot—or rather must not—stand you have no need of sail. With Dacron you worry not so much about your canvas as about your masts and rigging. But bilges can always worry.

Steve French, Pip Davies and Ray Pearson were salvaged from the gay life of a *Queen Mary* crossing; David Fairhall arrived the following day by air even though one of the four engines had packed up *en route*. The ship's company was complete. Steve is a young professional yachtsman, chock-full of experience, including several seasons' ocean racing, yacht voyages to the Mediterranean, and hard years in North Sea and distant water trawlers. Bill has sailed thousands of miles with me. Pip is an experienced amateur yachtsman with great ability and boundless enthusiasm; and so is Dave. Ray was newest to the game.

Readers who have waded through these notes to read about the Atlantic in a traditional mood must now be disillusioned. This was 1959, the good weather year—despite "Gracie" and "Hannah" and doubtless other exceptions "proving the rule". But this is not to say that we had no good sailing. We had just that: fair winds mostly, light at the start, good and vigorous later. The strong breezes doubtless were cooked up by depressions. newly born, young and not too vigorous. The seas might have been those of the English Channel, ruffled by similar winds. There was never a great fetch.

Chauve Souris had no proper spinnaker pole fitting on her mast but carried a 22-ft. spar with a goose-neck fitting that could be fixed to the belaying pin band near the mast halyard winches. With this we were able to set an old mizen a-weather like a spinnaker, and it earned its keep in moderate following breezes.

Today there is a conspiracy to make mainsails without leech-lines. Without a robust cord or an additional thickness of canvas to house better aerodynamic surface is obtained—an advantage over your opponents if racing. I concede that with Dacron or Terylene the lack of a leech-line may not weaken a sail badly—though I would not say this with orthodox canvas—but lack of this valuable adjusting cord (that can pucker up a sagging leech) means that the sail must be 100 per cent perfectly cut and the sail stretching carried out properly. Our mainsail fell down here. We carried it happily for many hours in the initial light reaching breezes without reefing but, when we came on the wind for a brief spell, the leech, despite battens, commenced a desperate flutter in a breeze not even near Force 4. The sail had a high roach leech, further pandering to aerodynamic perfection and adding to the trouble. Many American yachts I saw sailing seemed plagued with leech flutter, though none as bad as that which now faced us. Such matters appeared to be shrugged off as a slight imperfection to be tolerated. My feeling was: "O.K., in Long Island Sound if you are prepared to put up with steady deterioration of your canvas, but it ought to be treated seriously on a long voyage." Good gear, no doubt, will stand up well to the treatment but aged stuff quickly will show signs of stress. The sound of any equipment hurting itself drives me demented and a flogging leech is such an obvious one.

We had to witness a steady deterioration or improvise a leech-line. The great reefing cringles, exceptionally well built into our sail, were crashing about like two hammers. To sew a complete covering for a cord down the leech would be lengthy but Steve put forward the easier proposition of securing the line with 1 in. rope eyes sewn to the sail—some thirty at intervals down the leech. The idea worked well and with occasional replacements our mainsail was safe for the voyage.

Fourteen days after Bill and I first left England we were off down calm, hazy Long Island Sound in humid sunshine. The New York summer with continuous 80°F. plus and dreadful humidity was late in departing in this bumper year of sun.

And that is about all there is to say of our Atlantic crossing. Mostly we carried a soldier's wind for 2,000 miles. The best day's run was 214 miles. Gybing, hoisting our makeshift spinnaker, occasionally taking in the first reef; these were our main activities during the comfortable long hop to the Azores. Twelve and a half days out, we passed 20 miles south of Flores. Then calms and a headwind that strengthened into a vigorous easterly lengthened the passage to Ponta Delgada by a further 3 days. However, we could not grumble at the progress and after 4 days in port we continued towards Gibraltar. The headwind persisted and at first we made little way. The best tack was to the south-east but I considered it better strategy to go north where, around Latitude 41 degrees we found a fair breeze, north-north-east. This backed northerly and we roared towards Cape St. Vincent in great style, making several daily runs of more than 200 miles.

The first contact with the B.B.C. shipping forecast made us really feel we were home and the first sentence that came over told us of down-to-earth normal weather prevailing there again. The fabulous summer was over.

"Attention all shipping. . . ."

Gale warnings were in force for all sea areas except Finisterre and Biscay. Later the effect of the very deep depression that drifted into the North Sea was felt even as far as North Spain, but we were well south, going great guns in the spanking Portuguese trades, broad reaching for Cape St. Vincent. Nine and a half days from Ponta Delgada, as Steve indicated the anchor holding, I turned my best American on Bill.

"Waal, son, you're in Gibraltar!"

Stanley Jones, friend of the owner, joined us for the passage to Syra in the Greek Archipelago. Several years back he had sailed a yacht to the U.S.A. himself but he now assumed superannuation status and came as a passenger seeking Mediterranean sunshine. The ration was meagre, however, and the last 1,500 miles of our voyage were the least prosperous. A gusty Levanter clung to us along the Spanish coast. Then light headwinds off Africa, where polite interrogation and subsequent close shadowing by anti-gunrunner French naval patrols broke the monotony. Then the Malta Channel.

The fair breeze punctuated by squalls that carried us from Cape

Bon to the coast of Sicily backed east as the sun rose amongst the heavy thunder clouds. The foul wind restricted progress within the shallow bay by Gela until dusk, by which time *Chauve Souris* was standing S.S.W. on the port tack to give Cape Scalambri an offing. There were yet 30 miles of lee-shore to weather before clearing the south-eastern tip of Sicily. Ever cynical about the weather sages who delight in unsolicited dismal forecasts for "outward bounders" (their odd successes remain immortal; their failures fail even to reach recognition), I had to admit that, if ever the omens were bad, the green hue and cirrus blasted grey streaks above hinted violence. I noted the barometer and thought about sail reductions.

An hour later, jokingly infusing deceit, every cloud vanished, leaving a clear, star-studded sky. Next the wind freshened rapidly and before we had pulled down the first reef, heavy clouds and almost continuous lightning closed in from the south. We put about and were able to lie a course that would clear Isle delle Correnti; the southernmost danger of south-east Sicily. Visibility became variable when the rain squalls arrived but I was able to take a bearing of Scalambri's light.

Within 30 min. Bill sent word that the wind was strengthening further, quickly. Already my ideas of bed were postponed: the sudden angle of heel screamed for less sail. I poked my head into the bluster, solid with rain and instantly knew the whole main must be lowered. The stand-by watch scrambled out scantily clad. Lunging on the winch releasing lever, the halyard was freed but the sail took some hauling down against the weight of the wind that held the slides hard against the sides of the track. Luffing would have hurt even Dacron. My pyjamas were soaked from the start; Steve sported only a jersey shrunken by spray, and looked horrid in the continuous lightning flashes as he hauled the sail up to the boom; Ray hardening the sheet alone looked the seafarer, being with the duty watch and fully found with oilies and seaboots. The night was a black aura of airborne water but the wonderful spreader lights showed the yacht roaring before a gale abaft the beam. Either Bill at the helm was taking pity on the sail shifters and had run her off the wind, or a welcome veer had come through. In fact he was steering N.W. squandering our precious sea room in carefree abandon. He told me his course and I bellowed back:

"Bring her tight on the wind—we can't spare a yard to leeward. Never mind people running round the deck half starko. That's their worry."

He had thought that once the main was stowed we would wear round and take the port tack, that would best increase our sea room but, though very concerned about our distance offshore, I wanted to stand on for those 25 miles to Cape Passero, where the coast bore away to the north. Once there we could heave-to in comfort or even lie a-hull if necessary. The alternative tack admittedly would carry us seaward better but if the blow were prolonged and veered slowly—both not unlikely events—we would be in for a long struggle, never able to let up, always fearful of giving an inch down wind. Apart from the general lee-shore stretching west-north-west a persistent easterly tinge to the wind would find us worrying about shoal ground to the west where such names as Terrible Bank defiled our chart.

Besides, Greece was to the east.

That tells the story—what we were up against—except that half an hour later it all seemed a storm in a teacup. The lightning and thunder passed away to the Sicilian mountains, the rain stopped and the sky cleared, but even as we hoisted the reefed main I noticed the sky to windward darkening again. It was the last lull. Within a quarter of an hour the main was dragged down once more with the same hurry and flurry. Jib, staysail and mizen were reinforced by the engine in a determined effort to make easting tightly to windward and clear Sicily. It was a tough proposition, a thorough test for the gear—on which our safety and that of our ship depended. Given sea room it would have been time to heave-to but in our predicament that was out of the question. During the lull the shore lights had shown up briefly, closer than I had expected.

The lightning became less frequent but the wind seemed to be really getting down to it. To gauge its strength with conviction was beyond me. It also backed a little until there was scant margin for clearing the land. I consoled myself with the fact that we had gained a little offing just after the lull. We hung on, the helmsman coaxing the yacht as near to the wind as possible without permitting progress to falter. We had to keep her sailing; the engine alone could have done little but give steerage way. We crashed to windward, lying over, lee bulwarks rolling under the seas, a

189

mantle of hissing spray, first green then red, tearing past the navigation lights in ungovernable ferocity.

She dived into a classic trough, the steep creamer beyond inadvertently covering her foredeck, singing along the lee-side, burying the shrouds, light boards, the dinghy. The yacht struggled up, buoyant again, and a great residue of solid sea was immediately ripped from her and hurled to leeward. The obvious damage was to the port navigation light which was washed out of the light board and dangled over the sea, lighting the waves in brilliant red. I hauled it aboard and replaced it in its bracket, still working, but neglected to lash it down. I thought the episode must be a freak performance but very soon afterwards another sea carried it clean away. Later we found that the dinghy skeg was pulled out, the boat having been shifted sideways on its cradles.

The trial of strength continued for $5\frac{1}{2}$ hrs. Then, with Cape Passero's bright light flashing on the quarter, our sea room was secure. Apart from the minor damage mentioned (Bill King repaired the dinghy before we reached Syra) and a few parted seams on the leech of the jib, prompting its stowage, the yacht was in good order. We had earned a respite and when the jib was safely secured I dropped the mizen. We bore away E.N.E. under staysail alone.

The rain stopped—temporarily—but for an hour and a half the wind blew harder and harder, as if livid at seeing us out of danger. I wondered whether our mizen could have stood it but was thankful to leave it just a thought. The Dacron would not have flinched but what about the mast and rigging?

At 0630, Friday, 13th November 1959, all wind vanished off Cape Passero. *Chauve Souris* wallowed in a violent swell from two directions and it rained—cascaded. The barometer had fallen only $\frac{1}{10}$ in. during the night; therefore I hesitate to liken this to the eye of a hurricane, nevertheless after 3 hrs. of utter calm and torrential downpour a smart breeze came from the west. A very vigorous, though barometrically shallow, storm typical of the Mediterranean, had passed us towards the Ionian Sea.

We carried this fair wind for a day and a half. Then we motor-sailed with light reaching breezes, in 24 hrs. bringing Cape Matapan abeam, the Archipelago just round the corner. New York was exactly 6 weeks behind us. The next evening we tied up in Syra.

CHAPTER 21

Round the Med. Getting Nowhere

THE next job seemed to fit in well: a delivery to England from the South of France. By steamer and train four of us rode the crest of success to the Côte d'Azur. Then progress figuratively sank into the trough, enforcing a rest on our laurels. We had joined an auxiliary ketch, of traditional Scottish design, approaching the age of 40 yrs. Though 20 tons T.M. is a good size considering modern high costs, it was a down-to-earth shock for the luxury-reared yacht crew that clambered aboard. Yacht size is governed by comparison more than dimensions: I have experienced similar dismay when collecting a $2\frac{1}{2}$-ton auxiliary gaff cutter after a trip in a modern 20-tonner. It is as if a lady of leisure were suddenly confronted with hard times.

Bill King now claimed that age and our sad fall down the ladder of class permitted him to contract out of the project. He assisted in the preparation for sea; then vacated his berth for Bob Mc-Fadden, a young Middle West American with valuable mechanical knowledge, little yachting experience, but a great capacity to learn. He had the knack of spotting the essentials of any practical problem and would be on the job as quickly and as effectively as many a more experienced crew. His dry American humour was entirely unstifled by monotonous British banter.

We soon made ourselves comfortable aboard our stiff old-timer. There were rigging jobs outstanding and an obvious need to caulk beneath the covering board, where daylight was coming in. The owner had conceded that the laid decks needed re-paying;

therefore we rigged extensive anti-drip arrangements with polythene sheets to ensure that water would be carried clear of all bunks. Given a dry pitch to rest his limbs, a man's morale stands a chance. We wired up the electric navigation lights, and, influenced by the exceptionally efficient spreader lights on our last commission, the thought of working on deck in all the darkness a wild night ensures appalled us, and we rigged a working light on the mizen jumper strut. I was concerned to note that two out of every three shroud plate fastenings were wood screws, some showing signs of pulling out. Without interfering too much with the panelling, we were able to replace each one of these with proper through-bolts.

After 6 days of preparation we sailed. The meteorological chart, displayed in Cannes High Street, indicated an easterly drift but this was out-of-date information and, before we had spent a day at sea, the south-east breeze began to veer steadily. Besides her adequate gaff sail plan, our vessel had two new petrol motors in excellent order and these helped considerably in the light weather. However, our passage across the Gulf of Lions ended in a dead beat to clear Cap San Sebastian, the western end of the region so renowned for storms. As the darkness of the second night out approached, I realized that the slight leaking which had commenced in the morning was quickening its tempo. We were now close-hauled against a more serious wind.

Rudder trouble—an inability to give full port helm, owing to the blade riding upwards on its pintles—made us wonder how secure was the lowest gudgeon. An early port of call was indicated but, after settling for Rosa, a lull in the breeze tempted me on towards Barcelona where I thought better repair facilities would be available.

The whole night was spent rounding Cap San Sebastian. At midnight we had sufficient offing and put about to lie for Cape Tossa, clear of the notorious Gulf, but within minutes a violent squall struck our yacht, complete with the usual Mediterranean storm brew of thunder, quick-fire lightning, torrential rain and wind beyond the civilized yachtsman's ken. I left the wheel, bellowing "All hands!" down the main hatch on my way forward to drag down the mainsail. Smugly I knew that if anybody below reckoned the order an unnecessary imitation of Captain Bligh he need only poke his head out. I soon had assistants, dressed to keep dry, but before the main was stowed the staysail sheet carried away, bringing about a desperate pandemonium of flogging rope, canvas and dead-eyes. It was like a rifle brigade in action. The sail was new but I was amazed to get it down undamaged.

Instead of grappling with the diabolical scissors-type crutches with which our yacht was blessed, we dropped the main boom to the deck. Being flush-decked in design and having exceptionally little clearance anyway, the boom was best secured in this way. However, the peak halyard was not really long enough for this purpose and in the excitement the fall was lost. The wild motion and roaring gale soon snarled it round itself aloft, well out of reach. Steve French refused to accept the situation and made a gallant but unsuccessful attempt to reach it by climbing up a loose rope. Relief at seeing him safely back on deck after he had disappeared into the darkness like a bird-man made me forbid his second attempt.

The weather was a minor repeat performance of the *Chauve Souris* off Sicily, but with the lee-shore a good 9 miles off. We spent the next 4 hrs. with all sail stowed, heading straight into the seas with the engines giving steerage way: "dodging", the fishermen call it.

The storm vanished as quickly as it had come and at dawn we were motoring under headsails and mizen. At noon the swell had gone down and we were able to sort out the main halyards and set the main. The leaking had been bad during the first part of the night but after stowing the sails, despite the heavy sea that had developed, very much less attention to the pump was necessary. Without the tremendous strain that is always put on a yacht thrashing close-hauled to windward the hull had begun to "take up".

We made comfortable progress along the coast all day but with nightfall the wind began to harden again and soon another storm was on us. It built up more slowly but, if anything, seemed more severe. Or perhaps it was just that we hung on to the mainsail to drive our yacht towards Barcelona's welcome harbour, now broadening on the bow. Anyway, the poor old ship groaned at her timbers, her bilge filling with dismaying speed as soon as it was pumped dry. Investigation showed a good deal coming in under the forecastle floorboards but even that healthy flow hardly accounted for the total, and doubtless there were other leaks all along the garboard strake where inaccessibility or sluicing water defied detection.

The last hour was an anxious time, each of us suffering for the gear as it took harder and harder punishment. Compared to the way many yachts would have lain flat in such a wind, our stiff vessel stood virtually upright, her canvas bearing the full brunt of the gale. The strain on her hull and equipment must have been enormous and that small resultant force, aerodynamically won from the untamed fury of nature which screamed past us, drove her hard into spume-covered waves. But the gear held and, with the harbour lights to leeward at last, we dropped the main and ran down into shelter under headsails. Just inside the entrance the big night ferry for Majorca thumped past, picking up speed for a rough crossing to Palma. Far to the east, on the Azure Coast we had recently left, a dam burst to engulf a village in tragedy. We were glad to be in.

Bob McFadden's skin diving prowess soon established nothing seriously amiss with the rudder. The trouble was due to a fractured securing pin in the top pintle. A bulldog clip was substituted and the rudder was then secure.

The rest of the tale is short. After "taking up" in Barcelona, serious leaking started as soon as the wind freshened on our continued passage towards Gibraltar. It became clear that to attempt delivery to England would be foolhardy and, with great reluctance, I put into port once more to acquaint the owner with the sad facts. Despite a reasonable estimate for repairs in a Spanish yard, I was asked if I thought we could take the yacht back to France and this was done. However, a change took place during the return passage. A moderate mistral in the Gulf of Lions produced leaking that no longer ceased on arrival in harbour, and before we left the yacht it was essential to slip her.

Thus ended 3 weeks' unproductive work—unless it can be looked upon as a lengthy trial in lieu of a survey. Basically the yacht was a sturdy seaworthy vessel, well able to look after herself in very bad weather. After proper repairs have been effected she will be so again.

CHAPTER *22*

Dead Beat to Gibraltar

SHE was a small yacht, yet she promised to be an excellent assignment. March can be a slack period, punctuated with short trips in craft that have somehow escaped their proper winter lay-up. It is when weak gear, doubtful sails and bottoms in need of a scrub are more commonly encountered. Of good pedigree and obviously well cared for, this time I could expect a well found little vessel; nevertheless my illusions were fewer than hinted by patronizing acquaintances who heard tell of the job:

"Aren't you lucky . . . the glorious Mediterranean. . . . How I wish I were coming!"

Tricky Mediterranean weather apart, the crux of the job would be to sail an 8-ton yacht up the eastern Atlantic seaboard at a bad time of the year. The South of France to Gibraltar would be by way of an appetizer; then would come the Portuguese coast and the renowned Bay of Biscay.

I admit it was most pleasant checking *Sharavogue*'s gear while this 35 ft. overall, 26 ft. waterline auxiliary yawl lay at moorings in the picturesque harbour of St. Jean Cap Ferrat. Sheltered from the raw winter mistral, the Côte d'Azur beneath the Alpes Maritimes certainly supports life more easily than does Britain in the same season.

"Of course," said the major, as he entertained us aboard his beautifully finished Hillyard lying in the same harbour. "One cannot go out now. . . . Nobody does. We shall start our cruising in 3 months or so."

I am not sure how he equated the remark with the avowed intention of his guests to take the sleek *Sharavogue* to England

195

right then; but standing in its own right the idea of a close season for Mediterranean yachting is not unreasonable. The Greeks and Romans of ancient times strictly curtailed winter navigation. From October to April the Mediterranean is vicious and squally. Calms or gentle breezes give way to furious wind with great suddenness. From the sailing point of view the song of different, more syrupy sentiments describes it: "All or nothing at all".

The Azure Coast particularly has interesting weather in winter. Normally the land is sheltered from the mistral by the high mountains inland, but just out to sea this north to north-west wind from the Gulf of Lions curves round west-south-west to follow the coastline towards Italy. Eastward the tramontana, a similar wind often blowing at the same time, funnels from the Alps across the Gulf of Genoa and skirts the French coast from the other direction. At times the two almost reach and fight with each other. Offshore between Monte Carlo and Cannes their opposing swells can be seen colliding one over the other in a confused jumble a little way off the sheltered coast. A well established mistral in the Gulf will pursue its business 24 hrs. of the day until done but the offshoot along the Riviera is often influenced by convection. The west wind tends to increase during the afternoon and ease during the small hours. In the morning only the swell may remain, horribly confused because of a similar state of affairs at the Genoa end.

While enjoying our visit to the Hillyard an unexpected message arrived. I must go the the Bar du Port to await a 'phone call from Marseilles. When I returned I sought to relieve pent-up frustration and picked on Bob.

"Where's that Yankee Jonah. He'll never make England in a yacht. If he comes along the trip is bound to fail!"

Bob McFadden, staunch crew member of the luckless Golfe Juan, Tarragona and back to France jaunt before Christmas, offered an inquiring look. But his conscience was clear and he said nothing.

"A potential buyer has got on to us," I explained. "We have to call at Marseilles and if he likes *Sharavogue* he will buy her, making us redundant."

The main purpose of our voyage was to bring the yacht home where craft of her size sell more easily. Generally the Mediterranean yachtsman prefers larger vessels.

Preparations were complete in 2 days. Spare fuel was loaded, stores, water, a water tank flushed out, limber holes cleared, stern tube hardened, its greaser soldered where fractured, main halyard winch overhauled. The yacht had laid at moorings since the summer, yet she was surprisingly clean under the water. She was a modern Class III offshore racer from the board of C. A. Nicholson and built in 1952 for Adlard Coles, as his *Cohoe II*. Accommodation was comfortable as far as a small racing machine permits. John Liley, our stoic third crew member, was referred to the port quarter-berth, leaving the starboard equivalent free to have the folding chart table permanently rigged. Bob and I commandeered the more sheltered saloon berths, appreciating their excellent canvas leeboards that would keep us in, snug and safe, whichever way the yacht heeled. We would be spared the problem of solid water from the main companionway as a bedmate—a real hazard for users of quarter-berths. We conceded there would be times when John would find his sleeping apparatus impractical and prefer to warm whichever saloon berth was vacant. There, only a few leaks round the coach roof coamings were anticipated, a common feature when a yacht has been in hot sun for a spell, and easily diverted from the bunks with old charts and drawing pins. Cooking was by "Camping Gaz", French equipment I had not previously met. Burners screw directly on to small bottles of butane gas and an excellent gas lamp also was complete with burner. The large size bottle fitted snugly into a non-returnable 4 gallon petrol tin and, lashed securely to a sideboard, made a deeply fiddled stove able to hold a pressure cooker even while sailing at steep angles of heel.

We set sail in the afternoon of Wednesday, 2nd March, delighted at seeing a faint breeze reaching into the Bay from the south-east. Motor round Cap Ferrat, we hoped, and a broad reach would see us to Marseilles. But I gave little for our chances, even though this gentle wind backed east when we set a course for Cap d'Antibes. An easy swell accompanied it but another from dead ahead, a message from the Gulf of Lions, shouted the facts. Steeper, more urgent, this latter began to stop our yacht in her tracks. Flogging and flapping robbed the sails of drive. The helmsman sat frustrated, at times with bare steerage way despite running the little auxiliary motor. Sufficiently schooled in Mediterranean sailing, I foresaw the inevitable and knew it would come with a rush.

Two squally puffs from the north-west then the wind hardened properly a little south of west. We handed the big genoa and set the working jib—or No. 3 genoa, the inventory would have it—stowed the mizen and very soon afterwards rolled down a reef in the main. *Sharavogue* was off, but in the wrong direction, giving her crew an initial taste of what they soon accepted as their just deserts: windward work, mostly tacking.

From Force 5 the wind settled on a gusty increase. We were lying the offshore tack and the land receded fast. I had a good idea of the possibilities. Each headland nearer the Gulf of Lions meant less shelter from the mistral. I began to modify my idea of a non-stop leg to Marseilles. Tucked under the lee of the long promontory to windward was the ancient town of Antibes, its enticing harbour stretching from old battlements built to frustrate the tricks of Moorish pirates. My crew were undertaking stomach adjustments; the cabin was a wet shambles. We had about one sea leg between the three of us. Nobody was yet taking 8-tonner windward work in his stride. Just under 8 hrs. out of St. Jean, *Sharavogue* foamed into Antibes Harbour and dropped anchor, having made good 12½ miles and some more to and fro.

We left at 1000 the next day. The diurnal weather factor was operating: locally the mistral had died during the night. Sunshine was supreme, wind a faint waft from the east. Under sail and power we rounded Cap d'Antibes and, wishing to carry a quartering breeze, crossed Golfe Juan to pass inshore of Santa Margaret Island beside Cannes. In the afternoon a more vigorous easterly carried us past Agay but died on us off Cap Drammont beyond, where the yacht lay rolling wildly in a confused swell. "Overfalls due to a current round the headland" was my hopeful explanation—for a while—but as we struggled on by auxiliary power the steep waves persisted, taking a more regular shape, the crests breaking despite the absence of wind. They stretched westward towards the land which was only 7 miles off. There was no wind here, yet what else could build such a sea?

While forming the question I knew the only possible answer: mistral out of the Frejus Gulf. The wind had not yet reached this far seaward but nearer the land, funnelling out of the valley, it would be operating with vigour. Within an hour and a half we were lying the starboard tack for Cap Camarat, close-hauled, six rolls round the mainboom, the jib reefed. I logged Force 7 and later Force 8. Nearer the true mistral region, I saw little hope of a respite in the night; yet the wind was still offshore and shelter could be gained close under the headlands. We ought to try and beat as far as Hyeres Road, where it would be best to await a change of weather. Beyond that anchorage through the Little Pass which divides Porquerrolles Island from the mainland, you enter the Gulf of Lions. There the mistral screams in your face across 80 miles of unsheltered sea.

We were able to point inshore of the headland though leeway ensured we could just claw up to its off-lying reef. *Sharavogue* drove into the steep seas through a flurry of airborne spray. As helmsman I had quite a sail and, had our destination been a harbour under the lee of the land ahead, San Tropez for example, there would have been no despondency. Tacking to windward is stimulating if distances are short, the next harbour chosen rather than dictated. I hate to be told where to go; yet Marseilles was like the moon that afternoon and *Sharavogue* was no Sputnik. I considered Saline Anchorage near Hyeres Road the best we could hope for.

Close to Cap Camarat at sundown, skirting the off-lying reef that reaches half a mile seaward, we found smooth water and so much less wind that more sail would have helped. But I kept the jib reefed and the mainboom like a furled blind. It was a brief evening lull, shelter from the high promontory, or both. We continued slowly, appreciating the comfort, keeping under the land as much as possible towards Cap Lardier; then back to work —windward, hard. It blew across Cavalaire Bay, maximum fetch $3\frac{1}{2}$ miles, yet for the wetting it gave John, now at the helm, we might have been in mid-ocean. By the way it heeled the yacht beyond her gunwale it was real wind, and increasing with each tack. Crossing that bay was a saga in itself but, having triumphed to reach its western arm, I relaxed my vow to anchor under its lee. We would struggle on to Lavandou which seemed to have better facilities and a little harbour.

That was at 2030: several times before 0100 I wondered about the size of this mouthful. Could any mast and rigging stand up to dragging a half submerged, bucking hull through such hostile seas, lee rail permanently under, even the cockpit coaming dipping? I wondered about the cotton foresheets, stretching visibly where they passed through the fairlead dead-eyes. I wondered about the canvas, particularly the mainsail with its necessary battens that beat furiously in their pockets each time the 8-year-old sail flogged through stays. Should anything fail we should be blasted clean out to sea, helpless as butterflies blown from their flowers. Yet the gear held while *Sharavogue* progressed slowly against that tremendous wind, a true mistral that had left Admiral Beaufort's Force 9 behind. We clawed up to our shelter, 10 miles short of Hyeres, but honourable progress indeed.

Lavandou is an attractive, but small, harbour, and I had no detailed chart. The auxiliary motor might have helped us to sound our way in, but the sea had gained access to its cylinders via the exhaust. This pipe leads up to the deckhead before bending down to the skin fitting, an arrangement making it normally unnecessary to close the outlet sea cock. The after part of our yacht must have been deeply submerged at times. After some fruitless work with the starter motor we sailed close inshore, south-west of the breakwater and dropped anchor. Then we slept in wet bedding.

Cylinders cleared and plugs heated, we started the engine in the forenoon, motored gently into the harbour and found how shallow it was. No tide to help but, hoisting a little sail, the squally mistral heeled the yacht lifting her keel from the mud and off she came.

The next morning, Saturday, we motor-sailed to Marseilles in fluky breezes or complete calm.

Monsieur Billaud came aboard with his sailor. *Sharavogue* is a pretty little vessel, fast, a joy to sail and, considering her size, the accommodation with four berths plus a "sail bunk" in the forepeak was neatly fitted into her 26 ft. waterline length. However, conflict between living quarters and sailing qualities was apparent. Our client was used to thoroughbred racers and would have enjoyed sailing her but his wife's idea of comfortable cruising demanded more elbow room below decks. Only a larger hull could solve the problem. The yacht must sail 2,000 miles to her next showroom.

Preparations included replacing the old cotton foresail sheets and attention to the compass which had suffered a crack in its Perspex face. Bob made an excellent repair job with clear Bostik—an efficient all-purpose adhesive. Additional cooking gas was purchased, stores and water. We left just before midnight on

Monday, with a moderate south-easterly breeze promising a fast passage across the Gulf of Lions—to start with at any rate. Clear of the Chateau d'If and Pomeques Isle, sheets free to a good breeze, the yacht showed what she could really do, careering vigorously over a most unpleasant sea, chilly rain squalls blotting out the moon.

The waters of the Gulf mirror the diverse winds that ruffle its surface. Three distinct swells were disputing stardom. There was one from the north, the effect of a mild mistral probably localized around the Rhône and its delta; then there was the present "marin", south-easterly, a common feature on the eastern side of the Gulf and the Riviera following prolonged mistral weather. This was contributing a bumpy little sea of its own. Finally, there was a swell from the south-west, just the way we wanted to go, confirmation that the prevailing wind off south-east Spain was functioning, waiting to test our yacht's windward ability. Clearly our fair wind was to be a brief interlude between more vigorous seagoing, and each bumpy mile before it was savoured.

Shortly after dawn the rain vanished and for a while the sun appeared. The wind dropped light and rapidly backed a little west of south. Soon we could not lie the course for Cap San Sebastian, the south-western exit from the Gulf. The night that followed was occupied in beating south across Rosa Bay. We cleared the Gulf of Lions at dawn to commence a beat into the fresh dead muzzler that was blowing along the Spanish coast. Progress was painfully slow, but all we could do was plug into wind and weather.

I have heard people say they like tacking, claiming it the invigorating, best part of sailing. Protest that it is desperately uncomfortable, conducive to a shambles below decks, wet bedding and the most severe test on the tummy, all making for depressingly slow progress, and they reply that a heeling yacht is steadied by the wind and pitching does not worry them at all. Just how steady, as a thrashing sailing craft falls from one big hole to the next is not indicated. A trip in *Sharavogue* that March would have helped modify such opinions. Of the 744 hrs. in the month we spent 466 hrs. under way at sea. Of this seatime, the wind headed us for 426 hrs., often forcing us to tack. The distance made good, as opposed to mileage sailed through the water, was 1,320 miles making an average speed of 2.8 knots.

With apologies to Masefield:
"All I ask is a fair wind and sails to goose-wing by . . ."

A hard day's sail; then the breeze eased, affording a slower, more comfortable beat past Barcelona. Tacking to weather its outer breakwater, we passed close under the stern of cruise liner *Britannic* as she picked up the pilot to enter that harbour at dawn. Then we lay the starboard tack, hoping to clear Ibiza but soon to be headed eastward towards Majorca. During the night, in clear silhouette against the moon, the 28,000-ton *Britannic* was with us again; passing swiftly towards the largest of the Balearics. Doubtless her passengers were sleeping off Barcelona, preparing for Palma.

Strong headwinds the next night found us thrashing into a wild sea to bring Ibiza to leeward at last. Respite at dawn, and the port tack changed to be the more favourable. More hard sailing, now in brilliant sunshine, and we clawed up just down wind of Cape San Antonio. We rounded this headland and its twin, Cape Nao, at dusk, 5 hrs. light weather following. Then came more wind.

The peaceful spell was ending as I handed over to Bob at 2300. We took the opportunity of removing the big genoa, setting the working jib in its place. Particularly during the hours of darkness sail changing is best done with two people on deck, and the change of watch provides a good opportunity without somebody turning out specially. The yacht thrashed through the night, as usual not quite in the required direction, tightly close-hauled, working hard for her slow pace, the elements hating to permit progress against the wind using the wind.

More sail came in when John took over and his 3 hrs. were wild, wet ones. Below, warm and comfortable, lying hammock fashion, more on the canvas leeboard than the mattress, the noisy progress infiltrated into my sleep, keeping me aware of matters on deck. Around 0300 the helmsman crawled forward to operate the roller reefing further. I could sense him fumbling as the handle fouled the already bulging canvas on the boom. Mumbled curses confirmed that a reduced angle of heel meant the yacht was paying off; then came the pandemonium of a panic rush aft to prevent a gybe. Eventually she was sailing again, with less flurry but still going great guns.

A slow veer came at the height of the blow—Force 7 was my

reckoning. Then the yacht could lie the course for Cape Palos; soon, amazingly, the sheets could be started a fraction.

I was up at 0500 and sensed the rapid decline in wind while struggling into oilies. John remained with me while much of the main was unrolled, but after he went below I continued the race to carry suitable sail in keeping with the fast vanishing wind. Sometimes a blow will persist in squally strength behind a passing front and, because the veer brought *Sharavogue* a fair slant, this would have suited us. But it was not to be, probably because the mountainous Spanish coast here discourages sea level winds from the north-west. The remaining breeze was good to use but was soon gone. The big genoa and full main greeted the dawn: wild night gave place to benign day. Progress lapsed to ghosting pace.

In the afternoon we were back to a southerly breeze once more and the barometer, which had achieved a faint rise around dawn, continued its slow fall. Cape Palos and its off-lying Hormigas Isle came up on the port bow and even though the wind freshened we felt the shelter of the land. All signs of a strong blow returned and I reviewed possibilities for shelter.

To windward, 20 miles off, Cartagena represented an 8-hr. sail. To make harbour called for a third successive night of hard beating, our seventh out of Marseilles, by which time a real veer might come, bringing a fair wind too precious to waste. It would be better to anchor under the comfortable lee of Cape Palos now, while a headwind was blowing. We sailed towards the long sandy beach that narrowly divides the sea from an inland lake and dropped anchor in crystal-clear water. Close to windward, the mountains were taking the sting out of the wind.

It was an admirable decision. The strong blow of the night piped into full gale the next day. We caught up with sleep and appreciated the shelter. Progress to windward would have been impractical, seagoing of any kind in a small yacht a desperate struggle.

The following morning we continued our way, though no real veer came when the gale ended. It remained a dead beat to Cabo de Gata, the often hard-to-get-around gateway to the Gibraltar Strait approaches, 80 miles away. Thoroughly resigned we plugged on, using the motor when the wind died. We rounded the corner and entered Almeria in 33 hrs. More fuel was loaded but the improved weather—no wind instead of headwinds—

made me think the food would see us to Gibraltar. I did not cater for the slight popple kicked up by even faint westerly airs, which found our 6 h.p. auxiliary wanting. Fuel was short before we had covered half the distance. The brisk breeze on the second night out was therefore most welcome and I resolved to use it to the full, driving the yacht into the steep seas characteristic of the region. Lee rail awash, spray covered us continuously. John abandoned the quarter-berth with its heap of soaking gear. His complex anti-splash arrangements had broken down. We were attempting a sprint finish but, with 40 miles to go, our steady triumph over the strong east-flowing current petered out at dawn.

Then we eked out the fuel, making up to the east side of the Rock, but there, with only a pint in hand, we could not expect to make Gibraltar Bay. We lay becalmed all night and ghosted into harbour the next noon. The last potato had been eaten and John's scavenge through bare cupboards brought to light only a drab box of lump sugar.

Even as we dropped anchor the Levanter began and a subsequent visit to the R.A.F. meteorological office showed an easterly had become established from Italy, all along the route where we had bucked headwinds.

CHAPTER 23

Home in "Sharavogue"

THOUGH the worst of the Levanter was gone before we sailed, a moderate easterly breeze remained to carry us through the Straits and beyond. After solid windward work it seemed a strange delight to reel off 90 miles with so little fuss. Then came squally weather from the west, steadily increasing until we were plugging into the familiar headwind, mostly strong and gale at times. In a region where I have often found light breezes and sunshine, the vicious rain, coupled with squally and gusty winds, a disappointment. So, too, was our slow progress towards Cape St. Vincent. Paying off to the north, we closed the coast and beat a painful path along an open seaboard until we reached the sheltered Portuguese village of Lagos. Some 18 miles ahead lay the St. Vincent corner, beyond it a turbulent Atlantic now covered by a very wide storm area. Progress towards England would mean close-hauled work against a mighty ocean equipped with fierce contrary winds. Having made good 170 miles in 37 hrs, we joined the twenty-five coasters and fishing boats already anchored in the bay.

We continued on Sunday, wind west-north-west fresh, barometer rising slowly. Midnight found us round St. Vincent, commencing a slow plug against the continuing veer. But the breeze was dying, the disturbance and its associated fronts having passed to the north-east. To sail a yacht home from Gibraltar is to court a struggle against the Portuguese trades. Alternatively, mostly in winter, westerly or sou'westerly depression type weather may be met, and a third variety is light breezes and poor visibility or even extensive fog. Thus the foul stuff will be a fair wind and a good-weather wind a dead muzzler. We counted ourselves fortunate when the nor'westerly gave place to light airs. No anti-cyclone was developing over the Azores, that essential requisite for spanking Portuguese trades, friend of the Mediterranean bound yachtsman, *bête noir* of those on a reciprocal course. *Sharavogue* was being blessed with a lull between the last two upheavals of North Atlantic winter weather.

Often the radio announcer will read shipping forecasts rather more quickly than at dictation speed, making it difficult to note all the details accurately. The use of *Burman's Weather Charts* helps you to overcome this. These are pro-formas devised by a staunch shipmate of mine, which facilitate a complete record of the B.B.C. reports. However, on that last day of March, when *Sharavogue* had brought Oporto abaft the beam, even if I had made no use of my Burman's Chart, I would have remembered the final telling comment given in the morning "general synopsis":

" . . . a complex area of low pressure in mid-Atlantic will affect western sea areas later."

Appreciation of the overall picture of Atlantic weather briefly outlined in the "general synopsis" of the B.B.C. forecasts is a necessity if one is to form a reasonable opinion of events to come. Simple depressions, even with several attendant frontal systems, generally boost winds to gale force for brief periods only. Distance from a disturbance and its point of nearest approach will govern persistence and severity, but it is when widespread low pressure runs to more than one centre that you should sit up and take note. The overall weather system slows: the meteorologist watches one depression standing still, another describing a satellite circle round it. Gales, severe in places, will persist over wide areas. Elsewhere an uneasy balance between the two "lows" may cause calms. Furious winds are opposing each other balanced on a fulcrum. A vast sea area is gripped by stubborn bad weather, slow moving basically, fickle locally, meteorologically interesting, navigationally hazardous.

Had *Sharavogue* enjoyed average conditions recently, had we been endowed with more periods of free wind progress, I should have viewed the forecast gravely. Our distance from Cabo Silleiro and the virtues of Vigo Bay would have been considered. Should we contract out of the whole affair, bottle ourselves up south of Cape Finisterre as quickly as possible, or should we attempt to reach round-the-corner Corunna before seeking shelter? The question was never formulated. Only one thing sank in: a wind abaft the beam was coming, a wind that would really shift us in the desired direction. We should scud before it, home to England. No more lying on our ear, stamping about in the same hole, painfully putting astern too few miles in the wrong direction. I was light-headed, spreading the news to my crew in one track delight.

"Tomorrow we shall go like a bomb!"

It began that evening, slowly, without fuss. No Mediterranean style, sudden onslaught this, but dignity as fits the higher latitudes and great oceans. The sheets were free when Islas Cies'light, outpost of Vigo Bay, cut the haze on the starboard beam. Mostly holding the port tack, but always tightly close-hauled, we had successfully weathered all Portugal; now the wind permitted a broad reach that would clear Cape Finisterre, 45 miles distant. Beyond lay Biscay, *Gascogne*, *Biscaya*—whatever the name, every sailor in Europe knows its challenge. Our speed increased. Some coasters on a similar course found overtaking a slow business. Puzzled by our weak torch stern light, a close one exposed a searchlight as she thumped past. The sea became a floodlit stage, white horses glistening, *Sharavogue* the star, thrashing out her piece confidently, still with her full spread of canvas.

When Bob took over we changed the genoa for the working jib. As I dived below to sleep, I placated my shipmate's passion for the big headsail by promising to have the smaller one a-weather on the spinnaker pole at dawn. Three hours later, warm in my bunk, with every sound in the ship screaming progress I heard Bob on the foredeck goosewinging her.

A skipper who likes his finger on the pulse, inclined to play the indispensable, yet loath to leave his sleeping bag, I poked my head into the nasty fresh air, grumbling.

"You'll drop that pole end into the drink and see it snap in two. . . ."

He didn't.

By 1000 Cape Finisterre was abeam, dim in the murk. A hard wind was established and a big sea was piling up from the south. There was plenty of shipping about and, as one small, southbound freighter passed close by, her crew lined her deck and gave us a rousing cheer. We never heard them, of course, but the waving looked like that. Punching into it, no doubt this 4,000-ton vessel was beginning to feel the rising sea. *Sharavogue* must have been quite a picture as she rose bodily to the big ocean waves, her full main and boomed-out working jib pulling like a team of war horses. Doubtless an ocean racing man, to whom that extra fraction of a knot is so essential, would have hung on to this canvas—if he had already relinquished his spinnaker—but at 1100 my log read:

"Wind south by west Force 6. Moderate visibility. Barometer falling. Excellent progress but vessel yawing heavily at times. Reef main to first reef points—three and a half rolls."

Lately our little auxiliary motor had not been popular, being in the habit of discharging much of its exhaust gases into the bilge. Repairs to exhaust and silencer at Gibraltar had been ineffective and, while using it off Portugal in light weather, we had arranged a sail over the open forehatch as a wind scoop which sent a current of very cool fresh air through the yacht, carrying the deadly gases out via the main and aft peak hatches. Now, faced with prolonged bad weather, I wanted to charge the lighting battery. We opened all hatches and this time a blast from the following wind rushed through the yacht in the opposite direction, a less satisfactory arrangement because the exhaust gases were carried into the accommodation before being ejected through the fore hatch. Watching the big seas as they came up astern, spray often cutting over the quarter, I knew I had left the job too late. On two occasions a deluge on deck sluiced down into the aft peak. I hung on for a quarter of an hour, the motor generating its precious power at 15 amps. the yacht naked. Then the change rate eased and we cut the engine. I wanted to leave the hatches open for a while to allow the air below to clear thoroughly but a heavy squall soon prompted a hasty shut down, and more than a hint of obnoxious fumes had to find their own way out.

No longer dancing white horses, sombre crests were sometimes torn from the higher seas. Those which escaped the grasping wind long enough would grow into high creamers to tumble explosively down the wave slopes. The mainsail was dropped, the spinnaker pole stowed now that only the foresail remained set. The full gale was on us with the usual high latitude trimmings of driving rain and poor visibility. It was time to take the weather seriously. The honeymoon stage of our newly found following wind was over. In accepting Biscay in her classic dress, the dainty *Sharavogue* was wedded to a tough old man with an ungovernable temper, capable of ranting and raging for long spells. To harness his strength, yet avoid his brute wrath, she must use all her feminine wiles. We must help her come through unscathed. The spare fuel cans at the mizen shrouds were lashed more securely; all other gear on deck was checked and made fast. I was concerned with the doghouse doors, the main companionway. One man-size wave in the cockpit could smash them in, opening the cabin bare and water-logging the yacht. The winter awning and various sails were hauled from their stowage forward and lashed in a heap over the entrance so that they would take some of the force of a pooping sea. The dinghy paddles were lashed between the doors and this dunnage to transfer the shock to the bulkhead and dog-house coamings. This done, access below was restricted either to the sliding doghouse hatch above the doors or through the fore hatch.

By nightfall less sail was advisable; perhaps later it would be essential. I decided to double-reef the jib before turning in. *Sharavogue* did not have a storm jib but we had had a second set of reef points sewn into our working foresail at Gibraltar for just this event. When tackling the job, in order to deal with the great mass of canvas that must be furled down and tied with the reef points, more than half the total area of the sail, I realized that it would be best to lower away completely. This I did, putting the yacht under bare poles temporarily and immediately a disadvantage of yawl rig was apparent. Having a modern, cut-away fore-foot the wind in the bare mizen made her yaw off until she fell away into the trough. I yelled to John to keep her running but he replied that the helm was hard up. Eventually she paid off, but immediately careered round the other way and, as she did so, a heavy sea broke over her, the cockpit taking most of it. When running under bare poles, streaming ropes aft would probably be essential. Soon I completed the reef and hoisted the foresail again, now storm jib size, and proper control was regained.

I went aft and found John swearing at the compass light which had suddenly gone out. He fiddled with the plug and the card was illuminated again but as he did so a warning hiss astern told us of something big and unstable very near. Then we were hanging on amidst confusion. The yacht seemed buried. John remembers the compass light glowing below the foam. She heeled over to port and freed herself. Further smaller waves followed the first onslaught like infantry surging in behind tanks. Empty fuel cans, lightly lashed and stowed in the cockpit, jilled around us. I was surprised how the latter waves washed over us with so little fuss. There was less of the explosive torrent about them. Probably it was because the cockpit was full and, with some 20 gallons of spare fuel at the mizen shrouds and plenty of gear in the aft peak, she was somewhat heavy aft. At the time I wondered whether she was water-logged; yet I could see no damage and all hatches appeared secure. The cockpit was not absolutely watertight, having three small holes where the engine controls lead below and two lifting locker lids with access to the bilge, but this could hardly account for serious flooding. I went below through the forward hatch to inspect and to find a bucket to bail the cockpit. I could not reconcile my fears with the stories of those yachts that have survived pitch-poling, complete capsize or being more thoroughly buried. Down below I was reassured to see the cabin floorboards all in place instead of swilling about bunk high. Bob snoring his head off completed the soothing picture. I grabbed the bucket and rejoined John, who was pumping the bilge.

Clear of that bevy of big ones the yacht continued. Not very much water had got in and we were soon back to normal. Ensuring that the helmsman was securely attached to the yacht by his safety belt I went below for a short nap before being due on watch myself.

My turn at the tiller was raw, spitfire jib stuff, with heavy tumbling creamers astern arrayed in threes and fives, interspersed with lesser fry and hissing areas of foam—the residue of breakers that had exploded farther from us. The poor visibility of driving drizzle prompted a vigilant look-out. The wind was right aft, causing occasional gybes, not entirely harmless to our close-reefed jib but difficult to avoid at times. Guarding against this I frequently yawed towards the wind, putting approaching vessels on not exactly a reciprocal course. An early decision on the best side to pass became the responsible problem. On one occasion, while surf-riding between a tanker and a large liner, there seemed little room to spare. The darkness was playing its worrying tricks and each sandwiching vessel seemed only one wave away.

Soon after Bob came up a couple of heavy squalls heralded the passage of the cold front. The wind veered four points and began to ease; the rain gave way to squally showers. At intervals, an American voice filtered below decks, sometimes a low mutter, sometimes a clear announcement to all in earshot as if unable to give credence to the sudden change:

"Jeeze . . . but it's cold!"

By dawn a double-reefed jib was out of place and *Sharavogue* was slopping about in the swell with bare steerage way. Feeling like a chronic rheumatic, I relieved John and slowly sorted out the gear, setting the full main and finally the whole of the working jib. Then broad reaching in comfort enabled a weary crew to improve on the night's poor quality sleep.

Broadcast gale warnings were discontinued for our area that afternoon but by nightfall the meteorological men were promising more. After a quiet night dawn found the wind piping up again, though except for heavy rain squalls the sunshine and good visibility remained with us. Just the weather for photography. I captured some good shots, mostly of helmsman Bob in front of some sizeable creamers.

We believed that this blow would not attain the severity of our first night in Biscay, when I had entered Force 9 in the log. Having caught up with sleep during the lull, we felt fit as fiddles and in a holiday mood. I hung on to the main, though by noon it was prudently reefed. *Sharavogue* was really going, creaming down the big ones, scudding before the tumbling crests, yawing somewhat but always thrust back on course by resolute helmsmen, now fully equipped with sea legs, stomachs and nerves with Biscay thoroughly measured up. We would be past Ushant in the morning, England the day after.

Probably we were smug mariners still with lots to learn, but that was our mood, buoyant and confident, the bit between our teeth. Certainly we had "the channels"—that exultation of approaching our home port (not strictly true for Bob, being a Yankee far from home, but he had been trying to sail to England since the previous November). And why not? We had brought some tough lessons from the Mediterranean; later we could apply ourselves to more.

In the evening, the weather easing, John yelled: "Come and have a look at this!" A modern liner passing some 2 miles to port suddenly made a sharp turn and was heading directly towards us, probably suspecting we could be survivors of an accident. Steering close under our stern we made out her name—*Felix Dzerjinsky*—and noted the hammer and sickle of the Soviets on her funnel. Personnel on her bridge gave us a friendly wave—a refreshing change to the usual stony stare from passing Russian seamen. Having established all must be well aboard our 35-ft. craft, with her rag of sail, the liner careered off towards Finisterre, heeling over as she turned tightly at speed.

Thus nothing was to douse our spirits; not even East-West politics. Two days after we entered Weymouth to clear customs and a little later *Sharavogue* was back in the beautiful Beaulieu River, and here in tranquil surroundings end these yarns of yacht deliveries in all seasons.

CHAPTER 24

Passage Making To the Mediterranean

DESPITE the attractiveness of the coasts of Britain, many yachtsmen dream of taking their craft to the Mediterranean. Unless the French canals are favoured and are suitable, the project means crossing the Bay of Biscay—first, of course, having brought the yacht to the south westerly end of the English Channel from her home port.

The route and time of departure are important in planning a voyage. Around the UK and North Europe, in particular, they should be considered in relation to prevailing weather and tidal streams. Before offering ideas on strategy, it is assumed that the skipper will be confident about the seaworthiness of his vessel, the quality and quantity of her stores and equipment and the suitability of the crew.

The proximity of a coastline is a blessing or a curse. It can mean a respite from a wild sea, a threatening lee shore or a particular hazard during fog. A judicious route may enable good use to be made of sheltering land. Alternatively, the prudence of avoiding a coast that may be dangerous during on-shore winds should be taken into account. If fog is a possibility it is worth noting where the coast is steep-to and free from off-lying dangers. In such areas, providing it is not too dense, fog need not exclude a yacht from cautiously closing with the land to confirm her position.

Tides and tidal streams warrant attention, not least during the planning stage of a voyage. The time of leaving could have a considerable effect on the amount of fair or foul tide that may be encountered. An obvious option is to leave the moment the tidal stream is with you because that will give six hours' initial advantage—whatever else may befall. However, depending on destination and port of departure, it may be better to plan leaving so that you are off a particular headland or entering an area of particularly strong tides at the time the stream turns in your favour.

From the Clyde

As an example, consider sailing a Clyde based yacht to the Mediterranean, from her home port at Rhu Marina at the entrance to the Gareloch. Tidal streams are weak in the Firth so it is of little consequence whether you set off on the ebb or the flood. However, some 62 miles on, approaching Corsewell Point at the entrance to the North Channel, which separates S.W. Scotland from Ireland, you will encounter the first really strong tide. Plan to arrive there just as the south flowing flood begins. Consider the present wind and the forecast and work out just how long it will take to make those 62 miles from Rhu. Successfully timed, you will then surge down the North Channel at up to half your speed again, perhaps past the South Rock light on one tide. Given a good, free wind and a yacht of some performance, you may even draw clear of Strangford Lough entrance before the inevitable ebb.

On the other hand, if because of unpredictable weather or other difficulties you are entering the North Channel precisely when the ebb is starting, your fortunes will be less appealing. Even with a good fair wind, a small yacht will be lucky to make 15 miles in the next six hours, and if she has to tack she will be lucky to hold her own. If you have the option, a judicious starting time should avoid this worst of all scenarios, but if tacking is expected your ETA Corsewell Point will be more difficult to estimate.

The N.W. sector of the Irish Sea, the area embracing Strangford Lough to the Rockabill light and its eastern approaches, is remarkable for its slack tides. Everywhere else is a sluicing stream. Having enjoyed a favourable strong flood down the North Channel, you should head for this benevolent region. In doing so you will avoid the turn of the tide wiping out your bonus. Head S.W. by S. for the Rockabill, 54 miles from the South Rock across fairly open sea. As you approach across the bight strong tides will be with you again but now, depending on the precise weather, you may find a sheltering shore extending as far as the Tuskar Rock, S.E. Ireland. Unless you succumb to the delights of an Irish port of call, perhaps with the excuse of avoiding six hours of contrary tide, you must now take ebb and flow as they come, fair or foul, just like the wind and weather.

Planning a starting time to gain a tidal advantage is not always an option. A fault discovered at the last minute, the tardy arrival of a crewman, or a sudden fear on Saturday evening that the baked bean supplies are gravely insufficient may make it essential to set sail as soon you are finally ready. In that case, regardless of tides, the quicker you leave the quicker you will arrive, although your actual sea time could be longer.

The rhumb line from Corsewell Point to Land's End lies closer to Ireland than to most of Wales. Admittedly it goes near the tidal, overfalls-infested area of Skomer Isle off S.W. Wales, but unless you are bound for the Bristol Channel that is a place best given a wide berth anyway. Unless you pass west of the Smalls light, careful pilotage is required off that peninsula. It therefore surprises me that when the aim is a fast passage from Scotland to Land's End some yachtsmen route themselves down the Welsh side of the Irish Sea.

The Irish side is the weather shore. From the Rockabill light to the Tuskar Rock S.W. winds through W. to N.N.W. will give sheltered water, and despite the strong tidal streams the rise and fall of tide is remarkably small—in contrast to the phenomenon 60 miles to the east. Even during easterly winds a series of well marked, off-lying banks will break up the worst seas and offer a degree of shelter near the shore. Navigation inshore of these banks is not difficult, although you should be aware that the tides tend to run across the sands in places. The coast has good harbours, particularly Howth, Dunlaoghaire, Wicklow and Arklow with its sheltered dock. Skerries inshore of the Rockabill will offer shelter and Ardglass in Co. Down could be a port of call just after clearing the North Channel. If you have to await weather, particularly headwinds, before making the crossing to Land's End, Cornwall, Rosslare may be the place to stop.

On the eastern side of the Irish Sea it is different. Unlike that benign area off Dundrum and Dundalk Bays, there is no respite from the strong tides. With the exception of the Menai Straits and Pwllheli, facilities for yachts are few. Holyhead and Fishguard are mainly for ferries, and pleasure craft have a hard time, although I must acknowledge that local yachtsmen offer friendly help to visitors where they can. Unlike the Irish side the tidal rise and fall is enormous, and most of the Welsh coast is rugged, beset with tidal races and overfalls and often a dangerous lee-shore in the prevailing winds. Worthy of reiteration, it is also, mainly, further from the rhumb line of your voyage to S.W. England. For all that the Welsh coast has its adherents. Can it be the Sunday temperance?

Unfavourable weather may find you sheltering in Rosslare, using the safe anchorage for foul weather from the southerly sector. You cannot lie at the ferry piers so you will need a boat to go ashore. There are village shops and a pleasant hotel. You will await moderate weather or a good fair wind. Then, ideally, you will head to windward of Scilly, keep well clear of Biscay and make for N.W. Spain, but you could use a brief lull to make for Land's End, knowing that Penzance, just round the corner, is a better place to lie storm bound. Rosslare is not always safe. In fact, when the wind veers beyond west the message will be a clear—"go!" The wind will be fair for your voyage and uncomfortable if you remain in the anchorage. If it remains stormy after the veer you should seek a more sheltered anchorage. Perhaps a hard sail round the Coningbeg light to Dunmore East at the entrance to the Waterford River will be best.

The East Coast of Britain

There are areas round the British Coast where the tides meet, or partially meet. In these vicinities it is possible to win a bonus of up to three hours' favourable stream. Alternatively, if your timing is wrong you could be faced with a marathon slog against a seemingly everlasting foul tide. Land's End, Dungeness, and the Wash approaches offer these possibilities. The tidal stream charts should be consulted.

The east of Britain has a character of its own. Prevailing winds being westerly, it may be thought of as an easier proposition than the west coast, with its 130 mile-passage of open Atlantic between Ireland and Land's End. In fact, by comparison, the North Sea is probably more prone to winds from an easterly sector which, when they occur, will offer you a dangerous lee-shore. North of the Firth of Forth, winds N.N.E. through S. to S.S.W. expose the coast to the full fury of the North Sea, and south of the Firth the shores are barely less exposed to easterly weather. During on-shore gales, some of the harbours are dangerous to enter, and if you are safely sheltering, the breakers on the bars can continue to bottle you up in harbour when the general weather at sea is reasonable.

My favourite ports of call or refuge, largely based on convenience, are Fraserborough, Berwick, Blyth, Scarborough and Lowestoft. There are other, more attractive ports worth visiting but be sure you have good pilotage information. Often the larger commercial ports have few facilities for yachts but changes are taking place and new marinas are being built, sometimes in old docks, such as at Hull. In general, during the prevailing westerlies, much of the coast is a sheltered weather shore and good progress may be made by keeping close to the land. The passage from Flamborough to Norfolk, crossing the approaches to the Wash, where shoals demand careful pilotage, can be boisterous for small craft in strong winds from any sector. The Norfolk coast itself offers shelter inshore of the Scroby Sands but the approach from the North via the Cockle Gat, though well buoyed, concentrates the mind during thick weather. Yarmouth Haven boasts a fierce tide across the entrance—and in and out of it. During strong easterlies the result is a boiling cauldron, and Lowestoft is a better option for yachts.

Bound south from the Suffolk coast, with the Thames Estuary to be crossed, the best and direct route takes you outside the Kentish Knock bank. However, during headwinds it will be possible to gain a tidal advantage by tacking amongst the shoals —inwards with the flood down the East Swin and the Barrow Deep; then crossing the shallows by the Knock John, through the North Edinburgh Channel, hopefully now helped by the start of the ebb, and onwards holding a course towards the North Foreland. Timed right you will gain two hours' fair tide, and soon afterwards enjoy a full six hours' stream in your favour through the Dover Strait.

If a strengthening S.W. blow is developing as you approach the Kent coast—a not unknown occurrence—you have Ramsgate as a port of refuge. Its facilities for yachts are better than at Dover. You can tie up to pontoons in the outer old harbour and go ashore without having to await the tidal gates to the inner pool. The new Ramsgate ferry terminal is entirely separate and its recently built breakwater has eliminated the strong tidal stream that used to sluice across the outer piers of the old harbour.

With S.W. winds prevailing, patience may be required when bound down the English Channel. Ramsgate Royal Harbour was built to provide for a thriving fishing fleet, offer a port of refuge and sustain the many sailing ships that used to await fair winds anchored in the Downs off Deal. Bound westward, modern yachts also find it prudent to await favourable weather and not a few will congregate in Ramsgate, their skippers absorbed with weather forecasts.

To make down Channel I offer a few suggestions for dealing with prevailing sou'westerlies: keep close to the coast; keep to the English side; use the bights and bays to gain what shelter they offer; try to approach prominent headlands when the tide turns in your favour.

Meteorological considerations will help explain the need to stick to the English coast. Most of the depressions associated with our prevailing winds pass north of the British Isles. For this reason winds that I call depression top easterlies are usually far north of the UK. Because these higher latitude depressions that frequently dominate our weather move N.E. or E., the S. to S.W. winds of their southerly sectors must eventually veer west or N.W., sometimes northerly. Trailing fronts are known to confound the theory, but substantial veers can be anticipated, if not as often as prayers for them are offered!

Over the southern UK, S.W. winds seldom back S.E. unless a depression moves into France, but that is a fairly rare event, even if a sometimes stormy one when it happens. In the English Channel an established S. to S.W. wind is more likely to veer than back and this is why the advocate of long tack, who likes to cling to the starboard tack all the way to France, frequently finds the cards stacked against him. He may complete his crossing, perhaps a good sail against a steadily rising W.S.W. wind, making good S. by W., only to fall foul of the nearly inevitable veer. After happy anticipation of the new tack giving real westings, perhaps a course W.N.W., he will be vexed if the cold front crosses just as France is sighted.

A frustrating scenario will unfold. A strong squall and driving rain will necessitate further reefing. At the same time the wind will rapidly veer, perhaps to the west, perhaps further. After lying into the Baie de Seine, for example, the wind shift may enable the skipper to head near Cap Barfleur, still on the same tack, but unable to weather it. Soon he will be obliged to put about and that will expose the whole exercise as a failure. The yacht will be heading back for England with very little progress to show for it.

Had she been in mid-Channel when the veer came through there would have been less trauma. Had she been kept on the English side the change of wind would have brought elation. She would be up wind and in a commanding position.

Following the short tack plan the worst outcome would be to lose one short board—a minor irritation compared to a total waste of about 24 hours' windward work. Here, now, is an encouraging pattern. A short port tack from seaward brings you inshore by Littlehampton and the wind veers just north of west so that the Selsey peninsula becomes a weather shore. Three tacks could now take you to the Mixon Beacon off the Bill, perhaps two hours before H.W. Dover (piling on the good fortune). With the commencing fair tide you could pass through the Looe channel and make good progress towards the Solent. If you could reach Cowes in six hours you would—by the nature of the tidal streams in the area—gain an extra two hours of favourable ebb. Choosing the sheltered water "inside the Wight" would probably be better than beating round St. Catherine's Point. Whatever the plan, sticking close to England until you truly have a free wind remains good advice.

Of course, at times there are enterprising alternatives. Immediately after the passage of a cold front a long board out into the Channel could be fruitful. The associated depression may be creeping smugly away north of the Lofoton Isles while another follows along a similar Atlantic track, though not yet influencing the British Isles. A bold skipper could plan accordingly, anticipating a short-lived ridge of high pressure before the next warm sector makes its inevitable presence felt. Holding the starboard tack he will head close hauled seaward, while the wind slowly eases and backs. Eventually it will steady in the S.W., perhaps even nearer south, slowly starting to pick up. During these changes early substantial westings will give way to a course more directly into the Channel. Judiciously, when he is sure the wind direction has settled and he is far enough offshore, the skipper will put about, hopefully to resume progress westward but probably heading diagonally back towards England.

Depending on its depth and gradient, heavy weather could come with the new depression. As the yacht closes with the land her skipper may consider it prudent to make for an appropriate port of refuge. The South of England enjoys many harbours safe to enter during S.W. gales—Newhaven, Portsmouth, Poole, Weymouth, Torquay, and Dartmouth to name a few.

Despite the lure of the masterly long tack, sticking firmly to the English coast is not to be despised. During persistent S.W., winds, with occasional only modest veers, it is sensible to tack towards each deep bight, gaining a period of shelter before once more beating seaward to tack round the next challenging headland.

For example, considerable shelter is to be found under the lee of Portland, but of course passing the Bill via the inshore route and avoiding the race requires careful attention to the tide. The alternative is a long beat seaward of the Shambles Bank and outside all the overfalls. Either way, once westward of the headland and with 50 mile wide Lyme Bay ahead, a fairly substantial tack seaward followed by a board deep into the Bay is usually a good plan. Once inshore, work your way to the shelter of the Devon coast under the lee of Start Point.

If the wind continues from the S.W. with little or no veer, continue westward towards the Cornish coast—Falmouth or even Penzance. From such a position, as best to windward as you may hope to be, you may remain until you consider it favourable to cross Biscay. Ideally, await a substantial veer that will see you sailing across the deep (sometimes thought notorious) bay dividing N.W. France from Spain.

When persistent south westerlies extend from the English Channel to Biscay, it is good advice to keep westward of your rhumb line for N.W. Spain. With this in mind, aim to make well to windward of Ushant. Remember the cautionary Breton adage—*Qui voit Ouessant voit son sang*. On the other hand, particularly in summer, a fair wind across Biscay may be your good fortune and anyway, whatever the weather, you may wish to enjoy a Breton port of call.

If your passage down-Channel is blessed with an easterly wind, you will probably prefer a direct route diagonally across to N.W. France from your English departure port. Under such favourable conditions in the Channel, Biscay is unlikely to be a windward challenge and it will make sense to pass inshore of Ushant. You will use Le Four Channel or the Passage Fromveur, depending on whether you wish to make a Brittany port of call or press on directly for N.W. Spain. My favourite harbour on the N.W. tip of France is Camaret, just west of the Goulet de Brest on the south shore. The charm of this place more than compensates for its labour-intensive fuelling facilities (you have to manhandle jerry cans from the local garage). On the other hand, inside the Goulet lies Brest Marina which has a proper fuel berth.

Serious pollution occurred some years ago when a supertanker ran aground in the area and now all traffic is monitored carefully up to some 35 miles west of Ushant. As you approach the area, call Ushant Control and report your intended route. Your nautical almanac will give you the details.

The tide runs up to 3.2 knots through Le Four Channel and it can reach 5 knots in the Passage Fromveur. Arrival at either entrance with a fair tide will be of great advantage. Both channels are well marked but be sure to carry a detailed chart. The Passage Fromveur must be approached with care, particularly at night. When entering from the N.E., having picked up Créac'h Point and Stiff lights, it is necessary to approach and identify the lights on Kereon marking the eastern side reef and that on Men Korn on the Ushant, western, side of the channel. This latter used to be the weakest navigational light in the world but recently it has been improved. (On the other hand the great lighthouse at Créac'h Point, the Atlantic side of Ushant, truly is the most powerful in the world.) As you approach, plot your progress towards the entrance with frequent compass bearings. The very strong tide can surprise you.

During bad weather, or even during a heavy swell, wind against tide will cause heavy overfalls at either end of the From-veur, particularly at the south west end. A stranger approaching at night may fear he has strayed near the dangerous reefs when in fact he is correctly in the channel approach. Even leaving the Fromveur, bound S.S.W., the sudden change from sheltered waters into wild tumbling seas can be alarming. The entrance to Le Four Channel is spared this kind of turbulence.

If you visit the Brest region you have two options when continuing your journey. When you leave the Goulet—or Camaret just outside it—one option is to head directly for the Saints buoy, the off-lying cardinal mark seaward of that slim island and treacherous reef that extends 12 miles due westward from Point du Raz. Monitor your progress carefully. If you blunder too close to the Ar Men light it could be Amen indeed! Once past the cardinal you set your course for Cabo Villano, in N.W. Spain.

Alternatively, you can negotiate the route to the Raz de Sein and initially enjoy 17 miles of semi-sheltered water until you pass through the tide-charged Raz de Sein and meet the exposed waters of Biscay. For this route, study the chart and the tidal streams carefully. Choose your time of departure to ensure arrival at the narrows when the tide is favourable or slack. If the weather is good, use the fair tide to boost you through the Raz, but if you have been bold enough to set off in the face of a fresh or strong S. to S.W. wind it is prudent to use the slack and minimize the overfalls.

Should the prevailing weather find you in doubt about the Biscay crossing you can always set off for the Raz, taking advantage of the sheltered water north of the Chaussée. In this way you can make your final decision helped by the latest BBC offering, paying careful attention to the general synopsis to help you judge beyond the precise 24-hour-only area forecast. It may be advisable to cut your losses, return to your port of refuge and try again later.

Particularly in temperate latitudes the changing seasons herald different weather, though with regional variations. The British Islands, exposed to the North Atlantic, experience less extreme temperature differences than continental Europe. Wet air predominates both in winter and summer. Sunshine is often intermittent, with occasional, not even annual, long spells. Heatwaves are rare but welcome. Cold spells in the winter do not reach the extremes that occur on mainland Europe. Though only a few miles south, more influenced by the continental land mass, France is more subject to seasonal changes than England.

In the summertime depressions often maintain their grip on Britain, even though the weather is generally less violent than in winter, but in Biscay a mere 2° of latitude southward, summer nearly always brings a marked change for the better. The influence of the Atlantic depressions is lost, replaced by that of the seasonal anticyclone which establishes itself over the Azores, a ridge from it frequently extending sufficiently far north east to affect Biscay.

A yachtsman setting forth from the UK at this appropriate time, having passed Ushant, should find himself in a changed and agreeable weather pattern. Clear of the depression trail, the wind is often N.W., light or moderate, and as he crosses the big bight towards Cabo Villano, N.W. Spain, it will veer, going round north and then N.E.

In contrast to the situation over the Azores, a static low often hangs over Spain. Northern Spain is seldom short of rain, even in summer, and this depression influences the Azores high as it extends into Biscay. The result is an easterly airstream along the north Spanish coast which will follow the rugged cliffs past Punta Candelaria, La Coruña, Cabo Villano and on to Cabo Finisterre, strong if the barometric gradient demands it, which is often. Addicted listeners to the BBC shipping forecasts will appreciate the typical summertime offering for sea area Finisterre: "N. to N.E., 3 to 4, but N.E. to E., 6 to 8 near Cape Finisterre."

In winter it is altogether different.

As autumn goes its way the Atlantic depressions grow deeper, larger and more persistent. Occasionally a particularly intense one becomes static in mid-ocean. It will lurk there stubbornly, its centre usually some 300 miles south of Iceland, nurtured, topped up—or *topped down*, I should say—by a supply of lows marching in from the S.W. Its pressure gradient will influence a huge area of the North Atlantic, often extending well south of the Azores, its associated fronts flailing across vast tracts of ocean in turmoil. Biscay is frequently within its dominance and gales and storms are commonplace. Yachtsmen who cross Biscay in winter need prudence, patience and judgement.

Back to summer. You can run into sou'westerly, depression-type weather, but here is a not unusual, happier sequence of events. Approaching N.W. Spain, gentle progress will become more lively. The wind will have veered east and from there will freshen steadily. The seas will increase in size with surprising speed. In fact, the wind is not rising: in the area you are entering it has been blowing vigorously all the time. The big waves that are chasing you were always there. You will make excellent progress as you ride before them towards Villano and Finisterre. And if life is becoming too exuberant you can take comfort in the knowledge that once past Punta Torinana, which lies 11 miles north of Finisterre, you will probably find a respite in both wind and sea. Here the weather often switches off like a lamp and you will continue benignly down the west Iberian coast, probably using your engine for a time.

A northerly breeze will soon spring to your aid and by the time you are nearing Portugal it will very likely freshen. Frequent in summer, less so in winter, these are the Portuguese Trades. Other winter winds in the region are often influenced by the big Atlantic depressions and alternatively, if less frequently, continental winter high pressure can bring cold north easterlies that are by no means benign. In summer, if the northerly wind is absent, light airs and widespread fog may occur. I recollect that on a number of occasions when I have encountered fog off western Portugal, I have gone on to experience a strong Levanter at the approach to the Gibraltar Strait.

There are other worthwhile comments about Biscay. If depression type weather persists and you decide to make the crossing, aim to keep to windward. If you stray to leeward into the Bay, the veering wind syndrome will hound you. In summer this is not critical because of the frequent easterly winds along the north Spanish coast. But in winter try to keep to the west of your rhumb line.

Aim to cross Biscay. Do not coast round it—unless, of course, you are cruising the area or making for the Canal du Midi. It is 380 miles from Ushant to Cape Finisterre and nearly 700 miles round. You are better advised to await good conditions at Brest or Camaret than embark on the tortuous coastal route. This applies particularly to motor yachts. Without carrying fuel in spare cans, some will not have sufficient bunkers to make the direct crossing, especially if they try to go fast. Cut your speed to the waterline length rule and your range will be far greater. Diesel oil is cheaper in England than in France (or Spain). It is worth taking on spare fuel in cans, arranging a proper fuel transfer system. By making it from, say, Dartmouth to La Coruña or even Bayona the motor yacht owner will save a lot of money. However, the prudent powerboat man will plan to have at least 25% fuel in hand at his next expected port. There are no service stations at sea.

Thinking of limited fuel for motor craft, La Coruña offers the shortest full Biscay crossing. It is 300 miles from Ushant. La Coruña and Bayona (see later comments) are now the only two N.W. Spanish ports that sell fuel to yachts. The reason for this restrictive development is not clear. La Coruña is a substantial commercial port having also a large fishing fleet. The marina for yachts is rather exposed to S.W. gales. Before approaching the Bay of Coruña the navigator is advised to study a large scale chart. In particular, he must keep clear of the Banco Yancentes on which the sea or swell can break. There are leading lights. The busy town is pleasant and offers plenty of amenities.

Less attractive since the Spanish fuel-for-yachts restrictions, but an excellent port of refuge in the strategic position tucked under Cabo Villano, N.W. Spain, Camarinas is virtually on the S.W. corner of Biscay. The chart must be consulted. There are dangerous reefs to avoid at the approaches but leading lights to ensure a safe entry. The interesting, somewhat primitive harbour is mainly for fishing boats but yachts are allowed to tie up if there is room, sometimes outside a trawler. Otherwise, there is a safe and sheltered anchorage. The village is a true example of the old Spain, but it is beginning to grow into a minor, national rather than international, holiday place.

There are several ports along the western coast of Iberia worthy of a call during a leisurely cruise. Some are tidal and some have shifting shoals. Full pilotage details should be obtained before entering without a pilot. I shall only mention harbours that offer relative ease of entry and certain shelter, or are particularly convenient for a brief call.

Bayona, 50 miles south of Cape Finisterre, still in Spain and lying at the southern end of Vigo bay, is the favourite yachtsman's port after rounding Cape Finisterre. There is an hospitable yacht club. When entering, study the chart carefully and do not stray close to the rocky shores. Fuel is obtainable at the yacht club. Bayona is an attractive town. In 1493 the *Pinta*, one of Columbus's ships, called here when returning from the discovery of the Bahamas.

Leixoes, the large, artificial, commercial harbour for Oporto is 60 miles south of Bayona. It is safe to enter in any conditions. Yachts are required to moor up in a complicated way in the small craft basin, on the Leca (north) side of the harbour, and use their own boats to go ashore. Short stay craft will sometimes not be moved if they tie up on the outside mole of this basin. You can dry out on a tide if you lie against the wall by the sloping hardway near the lifeboat station. Fuel and water are obtainable and there is a friendly sporting club which serves plain but inexpensive meals. The yacht club is more strictly for members only. On Leca seafront there is an excellent restaurant specialising in sea food and lobsters—choose your own from the tank.

Having had no radio news for several days and out of touch with earth shattering world events, I happened to come ashore at Leixoes just after England had beaten Portugal and went on to win the world cup. At the tiny post office in Leca I fumbled for change to pay for some stamps. The charming girl behind the counter contemplated me seriously.

"You are English," she said sweetly, with a hint of an accusation.

"Yes."

"You are not my friend!"

I walked out, extremely puzzled.

Just up stream of historic Belem Castle, Lisbon, on the north side of the Tagus, is a dock with facilities for visiting yachts. Fuel and water is available and there is an efficient train service to the city centre. The dock is usually crowded and mooring up is complicated; in summer, therefore, I favour Cascais, a picturesque town on the south-facing coast at the approaches to the mouth of the Tagus. Yachts must anchor and you need a boat to get ashore. There is a yacht club on the sea wall where you may find help with small repairs. A strong scend runs into the bay and to bring a dinghy to the yacht club needs competent boat handling. The fuel facility at Cascais is an oddity. First you have to row ashore and clear Customs; then enquire on the beach about fuel. You will be directed to a buoy close inshore. Back to your yacht, up anchor and carefully worm your way past closely moored fishing craft. Pick up the buoy and you will find an extra line attached. Haul on it and and—surprise, surprise—up comes a fuel gun! Fill your tank, row ashore and pay: then you can be on your way.

Another easy port of call in Portugal is the modern marina of Vilamoura, 40 miles along the southern coast round Cabo St. Vincent. It has full facilities and will make a pleasant, easy stop. If you suspect or know a bad Levanter is blowing in Gibraltar Strait, Vilamoura is the better place to be.

Levanter Barrier

In the main, Gibraltar enjoys a good climate, temperate with plenty of sunshine. There is just enough rain, mainly in the winter. A new desalination plant, now supplementing the large water catchment on the east side of the Rock, has eliminated the occasional water problems.

The more usual winds, sometimes called the Poniente, blow from S.W. to W. and are seldom more than a moderate breeze. Less frequently it blows from the east. That wind is called the Levanter and is usually associated with low pressure over Morocco. A flowing, moist airstream hits the Rock, is deflected upward and then condenses into an ever replenishing, permanent mantle of moving cloud that hangs continuously above the town and harbour, its off-white trails blowing westward and evaporating over Gibraltar Bay. When you see this characteristic Levanter cloud you will know the wind is in the east, and may be serious.

A strong Levanter causes turbulence as it eddies round the

Rock. Violent squalls, N. or N.E., blow over the harbour, particularly near the marinas. The wind similarly surges in eddies round the south side of Gibraltar. During a winter Levanter boats have to be tended carefully if they are not to be damaged at their berths. Whole pontoons have been known to break adrift, complete with yachts. However, the Levanter's main impact is upon yachtsmen trying to sail into the Gibraltar Strait from the west. The narrowest part—just under 8 miles—is between Punta Cires on the African side and the land immediately east of Tarifa. Westward of this line the easterly wind suddenly doubles in velocity. As if shot from a gun a moderate or fresh breeze in the narrows leaps into a gale as it reaches more open water. You may think that air will move faster if concentrated into a narrow gap, compared to when it breaks free. Tidal streams behave that way, but the Levanter adheres to a different rule. Turbulent air over the mountains probably creates a booster effect.

West of Tarifa, a vigorous Levanter may reach storm force. It also spreads out directionally in a spray effect. Along the Spanish side towards Cabo Trafalgar it blows E.S.E., while along the coast past Tangier the direction is usually E. by N. For this reason taking long tacks across the approaches to the Strait is not advised. However you approach, the wind will be dead against you. Keep close to the Spanish shore. You will find the wind slightly off-shore, and during daylight (or at night if you have radar) partial shelter can occasionally be found in some of the shallow bays.

The Levanter is a persistent wind and may last for days at a time. Folklore confidently tells you that it will blow three days, five days or seven days—but never two days, four days or six days. I have never researched that one. The worst Levanters are in winter but they may be an unpleasant challenge at any time of the year. Not infrequently they extend as much as 100 miles west of the Strait and their existence can be easily foretold, sometimes as far as 80 miles westward. Having rounded Cape St. Vincent, you may receive a benign warning, and the sooner it occurs the more ominous will its message be. You will encounter the typical short swell that has rolled westward from the Levanter region. The farther it has travelled, the more vigorous will be the wind that reared it. You could be broad reaching before a fair breeze with Sagres Point just abaft the beam, and notice tell-tale undulations rolling against your quartering sea. As the day goes on the typical, disagreeable motion will increase and eventually the following breeze will die. Later still it will be replaced by a faint easterly which will veer E.S.E., dead ahead, and increase with dramatic speed.

Quickly you will be reefing. Now—take the starboard tack, lie close-hauled to the north east, and you should begin to find easier conditions as you draw clear of the main blast out of the Strait. However, even close to the coast and well north of Cadiz a bad Levanter will offer you a stiff, slightly offshore breeze. Close with the land and tack south. As you pass Cadiz Bay it will be worth considering making for shelter. If you decide to continue, the weather will steadily worsen and rounding Cabo Trafalgar will be a tough proposition. There is a dangerous rock two miles off the Cape, and in bad conditions you should pass seaward of it, taking a long tack to ensure you are clear. You will now find the Levanter at its worst. There is some shelter to be found close inshore, and recently a marina has been built at Barbate, five miles east of the Cape. I understand it offers good shelter for yachts. I have not visited it myself.

A word about currents is helpful. There is a permanent inward east-flowing surface current at the Gibraltar Strait. During westerly winds it is fairly strong and when sailing in with a fair wind everything will be in your favour. During a prolonged Levanter, although the current slows down, there remains some help for the inward passage. It continues significantly for 170 miles eastward of Gibraltar, along the southern Spanish coast beyond Cabo de Gata. A tidal stream exists along the edges of the Strait. Of little importance for an inward bound yacht, it can be helpful when beating out of the Strait towards the Atlantic against a westerly wind. Keeping close inshore at the appropriate time will help. Judicious resort to the engine will gratify those with less patience.

Some years ago, after one of the round the world races had terminated at Gosport, I was bound for the Mediterranean at the same time as two of the Italian race contestants were making for their home port in Italy. I visited one of these yachts in Cadiz, where we were all sheltering from a fine specimen of the Levanter. She had just run back after a third attempt to beat into the Strait.

"I can't believe it," said the skipper ruefully. "Here we are, after racing all round the world, through the Roaring Forties, Cape Horn, the lot—and we can't even sail into our own little sea!"

I felt in good company.

These notes are for the passage from the UK to the Mediterranean. The return passage requires different considerations, and I hope to write about that on another occasion. I believe Levanter information must be recorded on any treatise about sailing to the Mediterranean, but lest it appear too large a dose of gloom and deters people embarking on such an enterprise, I must add that this wind is an exciting and effective way of starting the homeward passage from Gibraltar. The short, steep seas of the Levanter that are so troublesome to tack against are seldom a problem for a yacht running W.N.W. for Cape St. Vincent. Also, I should reiterate that the more usual wind in the Gibraltar Strait is S.W. to W, often light or moderate with plenty of sunshine. Indeed, many yachtsmen have sailed successfully and happily into the Mediterranean without ever having heard of the Levanter. It remains as unknown to them as a Tehuantepecer is to a Norfolk Broads sailor.

I may appear preoccupied only with headwinds, foul tides, cataclysm and catastrophe. Newspaper editors, similarly, face the accusation that they peddle only bad news. The truth is that plenty of favourable, exhilarating and enjoyable things occur during a voyage to the Mediterranean, but the prudent skipper will wish to have a sound knowledge of the possible hazards he may face.

Appendix

Beaufort Scale of Wind Force
(With open sea criterion for small or moderate size modern yachts)

Beaufort Number	Mean limits of Wind Speed in knots	Descriptive terms	Open Sea Criterion for small or moderate size modern yachts. Full details of sail changes not included
0	Less than 1	Calm	Becalmed
1	1–3	Light air	Ghosting
2	4–6	Light breeze	Gentle sailing on the wind
3	7–10	Gentle breeze	Comfortable sailing and good progress on the wind
4	11–15	Moderate breeze	Good sailing all points of the wind
5	16–21	Fresh breeze	Hard thrash to windward
6	22–27	Strong breeze	Cruising yachts well reefed
7	28–33	Near gale	Cruising yachts on the wind lie-to, shelter or run
8	34–40	Gale	Hard bitten off-shore racing skippers will continue to windward; others lie a-hull or run
9	41–47	Strong gale or severe gale	Yachts lie a-hull or run under spitfire jib or bare poles. Watertight cockpit advisable
10	48–55	Storm	Lying a-hull may become dangerous; running under bare poles probably safe, given watertight cockpit. Drag warps suggested
11	56–63	Violent storm	No proven techniques if this weather persists for long
12	Over 63	Hurricane	Not recommended

Index